Praise for *Welcome to Math Class* . . .

I have loved Marilyn Burns's work since the moment I started teaching. A favorite of mine has been *The Border Problem*. I have used it with many levels of students with such rich results. In the past few years, I have used the problem with teachers. It always ends with a rich discussion around the surprise that the lesson began with something simple like a grid and then turned into algebra!

—Amy Hurley, kindergarten teacher, Albuquerque Public Schools, New Mexico

Having Marilyn's voice in my ear brings new life and insights to lessons I've taught countless times—one of my favorites being *Consecutive Sums*. Congratulations Marilyn—you continue to be my guiding light through the wonderful world of learning, teaching, and mathematics.

—Brenda Mercado, early childhood teacher in Tucson, Arizona, and coauthor of *Teaching Preschool and Kindergarten Math*

I have used each and every one of the lessons in *Welcome to Math Class* in my own practice, either as a classroom teacher or as a teacher educator. My career as a math teacher—and math teacher educator—would not be the same without Marilyn Burns and Math Solutions.

—Julie McNamara, author of *Beyond Invert & Multiply* and Assistant Professor of Mathematics Education, California State University, Hayward, California

Marilyn Burns believes in the power of story, and she dug deeply into her collection of math lessons to choose her favorite for *Welcome to Math Class*. They are indeed the best of the best.

—Susan Ohanian, author of *Garbage Pizza, Patchwork Quilts, and Math Magic: Stories about Teachers Who Love to Teach and Children Who Love to Learn*

This special collection of lessons and reflections lets us explore deeply the thinking of one of the most insightful, creative, and effective teachers ever to step into a classroom. For decades, Marilyn Burns has been inspiring teachers and anyone who cares about mathematics teaching and learning. Every time we see or hear Marilyn's words, we are encouraged to take one more step toward excellence and move ever closer to helping every student become empowered as a mathematical thinker. Marilyn is truly a national treasure, and this collection is yet another wonderful gift from Marilyn to all of us.

—Cathy Seeley, NCTM Past President and author of *Faster Isn't Smarter* and *Smarter Than We Think*

Marilyn Burns is the master of finding simple yet challenging situations for children to investigate. From *Billy and the Pencils* to *Counting Pockets* and *Raisins*, Marilyn's lesson descriptions have shown tens of thousands of teachers how to launch and support children in their work with powerful mathematical ideas. This new collection is just what I want to share with my teacher candidates as they explore and celebrate mathematics with their students. Thank you, Marilyn.

—Ann Carlyle, author of *It Makes Sense! Using Number Paths and Number Lines to Build Number Sense* and Continuing Lecturer, Teacher Education Program, University of California, Santa Barbara, California

Marilyn Burns's books and workshops set me on the path to being a math educator and researcher who cares for the success of *every* learner. She challenges me to think about how students can actually understand math—rather than just parroting what teachers tell them. Her insight into math learning and the clarity of her writing voice changed me as an educator, and for that I am grateful.

—John Tapper, author of *Solving for Why* and Assistant Professor, Elementary Education, University of Hartford, Connecticut

Marilyn Burns does it again! *Welcome to Math Class* is the perfect resource for everyone, whether you are purchasing your first Marilyn Burns book or adding to your collection. Marilyn's continued work toward supporting teachers and students is remarkable.

—Jennifer Lempp, author of *Math Workshop* and Coordinator, Office of School Support, Fairfax County Public Schools, Virginia

Long before I had the pleasure of engaging in conversations with Marilyn, I was listening to her voice as she spoke through her writing. My classroom shelves were lined with Marilyn's books, and as I read them, I learned how to teach math. *Welcome to Math Class* is a gift of inspiration and know-how to teachers, but ultimately it is a gift to students who will benefit from math lessons that spark their curiosity and create a lifelong love of learning.

—Patty Clark, Math Solutions Director of Professional Learning, Manassas, Virginia

This book is a must-have for every elementary teacher. These lessons are truly some of the best that we have ever used, resulting in student engagement and deep understanding.

—Amy Herman and Connie Horgan, Math Solutions professional learning consultants

Marilyn Burns, the consummate mentor: wise, insightful, respectful, engaging, inspiring, joyful, passionate, clear, and concise. Marilyn shares her years of experience in this treasure trove of rich, problem-solving lessons.

—Maryann Wickett, math consultant, author, and retired teacher, grades PreK–6, San Marcos Unified School District, San Diego, California

It's not often that an educator has a profound influence on thousands of teachers and students. I recall starting my career as a young teacher when Marilyn and colleagues visited my class each month and taught lessons. Over the years, we tinkered with ideas together; Marilyn sparked my passion for math education and was instrumental in shaping the work that I do today. She has the rare gift of pressing teachers to think critically about their mathematics instruction while being supportive and empowering.

—Cheryl Cameron Rectanus, mathematics professional development specialist, Teachers Development Group, West Linn, Oregon

Welcome to Math Class offers teachers of all levels of experience access to the wisdom of a true math education treasure, Marilyn Burns. From the hands-on tasks to Marilyn's insightful views of student work, this volume complements any professional learning curriculum. I can't wait to try out the ideas with my preservice teachers.

—Carrie Cutler, author of *Math-Positive Mindsets* and Assistant Professor, Elementary Mathematics Education, University of Houston, Texas

Welcome to Math Class is truly the best of the best from Marilyn Burns. Every one of these lessons provides rich and engaging contexts that encourage students to think, reason, and problem solve, while providing teachers with exceptional activities to address today's standards. Marilyn shares her thinking behind her teaching, helping all of us improve our craft. Thank you, Marilyn!

—Rusty Bresser, coauthor of *Math Workshop Essentials* and Supervisor of Teacher Education, University of California, San Diego, California

Welcome to Math Class is a wonderful addition to all of Marilyn Burns's books of mathematics that have helped me learn how to teach mathematics from the beginning of my teaching career. Thank you, Marilyn, for helping generations of teachers learn to see themselves as math people so they can pass this gift on to students.

—Sue Chapman, Math Solutions professional learning consultant, League City, Texas

Marilyn Burns has hit another "mathematical home run"! These terrific lessons can help both teachers who are new and those who are eager to improve their teaching of mathematics. In each lesson, students' ideas and thinking strategies are elicited, discussed, and extended. Even if you are a superstar, Marilyn has written this book in such a way that anyone who reads it can become wiser. That's what she has once again done for us all; thanks, Marilyn!

—Ann Lawrence, coauthor of *Lessons for Algebraic Thinking, Grades 6–8*

The lessons in *Welcome to Math Class* gave me the confidence to experiment and definitely made me a better teacher than I otherwise would have been. The lessons give the mental images and practical information needed to try something new with students. You'll be excited—and your students will be too!

—Doris Hirschhorn, former mathematics teacher, District 25, New York City, New York

For almost five decades, Marilyn Burns has set the standard for outstanding math instruction. From rigorous, compelling word problems to sense-making approaches to unraveling complex mathematical ideas, this collection of lessons shares Marilyn's best thinking. *Welcome to Math Class* is a coffee-table book for devotees, and a must-read for every teacher who wants to positively impact their students in mathematics.

—Robyn Silbey, math coach and consultant, Montgomery County, Maryland

Welcome to Math Class is one of many ways Marilyn inspires us to delight in our students' thinking and to love teaching mathematics.

—Caren Holtzman, coauthor of *Math Workshop Essentials* and Director of USCD's Partners At Learning (PAL) Program, University of California, San Diego, California

What a wonderful resource for all educators and an ideal gift for new teachers! Marilyn shares thoughtful lessons and insights into students' thinking in ways that encourage and inspire teachers to incorporate meaningful activities into their classrooms. Kudos to an outstanding educator and friend!

—Jeane Joyner, coauthor of the INFORMative Assessment series

Welcome to Math Class

A Collection of Marilyn's Favorite Lessons

Grades K-6

Marilyn Burns

Math Solutions

Boston, Massachusetts, USA

Math Solutions
www.mathsolutions.com

Library of Congress Control Number: 2019955414

Math Solutions is a division of Houghton Mifflin Harcourt.

MATH SOLUTIONS® and associated logos are trademarks or registered trademarks of Houghton Mifflin Harcourt Publishing Company. Other company names, brand names, and product names are the property and/or trademarks of their respective owners.

ISBN-13: 978-1-935099-52-9

The Classroom Illustrations
The classroom illustrations have been preserved from the original Collection of Math Lessons series. They were drawn by the late artist Martha Weston, who illustrated more than sixty children's books, including seven written by Marilyn Burns, beginning with *The I Hate Mathematics! Book* published in 1975. She also wrote as well as illustrated other children's books.

Executive Editor: *Jamie Ann Cross*
Production Manager: *Denise A. Botelho*
Editorial Assistant: *Kirby Sandmeyer*
Cover design and art: *Belle Design (belledesign.org)*
Cover illustrations: *Martha Weston and Claire Rollet*
Author photo: © *Heinemann 2018. Photo by Michael Grover.*
Interior design and composition: *Wanda España, WeeDesign Group*

Printed in the United States of America.
1 2 3 4 5 6 7 8 9 10   0304   27 26 25 24 23 22 21 20 19
4510006708   ABCDE

A MESSAGE FROM MATH SOLUTIONS

We at Math Solutions believe that teaching math well calls for increasing our understanding of the math we teach, seeking deeper insights into how students learn mathematics, and refining our lessons to best promote students' learning.

Math Solutions shares classroom-tested lessons and teaching expertise from our faculty of professional learning consultants as well as from other respected math educators. Our publications are part of the nationwide effort we've made since 1984 that now includes:

- more than five hundred face-to-face professional learning programs each year for teachers and administrators in districts across the country;
- professional learning books that span all math topics taught in kindergarten through high school;
- videos for teachers and for parents that show math lessons taught in actual classrooms;
- on-site visits to schools to help refine teaching strategies and assess student learning; and
- free online support, including grade-level lessons, book reviews, inservice information, and district feedback, all in our Math Solutions Online Newsletter.

For information about all of the products and services we have available, please visit our website at *www.mathsolutions.com*. You can also contact us to discuss math professional development needs by calling (877) 234-7323 or by sending an email to *info@mathsolutions.com*.

We're always eager for your feedback and interested in learning about your particular needs. We look forward to hearing from you.

From Houghton Mifflin Harcourt.

CONTENTS

*The reproducibles referenced in this book are available in a downloadable, printable format. See page xii for the key code and instructions to access these online versions.

LESSONS BY GRADE LEVEL

The particular grade levels in which the lessons have been taught are included in the vignettes. However, these grade levels aren't meant to imply that the lesson is suitable only for those grade levels. Most are applicable to more than one grade level. Also, it's beneficial for students to experience these investigations more than once, perhaps in a subsequent year, when they have the benefit of previous experience and increased maturity.

	GRADE						
	K	1	2	3	4	5	6
1. BILLY AND THE PENCILS Making Sense of Word Problems			X	X			
2. THE BORDER PROBLEM Introducing Students to Algebraic Thinking					X	X	X
3. THE CONSECUTIVE SUMS PROBLEM Problem Solving to Support Collaborating and Making Conjectures				X	X	X	X
4. COUNTING POCKETS, BEANS, AND MORE Developing Understanding of Place Value	X	X	X				
5. COWS AND CHICKENS AND OTHER SUCH PROBLEMS Building Number Sense	X	X	X				
6. EXPLORATIONS WITH FOUR TOOTHPICKS Reasoning about Shapes and Their Attributes			X	X	X	X	
7. THE FOUR-TRIANGLE PROBLEM Exploring Geometry—An Investigation for All	X	X	X	X	X	X	X
8. MULTIPLICATION WITH RECTANGLES Connecting Multiplication and Geometry				X	X	X	
9. PATTERN BLOCKS, HINGED MIRRORS, AND MORE Understanding and Measuring Angles					X	X	X
10. PENTOMINOES EXPLORATIONS Investigating and Classifying Shapes					X	X	X
11. A PLACE-VALUE MENU Supporting Understanding of Place Value		X	X				
12. RAISIN MATH Estimating, Dividing, and More				X	X	X	
13. RIDDLES WITH COLOR TILES Building Number Sense				X	X	X	X
14. SHARING COOKIES Connecting Fractions and Division				X	X	X	
15. THINGS THAT COME IN GROUPS Introducing Multiplication with Real-World Contexts				X	X		
16. THE TWO-DICE SUMS GAME Reinforcing Basic Addition and Introducing Probabiity				X	X	X	X

CONVERSATIONS WITH MARILYN

To extend your learning, this collection of lessons also features nine audio episodes of conversations between Marilyn Burns and her Math Solutions colleague Patty Clark. Consider these your personal conversations, meant to support you further as you plan to use the lessons with your students.

HOW TO ACCESS ONLINE AUDIO CLIPS AND REPRODUCIBLES

1. Go to mathsolutions.com/myonlineresources and log in if you already have an account. If you do not, click or tap the Create New Account button at the bottom of the Log In form.
2. Create an account, even if you have created one with the Math Solutions bookstore. You will receive a confirmation email when your account has been created.
3. Once your account has been created, you will be taken to the Product Registration page. Click Register on the product you would like to access (in this case, *Welcome to Math Class*).
4. Enter key code **WTMC** and click or tap the Submit Key Code button.
5. Click or tap the Complete Registration button.
6. To access audio clips and reproducibles at any time, visit your account page.

> Key Code
> WTMC

A WELCOME FROM MARILYN

Thinking about teaching math has consumed my professional focus since I became a teacher in 1962. That was more than fifty-five years ago, and many of my ideas about teaching have changed from then to now. In my early years in the classroom, I went through a transition that I think is typical for many teachers, moving away from relying on the ways I had been taught and moving toward finding my own ways. I learned by going to conferences, attending workshops, poring over professional books, reading articles in journals, collaborating with teacher friends, and more. Always, the best support I've received has been from trying out lessons in classes and learning from students.

The first professional book I ever wrote for teachers, published in 1987, was *A Collection of Math Lessons from Grades 3 through 6*. It was a collection of classroom vignettes. To write them, I'd teach a lesson and then, as soon as possible afterward, chronicle what had occurred and include my reflections about what I experienced. I often relied on students' written work to help me think more deeply about what had happened, and I included their actual work throughout the book.

As I continued developing my practice in classrooms, I continued to write vignettes. In a way, I felt then and still feel now that vignettes are a way to welcome people into my classroom and bring alive for teachers what I've learned. I try when I'm writing vignettes to tell the stories of my successes and my failures. I try to share classroom moments that excited me and the bumps that I would have liked to avoid. And I try to reflect on what I had experienced to invite teachers into my thinking.

> **"**I try when I'm writing vignettes to tell the stories of my successes and my failures. I try to share classroom moments that excited me and the bumps that I would have liked to avoid. And I try to reflect on what I had experienced to invite teachers into my thinking.**"**

I'm sometimes asked if I videotape my lessons in order to write vignettes. I don't do this often. When I began writing vignettes, videotaping wasn't often accessible or easy as it is today. I learned to write soon after teaching a lesson and have continued that practice.

The feedback I've received from many teachers is that the vignettes I've written are helpful for envisioning how a lesson might unfold in the classroom. They've told me that they enjoy reading about the classroom interactions, that the accompanying student work is useful for getting a glimpse of how some students reacted, that a vignette can help them prepare for a lesson and create a plan for how to introduce it to their students.

After publishing *A Collection of Math Lessons*, I continued with two subsequent books with the same title, one for grades 1 through 3 and the other for grades 6 through 8. For these collections, I collaborated on teaching the lessons and writing the vignettes with two colleagues, Bonnie Tank and Cathy Humphreys. Other teacher friends also read drafts of the lessons, tried them, and contributed ideas from their experiences with their own classes.

ABOUT THIS NEW BOOK

To create this new book, I revisited all thirty-nine chapters in the three-volume collection. With the help of another colleague, Doris Hirschhorn, I decided on sixteen lessons to include in this book. For me, these lessons have weathered the test of time and have become permanent parts of my teaching repertoire. Doris and I revisited the structure of how those lessons were presented, keeping the vignettes but breaking them into sections that we think will make it easier for teachers to translate into their own teaching plans.

> **"**These lessons, for me, have weathered the test of time and are permanent parts of my teaching repertoire.**"**

There are differences among the lessons I chose to include. Some are appropriate in early grades and others are suitable for older students. They address a broad range of math content, some focusing on number and operations while others engage students with geometry, patterns, algebraic thinking, probability, and more. Some work for a one-day lesson and others are suggestions meant to span several days of instruction.

Sometimes the lesson involves students with concrete materials and sometimes students are asked to write in math class. Some lessons engage students in solving a particular problem and some engage them in playing a game.

This may seem like an all-over-the-place collection of lessons, but there are elements that thread though all of them. First, my guiding goal for all lessons is to engage students in thinking and reasoning mathematically. I try and design experiences that are accessible to all students and also have the potential to challenge students who are particularly interested. I structure investigations to maximize students' opportunities to talk so they have experience with verbalizing and clarifying their ideas. I encourage students to listen and learn from each other and work to build a community of math learners in the classroom.

I've taught all of these lessons multiple times over the years, to different classes and often in different grades. Even with multiple experiences, each time I choose to use a particular lesson, I go through a two-part process—preparing and planning. I prepare by understanding the mathematical opportunities in the lesson and I plan by figuring out the logistics so that the lesson can go smoothly for me and for the students. My hope for the vignettes is that they help reveal both the preparing and the planning that I think is helpful for all instruction. I've learned that the more opportunities I've had to teach the same lessons in different situations, the better able I am to anticipate students' reactions and responses and to manage the class experience successfully.

SOME NEW FEATURES

A new addition to this book is a collection of nine audio segments, titled "Conversations with Marilyn." They're each an audio reflection in which I'm talking about teaching math from a variety of perspectives with Patty Clark, a longtime Math Solutions colleague. Also in the book are references to six blogs I've written that are relevant to particular lessons. You can read these blogs and others I've written at *www.marilynburnsmathblog.com*. These two new features are testimony to some of the ways my professional life has expanded over the more than fifty-five years.

I hope that you enjoy this new book, *Welcome to Math Class*, and find it useful for your own teaching. As always, I welcome your thoughts.

—*Marilyn Burns*

CONVERSATIONS WITH MARILYN

What Inspired *Welcome to Math Class*?

THE VALUE OF STORY WHEN SHARING MATH LESSONS

www.mathsolutions.com/welcometomathclass1

> **"**I like stories. I like to be carried along with a story. What a story does is give me a way to make my own mental images of what's going on and encourages me to think in my own way while engaging me fully. What I've tried to do is write lessons in a way that tells a story.**"**

Overview

In this conversation, I share with my longtime Math Solutions colleague Patty Clark why I was inspired to write *Welcome to Math Class*. Also, I talk about how writing has played an important part in my growth as a teacher.

Making Connections

I find that reflecting on my teaching is helpful, even essential, for me to think about how better to serve students. Writing about my classroom experiences is one way to revisit my teaching decisions and reflect on my lessons. In *Welcome to Math Class*, I share my writings in hopes they can be useful for you.

1

Billy and the Pencils

Making Sense of Word Problems

Taught in Grades 2–3

S tudents often struggle when they face solving word problems. "Do I need to add or subtract?" is a question I've heard many times from students when they're attempting a word problem. They more often wonder *What do I do to get the answer?* rather than *How can I make sense out of the situation?*

If the word problems students are assigned follow instruction about a particular operation and simply require applying that operation, students may not have too much difficulty. If, however, the problems on a page necessitate a mixture of operations, require using several operations in one problem, or contain extraneous information, many students are at a loss. Following are teaching ideas that I've found extremely useful and effective for addressing these difficulties and helping students demystify word problems.

OVERVIEW

Here I describe three days of instruction with fourth graders when we focused on just one situation involving Billy, a boy who has $1.00, buying pencils and erasers. I've used this same sequence of lessons in grades 3 through 6, and also with second graders, sometimes using an easier version of the problem. I always look forward to this teaching experience as the lessons engage students and I learn a good deal about their thinking. Also, I provide six other instructional suggestions for additional ways to engage students and prepare them for success with word problems.

MATERIALS

- paper, $8\frac{1}{2}$ inches by 11 inches, at least 2 sheets for each student
- paper, 12 inches by 18 inches, 1 sheet for each group
- folder, 1
- markers, 1 for each group

DAY 1

Introduce the information about Billy, the pencils, and the erasers.

I began the lesson by organizing the students into small groups so that they'd have the opportunity to collaborate in their thinking and to benefit from each other's ideas. There were seven groups in this class of fourth graders—one with five students and six with four.

Once the groups settled, I wrote the following on the board:

Pencils cost two for $.25.
Erasers cost $.10 each.
Billy has $1.00.

I explained to the students what I wanted them to do. "There are three parts to the directions I'm going to give you," I told the students. "I'll tell you what they are, and then I'll write them on the board, so you won't have to remember them." I knew that the directions were complicated and that having them on the board would give groups a reference for what they were to do. Giving the directions verbally first was a way to give the students an overall introduction. Then, when I'd write them on the board, I could involve them as I introduced the directions for a second time.

Explain the instructions for the three parts of the task.

"The first part is this," I continued. "I'd like each of you, individually, to write one question that you can answer from the information about pencils, erasers, and Billy. The second part is: When you've each written a question, take turns reading your questions aloud to the others in your group. After you each read your question, discuss as a group whether it can be answered from the information given. After that, you'll go on to the third part. For the third part, work together to think of other questions that can be answered from the same information. Write your group's questions on one sheet of paper. As a group, decide whether to include the questions you first wrote individually."

Write the instructions on the board.

I then wrote the directions on the board, asking students to contribute by recalling what I had said.

> ### Directions
> 1. By yourself, write a question that can be answered from the information posted.
> 2. In your groups, read your questions aloud, discussing whether they can be answered.
> 3. In your groups, brainstorm as many questions as you can that can be answered from the given information. Write them on your papers.

Circulate, observe, and offer help as needed.

The students got to work. For a few minutes, as students wrote their own questions, the room was quiet. Then, as students began to read their questions to each other and to brainstorm other questions, it became noisier. Still, it was possible for all the groups to work, and none seemed disturbed. Purposeful noise, such as the sound of students working together, never seems to be a deterrent to productive work.

> "Purposeful noise, such as the sound of students working together, never seems to be a deterrent to productive work."

Have groups share their questions.

After fifteen minutes or so, when I had noticed that there were at least six questions on each group's list, I interrupted the students. I told the students what we'd do next.

"Now groups will share the questions you've written. Here's how we're going to do that. Each group, in turn, will read just one of your questions. In a moment I'll give you a chance to decide which of your questions you'd like to read and who in your group will do the reading."

Before asking them to talk together about the questions they'd like to read, I asked a question, "Do you think it's possible, when we've gone around the class once with each group reading a question, that we'll have heard seven different questions?"

From the number of nods and murmurs, I could see they thought it was certainly possible.

"Why are you so sure?" I asked.

Alon raised his hand. "We have some really great questions on our list," he said.

"So do we," said Sofia.

"Do you think we'll be able to go around the room twice and still have each group ask a different question?" I queried again.

Some of the groups felt confident. Others weren't so sure.

"We'll try it and see," I said. "But this means that along with reading your questions, you'll have to listen carefully as others read theirs to make sure that you don't read the same question. It may be good to have a backup choice so that if a group asks your question, you have another to read. Keep in mind that sometimes questions can really be the same though the exact wording will be different."

I structured the activity this way to encourage students to listen to each other. Too often students are willing to offer their ideas, but have difficulty listening to each other's ideas. Giving them a reason to do so, such as not reading the same question, helps them focus when others are speaking.

> "Too often students are willing to offer their ideas, but have difficulty listening to each other's ideas. Giving them a reason to do so, such as not reading the same question, helps them focus when others are speaking."

I gave students a few moments to decide which questions they planned to read and who would do the reading for their group. I made one additional comment, "We won't worry about actually finding answers to your questions now, but I want you to think about whether it's possible to answer each of the questions read from the information."

Alina began by reading for her group, "If Billy wants six pencils and five erasers, how much more money does he need?"

"Can that be answered from the information?" I asked.

"Yes, I can figure it out," Mehir said.

"So can I," said Terry.

"I'm not interested in answers right now," I reminded them. "I'm interested in hearing the different questions you wrote."

Alina began by reading for her group, "If Billy wants six pencils and five erasers, how much more money does he need?"

Mehir read next for his group. "How many pencils and erasers can Billy buy for one dollar and not get any change back?"

"How about that question?" I asked. "Can it be answered?"

Some students nodded, but I realized that without having time to actually try to solve the problem, most were not sure if it could be done. I decided not to continue asking if questions could be answered. Instead, I decided to focus on whether what was asked was a new question or one we had already heard. I didn't announce this decision to the class, however acted on it after the next question was read.

Andrea read next, "If Billy has one dollar and he already bought two pencils, how many erasers can he buy?"

"Is this question different from the others?" I asked and was answered with nods. I called on the next group.

Marisol read, "Billy has to give his friend Mia twenty-five cents because Billy borrowed it. But Billy's teacher said that he needed five pencils by tomorrow. Will Billy have enough money to buy the pencils and pay Mia back?"

The class seemed impressed with this one and agreed that it was a new question.

Wengal went next. "How much does one pencil cost?" he read.

Alina raised her hand. "We didn't put that one on our list because we didn't think you could answer it," she said.

"Yes, you could," Wengal answered. "If you went into a store to buy one pencil, the store owner wouldn't send you away. He'd sell you a pencil."

Mehir chimed in, "But you can't tell for sure how much he would charge for it."

"I think it would be thirteen cents," Sara offered. "That's as close to half as he could get, and he'd charge the extra half cent because he had to break up a pair."

"But you couldn't know for sure," Alina insisted.

"Is the question different from the questions that have been asked so far?" I interjected.

My question was answered with nods.

"Let's leave it for now," I said, "and you'll have a chance to discuss how to answer it later. Who will read next?"

Andy offers to explain when Wengal challenges the question Esperanza read.

Manny read next, and he was very excited about their question. "If Billy bought one pencil and three erasers plus two more pencils and said to the clerk, 'Forget the half of a cent,' how much does Billy get back?"

Esperanza read for the last group, "If Billy pays one dollar for one eraser and two pencils, how much change will he get? Then if he sells each one for two cents more, what's his profit?" Esperanza was visibly pleased with her group's question. However, her face took on a look of dismay when her question was challenged.

Wengal said, "That's not one question—you asked two questions. That's not right."

"I know how to fix it," Andy said, who was in Esperanza's group. "Just give me a minute."

We waited patiently while Andy scribbled. Then he read, "If Billy has one dollar and buys one eraser and two pencils and then sells each one for two cents more, how much money does he have now?" He looked at Wengal and asked, "Is that OK?" Wengal nodded.

"So," I said, "it seems we went around the room and heard seven different questions. Could we make another round? Would you like to try?" The students were enthusiastic about trying.

I gave the groups a chance to look over their list again. I also changed the order in which the groups would read.

I changed the order of calling on groups and this time started with Marisol's group. She read, "Billy has a little sister who needs two pencils and two erasers. Billy needs four pencils and two erasers. Does this cost more or less than one dollar and how much change will Billy get if he gets any?" The class agreed this was a different question. Even though Marisol had read two questions, no one objected this time and I didn't comment.

Wengal read next, "How many erasers and pencils can Billy buy if the number of erasers and pencils has to be the same?" This question interested me, maybe because it was a question I don't think I would ever have thought of myself. (The uniqueness of students' thinking is part of what makes teaching fascinating to me.) I was now becoming more curious about what the students would do when I asked them to solve these problems.

Manny and his group needed a minute to scan their list again. Finally, Manny read, "If Billy bought six pencils and two erasers, how much change does he get back?"

Esperanza went next, "How many erasers can Billy buy and get ten cents change?"

Group 2

1. If Billy buys 5 erasers how many pencils can he buy?

2. If Billy buys 4 pencils and 2 erasers and Billy gives the clerk $1.00 how much change will he get back?

3. If Billy bought 6 pencils how many erasers could he get and what would be the amount of change he gets back?

4. If Billy bought 1 pencil and 3 erasers plus 2 more pencils and said to the clerk "forget the half a cent!" How much does Billy get back?

5. If Billy bought 6 pencils and 2 erasers how much change does he get back?

6. If Billy bought 4 pencils and 5 erasers how much change does Billy

In their fourth question, this group solved the problem of what to do if someone purchases only one pencil.

Group 3

1. If Billy has $1.00 and he already bought 2 pencils, how many Erasers can he buy?

2. If Billy bought 5 Erasers and 2 pencils will he get any change? And if he does how much will he get back?

3. How many Erasers and pencils can Billy buy, the number has to be the same? What is the least amount of change he can get back?

4. If Billy gave his friend .15 cents, how many pencils can he buy?

5. Billy thought he could buy 20 pencils. (He didn't know how much they cost) How much did he think they were?

Group 3 was especially proud of their fifth question.

Then Alina, "If Billy pays one dollar and gets twenty cents back, how many pencils and erasers did he buy?"

Mehir then read, "Billy thought he could buy twenty pencils. He didn't know how much they cost. How much did he think they were?"

And, finally, Andrea read again, "If Billy bought four pencils with a tax of three cents on each, how much would he pay?"

I then asked the class, "Would it be fair if I gave you the assignment of solving the fourteen problems that you've created about Billy and the pencils and erasers?"

The students indicated that they thought this would be fair.

"Would you rather solve them alone or in your groups?" I asked.

The answer was unanimously in favor of working in groups. Andrea declared, "You learn just as much or even more from helping each other."

Assign homework: Solve your group's questions.

This was the end of the time for math, so I explained their homework assignment. "For homework tonight, each of you will solve the problems your group wrote. Solve all of them, not just the ones you read. I'll give you time in a moment to copy them. Then tomorrow, in your groups, you'll compare your answers to the problems."

DAY 2

Have groups compare homework, create an answer sheet, and post their questions.

I began the class the next day by having the students compare their answers to the homework problems and resolve any discrepancies in their solutions. Then I had them focus on the two questions they had read aloud yesterday. I asked each group to write their agreed-upon answers for those two questions, writing each answer on a different sheet of paper and handing them in to me to review. My goal was to have fourteen corrected sheets in an answer folder to be available later to the students. Next, I had groups use markers to write each of the two questions they had read to the class on a large sheet of paper that I planned to post for everyone in the class to see. After I posted them, I numbered the questions so it would be convenient to refer to them.

Have groups sort the posted questions.

To begin, I wanted to provide an experience from which students would be alerted to the fact that there's more than one possible answer for some problems. Too often students quickly come to a conclusion and then stop thinking rather than investigate the situation further. To address this, I asked the students, in their groups, to decide for each question posted whether it had only one possible answer or more than one. I gave two examples, choosing from questions posted, "Here's a problem that has only one possible answer— How much change did Billy get?" There were murmurs of agreement. I continued, "And here's a question that has more than one possible answer—What could Billy buy with one dollar?" Again, they agreed. Then, as a class, we discussed the other questions to decide if they had one or more possible answers.

This was all we had time for this day.

> "I wanted to provide an experience from which students would be alerted to the fact that there's more than one possible answer for some problems."

Instruct groups to solve the posted questions.

I devoted the next day's class to groups finding solutions for the posted questions. I told them that they could work on them in any order. When they believed they had a problem solved, they were to check their answer against the solution in the answer folder.

I showed the class the answer folder that I had created the night before. I then explained that I had corrected the answer sheets they had handed in and numbered the answers to match the posted questions. I further explained that if their answer conflicted with the answer in the folder, they were to check with that group to resolve the difference of opinion. I would step in if they couldn't come to an agreement.

FURTHER EXPLORATIONS FOR OTHER DAYS

Ask students to write word problems for a particular equation.

For a first experience, give the class the same equation, perhaps a simple addition sentence, such as $8 + 6 = 14$. Ask each student to write a story for the equation that meets two criteria—it ends in a question and the question can be answered by the equation. Students read their stories to each other in their groups. Those who are willing then read their stories aloud to the entire class.

Ask students to choose their own equation and write a word problem for it.

Ask students to follow the same two criteria—the word problem ends in a question and the question can be answered by the equation. They read their stories aloud in their groups so others can figure out the equation. You can also post their stories and use as a class assignment or lesson for students to match equations to situations.

Ask students to write stories with extraneous information.

Again, ask students to write stories for equations, but this time including extra information in their stories that isn't needed. It's best to model this type of story for students first. Here's an example: *Nyah was planning a birthday party. She sent nine invitations. Seven friends replied that they could come. Nyah had $15.00 for refreshments. She bought a cake mix for $1.29, three six-packs of drinks for $2.39 each, and chips for $3.99. The day before the party one of the guests who had planned to come phoned to say she had an unexpected visit from her grandparents. How many guests attended the party?*

Ask students to decide, for word problems, whether in real life an exact answer is necessary or if an estimate would do.

Select word problems from the textbook and ask students, in groups, to decide for each whether in real life an exact answer would be needed or if an estimate would suffice or perhaps be even better. Ask them also to explain their reasoning, either in writing or in a class discussion.

Ask students to identify the operations needed to solve word problems.

Select word problems that you know require a combination of two or more operations. Ask students not to solve the problems, but to decide whether they will need to add, subtract, multiply, or divide, or some combination of these, in order to figure out an answer.

Use labels from cans or boxes of food to generate and solve word problems.

Ask each student to bring to class a label from a can of food or an empty box. Then ask students, either individually or in groups, to write word problems that could be answered from the information on the label or box. Students solve each other's problems.

 **FINAL THOUGHTS**

Many experiences are necessary to help students focus on making sense out of word problems. I've found that activities like these engage students' interest and prepare them to tackle word problems from their textbooks. Before I assign problems from their textbooks, I want to observe if students are able to focus on making sense of problem situations. When they do work on textbook problems, I still have them discuss their answers together rather than work alone on assignments. It's only when I need to assess their individual abilities to solve word problems that I have students work independently so that both they and I can find out what they understand. In classroom lessons, however, I'm interested in establishing a classroom environment that focuses on learning to think and reason, not on testing what they were supposed to have already learned.

> "In classroom lessons, I'm interested in establishing a classroom environment that focuses on learning to think and reason, not on testing what they were supposed to have already learned."

CONVERSATIONS WITH MARILYN

Marilyn's Math Story

MY JOURNEY TEACHING AND LEARNING MATH

www.mathsolutions.com/welcometomathclass2

> "I've had to change the way I think about teaching. It's not driven by my telling students where to go next, but by students' showing me where they might go next."

> "How do I get kids to be the stars in the classroom rather than me being the star in the classroom?"

> "When I tell people I'm a math teacher, they always say, 'Oh, you must be smart.' There's something about math that has a mystery to it; if you understand mathematics, you must be smart. I'm trying to break down that notion so every student I teach feels he or she has access to math."

Overview

In this conversation, I share with my longtime Math Solutions colleague Patty Clark why I became a math teacher, what my experience was like as a learner of math, and what has changed in my teaching over the years.

Making Connections

I think that an important aspect of being an effective math teacher is being a math learner. As you read the vignettes in *Welcome to Math Class* that describe lessons I've taught, some of the math problems or investigations may be new to you. I've learned, when reading about math, that it's important for me to make sense of the math for myself. I encourage you to take time to think about any of the math investigations that might be new to you or that you haven't yet thought about, perhaps the vignette about *The Border Problem* or *The Consecutive Sums Problem*, both of which appear in *Welcome to Math Class*.

2
The Border Problem

Introducing Students to Algebraic Thinking

Taught in Grades 4–6

Students often get their first glimpse of algebra from older sisters or brothers. They see problems that have more letters than numbers and typically seem very mysterious. Students are generally impressed, curious, and sometimes a bit fearful. This five-day investigation provides an introduction to algebraic thinking in a way that integrates algebra with geometry and arithmetic.

OVERVIEW

Cathy Humphreys taught this lesson, *The Border Problem*, to her middle school students. I've also taught the lesson to many classes in grades 4, 5, and 6. You can visit my blog to watch a video of me teaching part of it (www.marilynburnsmathblog.com/an-oldie-revisited-the-border-problem).

To begin the lesson, Cathy gave each of the students a 10-by-10 grid of centimeter-squared paper and asked them to figure out how many squares were in its border. After describing and comparing their different methods, students solved the same problem for grids of other sizes. Finally, they generalized their calculation methods into algebraic formulas. By introducing algebra as an extension of arithmetic and geometry, students were helped to see algebra as connected to their previous math learning. The experience is appropriate for students in grades 4 and up. For fourth and fifth graders, you may want to use the suggestions for only the first three days.

MATERIALS

*REPRODUCIBLES are available in a downloadable, printable format. See page xii for directions about how to access them.

- *The Border Problem* (**REPRODUCIBLE A***), 1 for each student plus 1 extra
- centimeter-squared paper (**REPRODUCIBLE B***), a large supply
- paper, 12 inches by 18 inches, a large supply
- chart paper, 1 sheet
- worksheet of student explanations, 1 for each pair of students (see page 17 for instructions)

DAY 1 PREPARATION

Create 10-by-10 grids.

Before I began the lesson, I cut 10-by-10 grids from centimeter-squared paper, one for each student and one for myself. On my grid only, I colored in the border to demonstrate that it was the outside row of squares on each side. Instead of creating your own grids, you may also use the one provided as **REPRODUCIBLE A**.

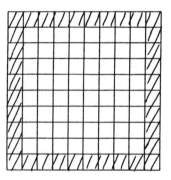

DAY 1

Ask students what they know about algebra.

"What do you know about algebra?" I asked the class. I was interested in learning what these students knew or had heard about algebra. My question was met with general silence.

Finally, Jesse raised his hand. "It has to do with using letters to stand for numbers," he said.

"Yes," I responded, "letters are often used for numbers in algebra. Does anyone have a different idea?"

Zack raised his hand. "My older brother learned it," he said. Others murmured that this was true for them as well.

No other students had ideas to offer.

Write on the board: *Algebra is a generalization of arithmetic.* Discuss the meaning of *arithmetic* and *generalization*.

I then wrote on the board:

Algebra is a generalization of arithmetic.

"What is arithmetic?" I asked.

Lots of hands went up to answer this question. "It has to do with numbers." "It's addition and subtraction and like that." "It's multiplication and division, too." "You do things to numbers and get answers."

I gave all the students who raised their hands the chance to contribute. Then I asked another question, "What's a generalization?"

Fewer hands went up. "It's the opposite of *specific*?" Quinn said, tentatively.

"It's like those statements we write about graphs," Krystal said, referring to their prior experience with interpreting graphs.

"They're like conclusions," Kamal added.

I confirmed that their ideas were all correct, that a generalization is a statement that's true for a collection of situations.

Tell the class how you plan to help them learn about algebra.

"In order to help you learn about algebra," I then said to the class, "I'm going to start from what you already know. I'm going to give you a problem you can solve using arithmetic. Then I'll introduce you to how to use algebra to make a generalization. We won't get to the algebra part today, but we'll focus just on the problem."

In general, students learn from connecting new experiences to what they know. I want students to see algebra in relation to what they've already learned, not as a topic separate from the mathematics they've been studying.

> "In general, students learn from connecting new experiences to what they know. I want students to see algebra in relation to what they've already learned."

Give each student a 10-by-10 grid of centimeter-squared paper (**REPRODUCIBLE A**). Ask, "How many squares are in the grid? How many are in the border?"

At this point, I distributed the 10-by-10 grids I had prepared and asked students to figure out how many squares were in the grid. It was easy for them to figure there were 100 squares.

"Now I'd like you to find out how many squares there are just in the border of your grid," I said, "the row all around the outer edge." I showed them the grid on which I had colored the border squares.

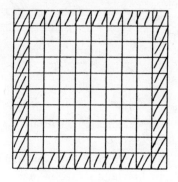

There were murmurs as students worked. "I know, it's forty." "It's got to be forty." "I'll count to check." "Hey, it's not forty." "Oops, I'd better count again." "I got thirty-six." "Yeah, I got thirty-six, too." "You could have fooled me."

When all the students had convinced themselves that there were thirty-six squares in the border, I asked for volunteers to explain how they figured it.

I called on Marek. "I did ten times four," he said, "and then I subtracted four and got thirty-six."

"Why do you think your method makes sense?" I asked.

"Because you can't count the corners twice," Marek answered, "so I subtracted them at the end."

I recorded Marek's method on a sheet of chart paper. I knew I was going to review their methods the next day, so writing on chart paper gave me a way to preserve their ideas.

$$10 \times 4 = 40$$
$$40 - 4 = 36$$

"Did anyone do it a different way?" I asked.

Roberto had a suggestion. "I counted the sides and added," he said. "The top has ten, then the next side has nine because you already counted the corner, and the next side has nine, and the last side has eight because you counted both corners."

Roberto and Isaac figure out how many squares there are in the border of the grid.

I recorded Roberto's method on the chart paper.

$$10 + 9 + 9 + 8 = 36$$

"Any other way?" I asked.

Tami reported next. "I just multiplied nine times four," she said.

"Why does that make sense?" I asked.

"Because I didn't want to count the corners twice," Tami answered. "I just said that each side gets one corner, so they each have nine squares, and I multiplied that by four."

I recorded Tami's method.

$$9 \times 4 = 36$$

Then I asked, "Any other ideas?"

I called on Zack. "There are sixty-four squares in the middle," he said, "because that's eight times eight. I subtracted sixty-four from one hundred and got thirty-six."

I added Zack's method to the chart paper.

$8 \times 8 = 64$
$100 - 64 = 36$

"Any other way?" I asked.

Quinn had an idea. "I added ten and ten for the top and bottom," she said. "Then there are only eight left on each side, so add eight and eight, and you add twenty plus sixteen to get thirty-six."

I recorded Quinn's idea.

$10 + 10 = 20$
$8 + 8 = 16$
$20 + 16 = 36$

"Another idea?" I asked again. There were no more volunteers.

"I have another method," I said. "I'll write it on the chart paper and then see if someone can explain what I was thinking." I wrote:

$8 \times 4 = 32$
$32 + 4 = 36$

Several hands shot up. I called on Juliette. "You took out the corners first and then added them back in at the end," she said.

"Where does the eight come from?" I asked.

Isaac explained. "That's how much is on each edge without the corners," he said.

I now had six methods recorded on the chart paper:

Method 1
$10 \times 4 = 40$
$40 - 4 = 36$

Method 2
$10 + 9 + 9 + 8 = 36$

Method 3
$9 \times 4 = 36$

Method 4
$100 - 64 = 36$

Method 5
$10 + 10 + 8 + 8 = 36$

Method 6
$8 \times 4 = 32$
$32 + 4 = 36$

Have students, individually, describe in writing one method and explain why it works. Collect their work.

I then gave students a writing assignment. "Choose one of the methods for solving the border problem," I said. "Describe it in your notebook so that someone who wasn't in class would have a way to figure out how many squares are in the border. Be sure to explain why the method works." (Students in this class had math notebooks, which they used for this assignment. With other classes, I distribute paper for the assignment.)

Having students write helps them find out what they know and what they don't know. Also, their writing gives me insights into their understanding. I knew that writing was difficult for many students in the class. They hadn't had much previous experience with writing about their thinking processes in their math classes.

DAY 2 PREPARATION

Read students' written work.

When I read through their explanations that night, I found most to be very poor, both in the thoughts they expressed and the grammar they used. The following are samples from about half the students.

Dante
You can figure it out by taking 9 from each side and multiplying it by four.

Sinead
All you had to do was add the top and bottom which is 10 + 10 = 20 and then add the two sides 8 + 8 = 16 and then add them together 20 + 16 = 36.

Quinn
take the bottom and the top and add them. then add the sides and theres your answer.
10 + 10 + 8 + 8 = 36

Algebra
Double stuff
'10
10
8
+ 8
——
36

take the bottom and the top and add them. then add the sides and theres your answer.

Aneitra
I think Marek had a good method because there are four sides and one of the sides has ten. You have to tell how many squares are around the border. So, you multiply 10 × 4 and come up with 40. Then I subtract 4 because I have to take out a corner and come up with 36.

Isaac
The easiest way to find out the number of squares in the border is 9 × 4 = 36.

Hasani

You can figure this out by multiplying 9 and 4 because it is easer then doing anything else.

> The border Problem
> The border has 36 squares.
> You can figure this out by multiplying 9 and 4 because it is easer then doing any thing else.

Zack

You can figure it out by 8 × 8 inside subtract 64 from 100 = 36.

Marek

You add the squares on the border then subtract the 4 corners that you don't use.

Jesse

You can figure this out by the Tami 9 on each side method. Each side has ten sqares but you can't count the corners twice. So, you just multiply 9 × 4.

Rachel

Take away the border and find how many squares are left 8 × 8 = 64 Then subtract 64 from 100 and you get the answer

Kamal

You can find this out by taking the number off the top which is 10. Then you add two sides which are 9 each and then add the bottom which is 8.
8 + 9 + 9 + 10 = 36

Juliette

You can figure this out by adding the 2 vertical sides and then adding the 2 middles which add up to 8 so 10 + 10 = 20 and 8 + 8 = 16 so 16 + 20 = 36.

I decided to focus the next lesson on helping students improve their ability to explain their reasoning in writing.

Copy five students' explanations verbatim, one for each method, each on a separate sheet of 12-by-18-inch paper. Copy a sixth explanation that describes one of the methods in a different way. Prepare a worksheet of other explanations.

To prepare for this day's class, I chose five of the explanations that students had written and wrote each on a 12-by-18-inch sheet of paper. I chose two explanations that I felt were fairly complete and then others that needed more revision. My plan was to use these examples to talk with the class about which parts of explanations they wrote were clear and which parts needed more information. I was going to model for students how to edit each of the explanations to make improvements. I also prepared a worksheet of five other of the students' explanations. I planned this to be for students, working in pairs, to revise.

Post the chart of all the methods recorded on Day 1. Then post one of the clear explanations you prepared.

I posted the chart of the six methods I had recorded the day before. Then I posted one of their explanations, choosing one of the more complete explanations to review first:

> You can find this out by taking the number off the top which is 10. Then you add two sides which are 9 each and then add the bottom which is 8.
>
> 8 + 9 + 9 + 10 = 36

Ask the class which method the posted explanation describes. Discuss. If appropriate, edit the explanation with students' help.

"Which method does this explain?" I asked, drawing their attention to the chart paper on which I had recorded their explanations on the day before.

Several hands went up. "It's like number two," Juliette said, "the one that Roberto said."

"That's right," I answered, "and the explanation is fairly clear. There is some missing information, however. The explanation doesn't tell where the nine and eight come from. Let's start with the nine. What does the nine represent?"

"I can explain," Roberto said. "It's because you already used the corner."

"That's just the kind of information that should be included," I responded and inserted *because you can't count the corner again* into the explanation.

"How can you explain the eight?" I then asked.

I called on Dante. "You already counted both corners for the last row," he said, "so you can't count them." I added *without the two corners* after the 8. The explanation now read:

> You can find this out by taking the number off the top which is 10. Then you add two sides which are 9 each because you can't count the corner again, and then add the bottom which is 8 (without the two corners).
>
> 8 + 9 + 9 + 10 = 36

I made one more comment. "Including the numerical representation is a good idea because it adds to the explanation."

Post another explanation, ask which method, discuss, and edit.

I then went on to a second explanation, also a fairly complete one:

> I think Marek had a good method because there are four sides and one of the sides has ten. You have to tell how many squares are around the border. So, you multiply 10 × 4 and come up with 40. Then I subtract 4 because I have to take out a corner and come up with 36.

"I didn't write that," Marek called out.

"No, Aneitra did," I answered. "She was describing the method you explained."

"It seems clear to me," Zack said.

"I think so, too," I said, "except that I have two changes to recommend." I changed *one of the sides* to *each of the sides* and *a corner* to *all four corners*. Although these were small changes, I wanted students to know that I expected careful reading and attention to all details.

Post a third explanation and repeat the process.

I posted another explanation that needed more revision than the first two:

> You can figure this out by multiplying 9 and 4 because it is easer than doing anything else.

"There were more explanations of this method than any of the others," I said. "Although it was a popular choice, none of the explanations have enough information. What's missing is an explanation of why it makes sense to multiply nine and four."

"I can explain," Tami said. She came to the board and drew just the border with ten squares on a side. She continued, "You count nine on each side by stopping before the last one so you don't count the corners twice." Tami illustrated this by counting and marking the squares she had drawn.

"Your explanation makes sense," I said. "How can I describe what you did in writing?"

Tami was stumped. Jaden raised his hand. "You take a corner off each side," he said, "and that leaves nine."

"Then what?" I said.

"You do nine times four," Tami added.

I rewrote the explanation on the chart:

Take one corner off each side. That leaves 9 on each side. Then multiply 9 times 4 to find out how many squares are in the border.

"This isn't the only possible way to explain Tami's method," I said. "There isn't one right way, but you have to be sure that what you write has all the information needed to make sense."

Post a fourth explanation and repeat the process.

I then posted a fourth explanation:

Take away the border and find how many squares are left 8 × 8 = 64 Then subtract 64 from 100 and you get the answer

I went through a similar discussion, talking with the class about explaining why multiplying eight times eight made sense and where the number 100 came from. Also, I reminded them to include a period at the end of each sentence.

Post the last explanation and repeat the process.

The last explanation I posted read:

Take the bottom and the top and add them. then add the sides and theres your answer.

10 + 10 + 8 + 8 = 36

First, I corrected the grammar, adding capital letters at the beginning of each sentence and an apostrophe in *theres*.

"Having the numbers included helps," I said, "but I think the explanation would be clearer if you explained why you added the two eights."

"They're the sides," Tri said.

"Why does eight make sense for the sides?" I asked.

"Because you can't count the corners again," Aneitra answered.

I edited the explanation to read:

Take the bottom and the top and add them. Then add the sides which are 2 less than the top because you can't count the corners again, and there's your answer.

Post the final explanation. Without any discussion, have each student write an improved version. Circulate, observe, and offer help as needed.

"Now I'm going to post one more," I said to the students. "This time, each of you is to write in your notebook an improved version of what I've posted." I posted an explanation that was another version of a method we had already discussed:

You add the squares on the border then subtract the 4 corners that you don't use.

The students' explanations showed improvement.

Krystal

There are ten squares on each side. You can't count any square twice. So subtract four corner squares. Now there are 36 squares. [Krystal included a diagram to illustrate her explanation.]

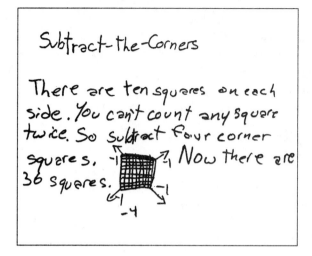

Isaac

OK you have 10 squares on each side and there are 4 sides so then you multiply 10 × 4 which is 40 but you have added the corners twice so you have to take out the 4 corners which makes it 36 squares. 10 × 4 – 4 = 36.

Juliette

You add the top which is 10 and then the next side which is ten (counting the corner you've already counted). Add the bottom which is ten and then the next side up which is ten. And then you subtract the 4 corners that you counted twice each.
[Juliette also included a numerical recording.]

> You add the top which is 10 and then the next side which is ten (counting the corner you've already counted) ~~count the to~~ Add the bottom which is ten and then the next side up which is ten. And then you subtract the 4 corners that you counted twice ~~ea~~ each
>
> $$\begin{array}{r} 10 \\ +10 \\ 10 \\ 10 \\ \hline 40 \\ -\ 4 \\ \hline 36. \end{array}$$

Tami

You count the 10 on each side and you get 40. Then subtract the 4 corners because you counted all corners twice and then you come up with the answer 36.

Hasani

You add the number on the top and then multiply it by 4 and then you subtract the corners that you used all ready.

Jaden

Assuming that the sides don't overlap on the corners, you multiply the 10 squares on a side by four for the four sides. Then you subtract the overlapping corners.

Tri

We count each side of borders are 10, we subtract 4 because we count twice on the corner. [Tri, a Vietnamese boy, has lived in the United States for only three years. Practice with writing is necessary for Tri to learn to express his ideas in more conventional English.]

Zack

There are 10 squares on each side. Multiply 10 × 4, then subtract the corners (4), because you counted each twice.

Give each pair of students the worksheet you prepared of five other explanations. Have students improve the explanations.

When I noticed that most of the students had written an explanation, I interrupted them to give additional directions. "I'm going to give each pair of you a worksheet I've prepared that has five other explanations taken from what some of you wrote in your notebooks. Start with the first explanation on the sheet. Separately, re-write it to make improvements and then compare what you wrote with your partner. Together, agree on one way to revise the explanation and write the revision on the worksheet. Do the same to write improved versions of the other explanations."

DAY 3 PREPARATION

Read students' worksheets.

When I read the worksheets that night, only one pair of students had rewritten all five explanations. It's typical for some pairs to work more quickly than others. I wanted to give the others time to finish their work while keeping them all moving toward describing the methods algebraically. But before having them return to revising the explanations on the worksheet, I decided first to give an additional problem to extend their work into figuring out the borders of squares of different sizes.

DAY 3

Present a new but related problem. Draw a 5-by-5 grid on the board. Ask, "How many squares are in the border?"

I began the class by drawing a 5-by-5 grid on the whiteboard. "How many squares are in the border of this grid?" I asked.

I waited, giving students a chance to think about the problem. When more than half the hands were raised, I called on Isaac.

"Sixteen," he said.

"How did you figure that out?" I asked.

"I did it by Tami's method," he said. "I multiplied four times four."

"Who did it a different way?" I asked. In this way, students again had the opportunity to describe different methods for figuring the border. I gave all who were willing the opportunity to explain.

> "Students again had the opportunity to describe different methods for figuring the border. I gave all who were willing the opportunity to explain."

Ask students to complete the worksheet from the day before. Then have them figure out the number of squares in the border of grids of different sizes, record their findings in a chart, and look for patterns.

I explained what students would do next. "If you didn't have time yesterday to finish rewriting the explanations, do that next," I said. "Then figure out how many squares are in the border of grids of different sizes and record on a chart like this one." I drew a chart for them on the board, filling in the answers we had already figured out.

Number of squares on edge	Number of squares on border
3	
4	
5	16
6	
7	
8	
9	
10	36

"Underneath your chart," I said, "write what you notice about the pattern in the borders as the grids increase in size."

"Can we draw the squares to figure them out?" Jaden asked.

"Yes," I answered, "making a drawing often helps in solving problems."

"Can we do this first before we finish the writing?" Halbert asked.

"No," I answered, "you need to complete the other work and have me check it before you begin this."

Circulate, observe, and offer help as needed.

There were no other questions, and students got to work. Near the end of the period, all but two had finished what I had assigned. I asked those two to finish their work as homework. I called the class back to attention and told them that tomorrow we would be talking more about how algebra can be related to the border problem.

"Oooh, that's going to be hard," Sinead said.

"How many of you think algebra is going to be hard to learn?" I asked. Sinead and Halbert raised their hands.

"I don't think it's going to be hard," Roberto said, "but I don't think it's going to be easy." There was general agreement with Roberto's feelings from the class.

"We'll see tomorrow," I said. I felt they were anxious but also interested and curious.

Review students' charts.

To prepare for the next day's discussion, I reviewed the charts that students had filled in and read what they wrote about the patterns they noticed.

Discuss the charts and the pattern you selected.

I began the fourth day's lesson by discussing the charts on which students had recorded the number of squares in the borders of grids of different sizes. They all had noticed that the number of squares in the borders increased by 4 as the number of squares on the edges increased by 1.

Number of squares on edge	Number of squares on border
3	8
4	12
5	16
6	20
7	24
8	28
9	32
10	36

"Why do you think this is so?" I asked.

"Because squares have four sides?" Krystal said. The upturn when she talked was an indication that she wasn't sure of her idea. But several of the others nodded in agreement.

"No, because they have four corners," Isaac said. More nodded or murmured their agreement with Isaac's thought.

"I think I know why," Zack said. Zack was respected by the others for his understanding of math and he had the attention of the class. "It's kind of like what Krystal said," he continued. "When the edge of the squares increases by one, the border increases by four because one square is added to each side."

"That's it," Isaac said.

"I don't get it," Rachel said.

"Look," Isaac said, "every time a square is bigger by one, you have to make each side bigger by one, so that's like adding four."

"Does anyone have another way to explain that to Rachel?" I asked.

"I can," Jesse said. "Adding one to each side is adding four altogether, and those four are on the border, so the border gets bigger by four."

"Is there another way to say that?" I probed. There were no other volunteers. Rachel and the others seemed satisfied.

I was pleased that Zack offered his idea. I much prefer it when ideas such as these come from the students instead of from me. Students always seem to be more curious about and receptive to their classmates' ideas than to mine. My ideas are taken more as pronouncements, laden with the authority of my position. (If Zack hadn't offered his idea, however, I would have offered an explanation. Then I would have asked for others to explain my idea in their own words.)

Ask, "How would you explain how to figure out the number of squares in the border of a grid if you didn't know its size?" Write a volunteer's explanation verbatim on the board. Ask, "Do you think this method will work for all grids?"

At this point, I moved ahead in my lesson plan. I said, "Suppose I told you that I had a grid in my pocket and that I wanted to figure out the number of squares in its border. Who could explain how to do it?"

About a third of the students raised their hands. Before calling on anyone, I asked them to turn and talk with their partner first. When I again asked who could explain, more hands were raised. I called on Jung.

"Go slowly, Jung," I said, "because I'm going to write down what you would do as you explain it."

"First count the squares on an edge," he said. I stopped him so I could write this on the board. Then I asked him to continue.

"Multiply that number times four," he continued, "and then subtract four." I wrote that on the board as well.

Isaac explains to Rachel why the number of squares in the border increases by 4 as the number of squares on the edges increases by 1.

"Anything else?" I asked.

"No," Jung said, "that tells you the answer." I wrote that as well. I had now written:

First count the squares on an edge. Multiply that number by 4 and then subtract 4. That tells how many squares are in the border.

"Do you agree that this method works for any size grid?" I asked. Students indicated their agreement.

Share with the class that the method on the board is a generalization because it works for all grids.

"Jung's explanation is an example of a generalization," I said. "It's a method that works for all sizes of grids, not just the ones we've explored. Algebra is a way of describing a generalized method. Let me show you how I could translate Jung's method to algebra."

Marek blurted out, "That wasn't Jung's method. That was my idea." Marek's need for attention was characteristic of him.

"Yes," I acknowledged, "Jung described the method you first reported in a more generalized way." That seemed to satisfy Marek for the moment.

Show the class how to represent the method algebraically. Explain why you use letters as well as numbers.

"Because I don't know yet how many squares are on the edge," I continued, "I'm going to use a letter instead of a number. I'll use e to represent the number of squares on the edge. What shall I use to represent the number of squares in the border?"

"B," several students called out together.

"So, I'll write Jung's generalization like this," I said, and wrote on the board:

$$e \times 4 - 4 = b$$

"This says that if I multiply the number of squares on the edge, e, by four and then subtract four, I'll know how many squares are in the border. That's an algebraic way to express the method."

There were positive reactions to this. "That's cool." "I get it." "That's not so hard." "Yeah, that's OK."

Introduce alternative ways to write the algebraic representation.

"Here are two other ways I could write the generalization," I said, writing them on the board. Now there were three formulas:

$$e \times 4 - 4 = b$$
$$4e - 4 = b$$
$$(e \times 4) - 4 = b$$

Then I explained. I pointed to the $4e$ in the second equation and said, "When a number and letter are written together like this, it's understood that it means to multiply."

"Could you write $e4$ instead?" Juliette asked.

"No," I answered, "the number is written first."

I next pointed to the parentheses and said, "Although it's not necessary, you could use parentheses as punctuation when you write the times sign." I continued, "Each of these three formulas describes how to apply Marek's original method to a grid of any size. This formula doesn't describe the other methods. Tami, for example, didn't multiply the edge by four in her method. She removed one corner from each edge first before multiplying."

"How do you write that in algebra?" Hasani asked.

"I know," Jesse said. "You have to use e minus one instead of e." I wrote "$e - 1$" on the board.

"Can you explain why that makes sense to you?" I asked.

"Because you take one away from each edge, and that's e minus one," Jesse said.

"I get it," Hasani said.

Have students, in pairs, write formulas for the remaining five methods that were posted on Day 2.

I continued with directions. "Working with your partner, try to write formulas for the other five methods," I said. "Though you'll work together, each of you should record in your own notebook. If you get stuck, try writing an explanation in words first and then translate it to a formula."

Left board:
① $4e - 4 = b$
② $e + e - 1 + e - 1 + e - 2 = b$
③ $4(e - 1) = b$
④ $e\ e(e - 2) \times 2 = b$
⑤ $2e + e - 2 \times 2 = b$
⑥ $e - 2 \times 4 + 4 = b$

Right board:
Border problem in Algebra
1. $(e \times 4) - 4 = b$
2. $e + e - 1 + e - 1 + e - 2 = b$
3. $(e - 1) \times 4 = b$
4. $(e \times e) - (e - 2)^2 = b$
5. $e \times 2 + e - 2 + e - 2 = b$
6. $e - 2 + e - 2 + e - 2 + e - 2 + 4 = b$

Working in pairs, students wrote formulas to describe each of the methods.

The students were willing to try this assignment. Their discussions were animated. Most found some way to write a formula for each method. The method that gave most of the students difficulty was Zack's method of removing the middle and leaving just the border.

I collected their notebooks at the end of class to see what they had accomplished.

DAY 5 PREPARATION

Read students' written work.

When I looked at their work, I found a wide variety in what they had written. Some formulas were correct and others were incorrect. As with any lesson, I now had a decision to make about what to do. It made no sense to belabor the work for those who understood. And it didn't make sense to belabor the work for those who did not yet understand. My goal for this instruction was to give students a beginning experience with algebra that I could build on over time. Although I would have liked each student to be able to write formulas easily and correctly, for the methods we had been studying, this wasn't the case. (It rarely is in a class.)

Prepare a list of the different formulas that students wrote for one particular method, such as adding the top and bottom edges and then the sides, each two less than the top and bottom.

What I decided to do the next day was to focus on some of the formulas that students wrote, and then have students write about their experiences with the lesson.

DAY 5

On the board, write the list of formulas you had prepared the night before.

I began class by writing on the board five different formulas that students had written for method Number 5—adding the top and bottom edges and then the sides, each two less than the top and bottom.

$$e + e + e - 2 + e - 2 = b$$
$$e \times 2 + e - 2 + e - 2 = b$$
$$2e + (e - 2) \times 2 = b$$
$$e + e + (e - 2) + (e - 2) = b$$
$$e \times 2 + e - 2 \times 2 = b$$

Ask students to identify what's the same and different about each of the formulas.

"What's the same and what's different about each of these algebraic formulas?" I asked.

"They all explain Chris's method," Dante said.

"Some use times and some don't," Isaac said.

"Some have parentheses, and some don't," Jaden said.

"What do the parentheses do?" I asked.

"They make it clearer," Juliette said.

"It looks neater," Jesse added.

"More than that," I said, "parentheses are sometimes necessary." I pointed out to students that in the last formula I had written on the board, it wasn't clear that I was to multiply the quantity of *e* minus 2 by 2. I added parentheses. Then I asked them what else they noticed about the formulas.

"They all work," Zack said.

"With the parentheses added to the last formula, I agree with you," I said. "However, all the formulas you wrote don't work."

Have students, in small groups, check if all the formulas they had written work.

I continued explaining, "I'm going to give you a chance to take another look at what you've done, this time with other students so you can get different points of view. I'm going to organize you into groups of three or four instead of partners so you have more formulas to compare."

I did this and had the groups work for about ten minutes.

Circulate, observe, and offer help as needed.

During this time, I talked with the groups that asked for help. There was much sharing of ideas and much erasing in notebooks.

Have students write a lesson log.

When I interrupted students, I asked them to write a lesson log about this experience. I asked students to describe what had happened during the lesson and what they had learned so that it would be possible for someone who hadn't been present to have a sense of what occurred. I asked that they include as many details and specific examples as possible. I also required that their logs be about one page in length. For writing logs like this, I give students a form to use. It helps to write this on the board as a guideline for them, even when they've previously written lesson logs:

> Date of lesson:
> General title: (Describing the lesson)
> Description: (What went on)
> Math content: (What you learned about)

> "I asked students to describe what had happened during the lesson and what they had learned so that it would be possible for someone who hadn't been present to have a sense of what occurred."

Circulate, observe, and offer help as needed.

This was students' third experience writing a lesson log, and their approach to writing was more purposeful than in either of their earlier attempts. I circulated as students wrote. When someone asked me if what he or she had written was OK or enough, I had a stock answer. "That's a good beginning," I'd say and I'd add, "Include more examples," or "Explain more about what you learned," or "Write more about the mathematics."

As with all their writing, I gained insights into their thinking. Their comments revealed their perceptions and understanding.

Juliette

We learned about the beginning of algerbra and how to take a normal problem and change it to an algerbra equation.

Chris

I learned about basic Algebra. How to make equastions and how to seperate algebraic promblems. I at first had a hard time figuring out what e &b ment but I figured out what they ment at the end. For example, e ment the question and b ment the answer.

Hasani

Algebra is not easy but its not as hard as people say it is if you put your mind in.

Krystal

I think algebra is finding new ways to write things and solve things, shortening things and extending things. I also think it helps you use your mind in difficult situations.

Jesse

Algebra is a way of generalizing mathematics. You substitute letters for numbers. When we did it we used E for Edge and B for Border. This activity was just right because we had small groups.

Dante

We learned about different ways to solve problems and there is no best way although one may fit you better than another. Some of us learned something about algebra.

Marek

Algebra is the way to write how to figure out the problems. There are many ways to write algebra. Algebra is a way of adding, subtracting, dividing and multiplying letters to mean something with numbers.

Alesia

I think algebra is letters that discribe numbers.

Jung

I think algebra is another way to find the answer to a math problem.

MATH LESSON LOG

Date: Oct. 13, 14, 17, 18, 19
The Border problem

Description: First Mrs. Burns had us try to figure out all the different ways to find the border of a square that has 10 on each side. First thing that popped into everybody's head was 40 but you have to eliminate the corners which we already counted. The way I found the easiest was to count the 2 horizontal sides which are ten (with corners) and then count the two vertical sides which is 8 which you multiply by 2 and add to the 2 tens which add up to 20.

The next day we worked on improving the way that Mrs. Burns had written problems on a sheet of paper so they were easy to understand. Next we wrote all 6 of the ways to figure the border out into algebraic equations for algebra. Zach's was the hardest to figure out. His was to multiply the two edges (10x10, exe) and then that gives you the area of the whole square and then he took the area and subtracted just the middle which was everything but the border which turned out the equation was exe - exe-2 =b. This unit helped us understand equations better. It helped us not just do the problem, but understand how we did the problem.

Math Content: We learned about the beginning of algebra and how to take a normal problem and change it to an algebra equation.

Math Lesson Log
October, 14, 17, 18, 19
ALGEBRA=
THE BORDER PROBLEM

Description: We try to find out the border of a square by counting the edge, add the four edges, and then subtract the four corners. Here is an example. We cut it down, shortened it into a different form.

$$(e \times 4) - 4 = b$$
$$4e - 4 = b$$

Math Content: I think algebra is: finding new ways to write things and solve things, shortening things and extending things. I also think it helps you use your mind in difficult situations.

Math Lesson Log.
Date: October 13, 14, 17, 18, 19;
Title: Algebra;
The Border Problem.

Description: We have been working on the border problem for the past five days. We had a square and we tried to figure out the area of the square, when we found it out it was 36. Then we had to figure out how someone got that.

Math Content: I learned about basic Algebra. How to make equations and how to spents algebra problems. I at first had a hard time figuring out what e&b ment but I figured out what they ment at the end. For example e ment the question and b ment the answer.

$$(e-1) + (e-1) + (e-1) + (e-1) = B$$

This equations means, edge-1 + edge-1 plus edge-1 plus edge-1, then B would be the final answer.

Logs help students reflect on their learning experiences and also help teachers assess students' understandings and misconceptions.

🧠 FINAL THOUGHTS

Looking at students' notebooks later, I noticed that although there was improvement in their formulas, there were still errors. Clearly, not all students had "mastered" generalizing arithmetic procedures to algebraic representations. This did not concern me.

I've come to understand that partially grasped ideas and periods of confusion are natural to the learning process. I've come to understand that students' mathematical knowledge is developed, elaborated, deepened, and made more complete over time. I've come to understand that I shouldn't expect all students to get the same thing out of the same experience.

I feel that students benefited from the lesson in different ways. Zack, Jesse, Juliette, Krystal, and others gained insights and facility with algebraic notation. Sinead, Quinn, and Rachel learned that there was more than one way to solve a problem. Jung and Halbert learned more about the benefits of working collaboratively with others. Tri gained experience with expressing his ideas about math in English. Hasani learned he could do something he thought was hard.

And I learned more about each of my students, which helped me better meet their needs as the year progressed.

> "I've come to understand that partially grasped ideas and periods of confusion are natural to the learning process."

3
The Consecutive Sums Problem

Problem Solving to Support Collaborating and Making Conjectures

Taught in Grades 3–6

Helping students develop the ability to apply their mathematics knowledge to solving problems is the over-arching goal of elementary math instruction. Students need to be challenged to use their math understanding and skills in new situations in which they make and test predictions, analyze patterns and relationships, organize information, and formulate generalizations.

Another important goal of elementary math instruction is to help students develop a positive attitude toward mathematics. A positive attitude is more than finding math experiences enjoyable. It includes feeling a sense of power and satisfaction at having successfully tackled a mathematical problem and feeling that the problem was mathematically interesting. Positive experiences leave students open and eager for more math.

This exploration serves both of these goals and is one of my longtime favorites.

OVERVIEW

Here I describe what occurred when I taught the lesson, *The Consecutive Sums Problem*, to fifth graders. On many other occasions I've used the lesson with classes from grade 3 through middle school. It's one of those "low floor, high ceiling" problems because access is easy (students have to find addends for sums up to 35) but the mathematical payoff is substantial (students are engaged in looking for patterns and making conjectures).

MATERIALS

- paper, 12 inches by 18 inches, 1 sheet for each group
- playing cards, 1 deck (optional)
- group labels made from folded index cards labeled *ace, 2, 3, 4, 5, 6*, 1 for each table (optional)

THE LESSON

Organize students into small groups.

Twenty-one of the twenty-four fifth-grade students were in class the day I taught this lesson. I had an hour and a half to work with them. I organized the students into small groups to work on the problem, which was the first experience students in this class would have working in this way. The benefit of working in a group quickly became evident to students as they explored what's required for this problem.

I began by saying, "I'm going to give you a mathematical problem to work on. Before the end of the class, I'll be interested in hearing what you enjoyed about solving the problem, what you didn't enjoy, what you learned, and any other reactions you had. Your ideas can help me as I prepare to teach other classes."

I continued, "Before I tell you about the problem, I'd like to explain how you'll be organized. I'm going to put you into small groups to work so that you won't have to solve the problem alone." I added, "We'll have to rearrange your desks." (The students' desks were in rows.)

I decided to put the twenty-one students into six groups—three groups with four students in each and three groups with three students in each. I wanted to group students randomly and used playing cards to do so. I took all four aces, 2s, and 3s, along with three of the 4s, 5s, and 6s from a deck and shuffled them.

I explained all this to the students and told them that we would first rearrange their desks, and then I'd assign seats. "For this lesson you may not be sitting at your regular desk," I told them and asked, "Will this be a problem for anyone?" No one responded, so I continued.

I directed students to move their desks into the six groups, and then I numbered each group—ace, 2, 3, 4, 5, 6. I asked students to come up in an orderly line so each could choose a card from me to find where to sit. "You'll need something to write with," I added, "so please bring that with you when you come up to pick a card."

Introduce consecutive numbers, giving examples and counterexamples.

Getting students seated in their groups took a little more than five minutes. When they were settled, I wrote on the board *Consecutive Numbers*. "Do you know what consecutive numbers are?" I asked. Several hands went up. I chose Nelson to answer. "They go in a row," he offered, and others nodded.

"Are 23, 24, and 25 consecutive numbers?" I asked, writing these numbers on the board. In response I got nods. "What about 59, 60, 61?" I asked and wrote those numbers on the board. More nods. I was doing this to focus them on me as much as to check their understanding. I continued in this same way. "How about 42, 43, 46?" Heads shake. "How about 14, 16, 18?" This caused some head nods along with shakes.

Lisl explained, "They aren't consecutive because they skip numbers."

Playing cards are useful for organizing students into groups of four.

Swaraj added, "You could say they are consecutive even numbers."

I agreed with both of them and shared that in this problem, we would be dealing only with consecutive numbers that go up by ones.

Pose a part of the problem.

I posed a part of the problem students would be asked to solve. I wrote 9 on the board and asked, "How can you write the number nine as the sum of consecutive addends?"

I gave the class a few moments to think even though several hands immediately shot up. Then I called on Valeria. "You can do four plus five," she said, and I wrote *4 + 5* on the board.

"Can anyone think of another way to write nine as the sum of consecutive addends?" I asked. This time I called on Seth. "I did eight and one," he said and quickly corrected himself by adding, "Wait, that won't work—they're not consecutive."

I had written *8 + 1* on the board when Seth offered it and now, before erasing it, I asked the class, "Do you agree with Seth that these addends aren't consecutive?" I asked this question for two reasons. One was to support my goal that they listen to each other's ideas, and the other was to reinforce the terminology of "addends" and "consecutive." There was general agreement.

I called on Maria. "Five plus four," she said. Students nodded. "I agree," I said, "but for our investigation today, if the addends aren't different, but are only in a different order, it doesn't count as another way."

After a few more moments, Akiko raised her hand and blurted out at the same time, "Two plus three plus four." I wrote *2 + 3 + 4* on the board, and the class murmured agreement.

"Any other ways?" I asked again. After some silence, I moved on with the lesson. I didn't confirm that these were the only two ways to represent nine as the sum of consecutive addends, but said, "You'll have a chance to think more about the number nine when you're working on the problem."

Present the task: *With your group, find all the ways to write the numbers from 1 to 35 as the sum of consecutive addends.*

I next gave the class directions, "What you're to do in your groups is to investigate all the numbers from one to thirty-five and find all the ways you can to represent each as the sum of consecutive addends."

I also gave some guidelines. "First of all, I'll give each group one sheet of paper on which I'd like you to record. How you organize the paper and who does the recording are decisions your group needs to make. Be sure to write your group numbers and all of your names at the top of your paper."

Offer hints about looking for patterns.

After outlining the logistical directions, I said, "Next, here's a mathematical warning: It's not possible to represent some of the numbers as the sum of consecutive addends. There's a pattern to those impossible numbers, so when you figure out the pattern, you can use it to predict all the numbers that are impossible." There was a buzz in the class as students thought about some numbers not being possible. I suspected that some students didn't have experience with problems that didn't have answers.

I continued, "Some of the numbers can be written only one way, and there's a pattern to those numbers as well. There will be other patterns you may notice as you work. I'll be asking you about them later."

I then gave another logistical direction. I said, "As you work, one rule that I'll follow is that I will give help only when everyone in your group has the same question and you've all raised a hand, so you'll need to discuss all that you're doing. Remember, you are to find all the possible ways to write each of the numbers as the sum of consecutive addends."

Ask if there are any questions.

> "I know that not all students will be clear about what is expected of them. Having them in groups helps enormously; students will pool their knowledge and clarify the task together."

Before I asked them to begin work, I asked, "What questions do you have?" I had given the class a great deal of information and realized that it was important for them to have the chance to ask any questions they might have. In that way, some of the directions will be clarified and others will be restated in different ways. Still, I know that not all students will be clear about what is expected of them. Having them in groups helps enormously in this situation because the students will pool their knowledge and clarify the task together.

Several students had questions. "You mean we can write our answers any way we want?" "How high do we need to go?" "Can we use scratch paper?" "How do we decide who does the writing?" "What if we don't find all the ways?" I answered all of these questions.

Marcie then asked, "Do we use zero?"

I didn't give a direct answer but instead responded, "It's up to your group to decide whether you want to include zero. You'll need to investigate to see if zero changes the patterns you notice." (When I teach this to third graders, I've found it useful to avoid confusion by simplifying the task and telling them not to use zero, but to use only the counting numbers—1, 2, 3, and so on.)

There were no further questions. I asked students to begin work on the problem.

Circulate, observe, and offer help as needed.

As I circulated, I noticed that groups got started differently. Several were engaged in discussion, heads together, spending time deciding how to organize before they started looking for consecutive addends.

One of those groups began by focusing on the recording. Karine suggested, "Let's number the paper from one to thirty-five." "I'll do it," Marcie said. "That's good," Seth commented, "my writing isn't too good." "But I don't want to just write," Marcie continued, "I want to find some answers too." "You can," Karine said, "because we can save the ones we find on scratch paper, and then every so often you can put them on the chart." And so they went to work, Marcie organizing the chart, Seth and Karine looking for consecutive sums in no particular order.

Marcie organizes the chart while Seth and Karine look for sums.

Another group wasn't at all concerned with the chart, but focused on organizing who was going to look for what. Jonathan made the initial suggestion, "Let's divide up the numbers so we're each looking for something else." The group accepted that suggestion, and they decided that with thirty-five numbers, they would each have eight, but there were three extras. "The person with the smaller numbers should have more," Mark said, thinking that the greater numbers would be harder or more work. They agreed that Lisl would do one to ten, Akiko would do eleven to nineteen, Mark would do twenty to twenty-seven, and Jonathan twenty-eight to thirty-five.

Other groups did not give this initial time to organizing. One group of three did not talk to each other at all. Instead, each student went to work independently, looking for sums on separate sheets of paper. I watched them for a while and finally asked them how they were organizing their effort. They looked up, seeming almost surprised at being interrupted. "You're each working hard, it seems," I commented, "but I noticed that your group chart is empty. How do you plan to collaborate on that?" They looked at each other for a few moments. Finally, Emilio said, "When we've each done all we can, we could compare." Swaraj nodded. "Not yet, though," Jessica said, adding that she needed more time.

"It seems you're comfortable working this way," I said, "but pay attention to the time so that you'll have your chart done before the end of the class." They nodded and immediately fell back to working individually.

Another group decided to work together, searching for consecutive addends for numbers sequentially. Suejin was recording. They called me over fairly soon after they had started. They had gotten to the number seven, having found solutions only for the odd numbers. Their chart looked like this:

$$1 = 0 + 1$$
$$2 = \text{impossible}$$
$$3 = 1 + 2$$
$$4 = \text{impossible}$$
$$5 = 2 + 3$$
$$6 = \text{impossible}$$
$$7 = 3 + 4$$

"See," Femi said, "we've already figured out the pattern. All the even numbers are impossible." Kathy, Suejin, and Doug nodded in agreement. It's not unusual for students to come to generalizations quickly and invest totally in them before looking more deeply. When such thinking is incorrect, my way of handling the situation is to provide a contradiction that allows them to see that they need to look further. "Do you agree that the numbers 1, 2, and 3 are consecutive?" I asked. They nodded. "How much is 1 plus 2 plus 3?" I asked. "Oh, no," Suejin groaned, "that shoots our theory," and she began to erase "impossible" after the 6. "What's the pattern?" Femi asked, feeling discouraged. I responded, "I'd rather not tell you that. I want to give you the chance to find out for yourselves." I left when they went back to work.

Several times individual students came up to me with a question. In each of those instances, I would accompany the students back to the group and have them state their question again for the group. In all but one of those instances, the group answered the question without my intervening. I reminded students to check with each other before seeking my help.

One group had a question that had them all stumped. They had found consecutive addends for many of the numbers and had decided that 2, 4, 8, 16, and 32 were impossible. But they were disturbed because they couldn't find consecutive addends for some of the sums. They were frustrated. I spent a bit of time getting them to focus on other patterns that might be helpful. I told them what David had shared with me (he was not in this group): he had noticed a pattern of the sums made with three addends. Starting with $0 + 1 + 2$, then $1 + 2 + 3$, then $2 + 3 + 4$, and so on, the sums went up by 3s—3, 6, 9, 12, 15, 18, and so on. They saw immediately that the pattern could be useful, and although it added another alternative in a few places, it didn't help with all of the holes on their chart. "What about looking at four addends and seeing if there is a pattern there," I suggested. They got started, and Kathy verbalized what they were finding, "First $0 + 1 + 2 + 3 = 6$, then comes $1 + 2 + 3 + 4$, and that's 10, and $2 + 3 + 4 + 5$ is [after a pause] 14." Jason got very excited, "Look, it goes up by 4s, and that takes care of 22. We found one for 22." I left them to continue working.

During this time, two groups came to me to announce that they were done, asking what they should do next. Each group had found one way to write each number and more than one way to write only some of them. I wanted them to search further and, for both groups, I pointed out another direction. I said, "I notice that you don't have any with four addends. Let's try one together. How much is $1 + 2 + 3 + 4$?" After a typical fifth-grade groan, they added it to their chart and were willing to keep looking for others.

Ask groups to report how they approached the problem.

I asked students to stop work so that I would have twenty minutes left for a class discussion. They weren't all finished, and I realized this, but I decided that I wanted to spend some time in a class discussion, then give them the chance in their next math period to continue and extend their investigation.

First, I asked students to report how they had gotten organized. I wanted students to hear the different ways groups approached the problem, thereby reinforcing the idea that different ways are acceptable. I wanted to stress that it's important to choose a procedure that's useful for the task. Some groups reported that they had changed their methods while they were working. The group that approached the numbers in sequence realized that their procedure wasn't very efficient since they were finding solutions for other numbers and didn't want to "waste" them. They then extended their chart so they would be able to add whatever they found. The group that had divided up the numbers so carefully found that they began to help each other with their numbers and wound up collaborating together more than they had planned.

I asked them to report how they had decided who would do the recording. A ripple of laughter went through the class. In most groups it was just one person who grabbed the chart or one who was given the job. Generally, very little discussion had contributed to making this decision. One girl complained that she would have liked to have written. I said that she needed to tell her group and pointed out that group members need to listen and to be sensitive to each other.

Discuss the pattern of the "impossible" numbers.

I then focused on the patterns that students were noticing. "How many groups figured out the pattern of the impossible numbers?" I asked. All hands went up.

"I'd like to hear how you would describe the pattern," I continued. Several raised their hands, and I had each of them give a description, each time asking if someone could explain it in a different way. "They double." "They are all times two." "See, you take one and then you add it to itself and you get the next one and you keep doing that." "They go by twos."

I was interested in seeing if I could get them to express the generalization more clearly and told them I'd like to write a statement on the board that describes the pattern. "What should I write?" I asked. This was very difficult for them. Although they knew what they meant, they had difficulty expressing themselves. We worked as a class on the statement for a bit. I didn't push it very far, sensing their difficulty and realizing that they needed a good deal more experience expressing their ideas.

Discuss other patterns that groups found.

I then shifted the discussion and asked the class, "What other patterns did you find?" Suejin responded that all the odd numbers could be written as the sum of two consecutive numbers, adding, "Like 1 + 2 = 3 and 2 + 3 = 5." Another group volunteered a pattern for adding three numbers like 0 +1 + 2, 1 + 2 + 3, and 2 + 3 + 4. "The numbers go up by 3, like 3, 6, 9," Seth explained. Doug offered, "The multiples of 3 are the sum of three consecutive addends." I continued in this way, asking students to describe what they noticed and asking others to explain the same pattern in different ways.

Ask for students' reactions to the lesson.

As a final question, I asked for reactions to the lesson, "What did you enjoy and not enjoy? How did you feel about working with a group? What was difficult about the problem and what was easy? What did you learn?" When I ask questions like these, I avoid asking questions that students can answer merely with "yes" or "no," but rather ask questions that prompt them to express their ideas. The students' reactions were positive. Suejin's comment was a tribute to the potential of cooperative groups, "Everyone could do something, even if you're not that good in math, and that was good."

> **"**I avoid asking questions that students can answer merely with 'yes' or 'no,' but rather ask questions that prompt them to express their ideas.**"**

I told students what I had observed, pointing out the strengths I had noticed and those areas in which I thought they needed more work. I told them that I felt they worked well together, but they seemed more interested in getting the answers and getting done instead of searching for the patterns. I told them that I thought they would get better at looking for mathematical patterns when they had more experience. I told them that I felt they were doing interesting thinking, but that it seemed hard for them to explain their thinking, and that we'd work more on the explanations in the future. And I told them I had enjoyed their enthusiasm and how well they stuck to the task.

The lesson was a good beginning.

CONVERSATIONS WITH MARILYN

What Makes a Good Math Problem?

THE IMPORTANCE OF GOOD PROBLEMS WHEN TEACHING AND LEARNING MATH

www.mathsolutions.com/welcometomathclass3

> "There are so many different kinds of problems.
> Sometimes there are problems for which there's more
> than one right answer. This was mindblowing for me—
> that a problem might have more than one answer—
> because growing up there was only right or wrong."

> "Teachers are under such pressure today. Kids are being tested,
> and teachers feel they have to get through and cover
> all the curriculum. Teachers say, 'There's so much to cover.'
> I respond, 'No, my job is not to cover, my job is to uncover.'
> I say it over and over again: we don't want to cover it,
> we want each child to uncover it for him- or herself."

Overview

In this conversation with my longtime Math Solutions colleague Patty Clark, we discuss what makes a good math problem and why good math problems are worth the valuable classroom instructional time we have.

Making Connections

For me, the essential ingredients for "good math problems" include that they engage students' curiosity, provide them with opportunities to think and reason, are accessible, and connect to important math concepts. Of course, not every problem will inspire every student, but I think it's important for students to have regular problem-solving experiences where there isn't always one right answer. It's another aspect of supporting the development of students' understanding and skills in math class, as you'll read about in several of the lessons in *Welcome to Math Class—The Consecutive Sums Problem, Billy and the Pencils, Raisin Math, Sharing Cookies*, and more.

4
Counting Pockets, Beans, and More
Developing Understanding of Place Value

Taught in Grades K–2

It's essential for students to learn about the place-value structure of our number system. To develop understanding of place value, students benefit from experiences in which they organize objects into groups of ten to count how many there are. Presented here are two separate but related lessons plus several additional suggestions, all of which use grouping by tens as an organizational tool for making sense of numbers.

OVERVIEW

In the first lesson, first graders investigated the numbers of pockets there were altogether in the clothing they wore to class, repeating the activity each day for a week. In the second lesson, second graders estimated how many beans filled a small clear plastic container, counted to check their predictions, and then counted again by grouping the beans into groups of ten. Bonnie Tank taught the lessons described, both of which are appropriate for helping students in kindergarten, first grade, and second grade learn about the usefulness of the place-value structure of our number system. Recommendations at the end suggest additional ideas. These lessons are also useful for preparing students for the independent work on the menu described in *A Place-Value Menu* (page 115).

MATERIALS

- interlocking cubes, a large supply
- small clear containers with lids that hold between 30 and 40 lima beans (e.g., empty spice jars or snack containers), 1 for each group
- lima beans, enough to fill the small clear container
- small shallow paper cups, a few for each group
- Tens and Ones Mat (**REPRODUCIBLE C***), 1 sheet for each group or construction paper, approximately 9 inches by 12 inches, folded in half on the short side, the left half labeled *Tens* and the right half *Ones*, 1 sheet for each group

ACTIVITY 1   How Many Pockets?

Ask, "How many pockets do you think we're wearing today altogether?"

"How many pockets do you think we're wearing today altogether?" I asked the class on Monday morning. These were first graders. I was interested in providing students with an opportunity to estimate and compare numbers that would also contribute to building their understanding of place value. To do so, I planned this experience to build their number understanding and present how we use groups of ten to make sense of greater numbers.

I gave students a few minutes to consider the question of how many pockets they had. Some started to count the pockets on their own clothes. Giancarlo was especially excited. "I've got ten just on my jeans!" he shouted. He was wearing jeans with pockets all over them.

Lamia went to her cubby to retrieve her jacket. "I'll have more pockets this way," she announced to the others at her table. Other students saw this as a good idea and began to get their jackets. However, I asked that they all leave their jackets in their cubbies. Lamia reluctantly returned hers.

When I asked the students for estimates, responses varied. "Maybe a hundred." "Fifty." "Lots." "I bet there's more than a hundred."

Have students put a cube in each pocket.

I then made a suggestion to the class about how we could find out how many pockets we had altogether. "I'm going to put a supply of interlocking cubes at each table," I said. "Then I want each of you to put one cube in each of your pockets." I demonstrated for the students by placing a cube in each of the six pockets I had—two in my skirt, one in my blouse, and three in my jacket.

"When each of you has put one cube in each pocket," I continued, "I'll come and collect the extra cubes. Then I'll give some more directions."

After I distributed cubes to each table, the students put cubes in their pockets and I collected the remaining cubes. I then gave further directions.

The students put one interlocking cube in each of their pockets.

Direct students to make trains with their cubes and compare their trains with each other.

"Watch what I do with the cubes in my pockets," I said to the students. I removed the six cubes from my pockets, one by one, and snapped them into a train. I had the students count how many I had.

"Each of you should now do the same with the cubes in your pockets," I explained. "Then compare your trains with one another at your table."

The students had made their trains almost before I had completed giving directions. As I circulated, I listened to the language they were using to compare their trains. "I have most." "My train has more than yours." "Mine is tallest." "Yours is the smallest." "Mine has the mostest." "Look, you have five and I have six. Mine's bigger."

Make statements about the students' trains.

I called students back to attention. "I'm going to make some statements," I told them. "Listen carefully to what I say. Then check with the person next to you to see if the statement fits you. If it does, hold your train of cubes up for me to see." For more than half the students in the class, English was not their first language. I used every opportunity I could to connect activities to appropriate language.

"If you have six pockets so you have six cubes in your train, hold it up," I said. Some students immediately showed their trains. I reminded them that they were to check with the person sitting next to them before doing so. Checking with another would help those who needed more language support.

"Hold up your train if you have more than four pockets," I said next. I had the students who held up trains call out how many cubes they had.

"If you have fewer than five pockets, hold up your train," I said next. I had to say this in another way for some of the students. "That means your train has only four or three or two cubes."

> "For more than half the students in the class, English was not their first language. I used every opportunity I could to connect activities to appropriate language."

I continued with other statements. "If you have more than two cubes, hold up your train." "Hold up your train if someone else at your table has a train that's the same length." "Hold up your train if yours is the shortest at the table." "Who thinks you have the fewest number of pockets in the whole class?" (Renata didn't have any pockets and had felt a little left out. She seemed thrilled to be able to respond to this last question.)

Have each group make trains of ten with their cubes.

I then said, "Now we're going to find out how many pockets we have altogether." I continued, explaining what they were going to do, "To do that, at your table, put together your cubes to make a train of ten cubes. If you have enough, make more trains of ten. Keep the extra cubes separate from the trains you make. When you've done that, I'll ask each group to report how many tens you made and how many extras you have."

Collect and display their trains and the extras.

As groups reported, I had them bring their trains of ten to the front of the room. Then I had the groups, one by one, bring up their extra cubes. I used their extra cubes to make additional trains of ten, counting out loud as I did so and encouraging students to count along with me. "I have four from Hassan's table. Tina's table has three extras. Let's count: four, . . . , five, six, seven. Kailani, bring up your table's extras."

I stacked the trains of ten on a table at the front of the room with the extras left separate next to them.

With the class, count the trains by tens and the extra cubes by ones.

I had students count the six trains by tens with me, moving each train aside as we counted it, "Ten, twenty, thirty, forty, fifty, sixty." Then, as I pointed to each of the extra cubes, we counted on, "Sixty-one, sixty-two, sixty-three, sixty-four, sixty-five, sixty-six, sixty-seven, sixty-eight."

As the students watched, I posted a sheet of chart paper. I said, "So we have sixty-eight pockets in all. I'll record this, and then we'll try it again tomorrow." I wrote on the chart.

How many pockets?	
Monday	6 tens and 8 ones = 68
Tuesday	
Wednesday	
Thursday	
Friday	

Repeat the activity each day for the rest of the week.

We repeated the activity daily throughout the week. Students came wearing more pockets on Tuesday, motivated to increase the Monday count. (Giancarlo wore the same jeans again.) On Tuesday there were 82 pockets. The count rose to 87 on Wednesday and to 95 on Thursday. (Giancarlo was still wearing the same jeans.) The students were hoping for 100 on Friday, but they were disappointed. The Friday count was only 89. Obviously, students had exhausted the pocket potential of their wardrobes by the end of the week. (Giancarlo no longer wore the same jeans. "My mother wouldn't let me," he explained.)

Fill small containers with lima beans and ask students for estimates.

To prepare for this activity with second graders, I filled small, clear containers, which were all the same size, with lima beans. The students sat in groups of six, and I prepared five containers, one for each group. I showed the class one of the containers and said, "Make an estimate of how many beans you think there are in this container."

Record students' estimates and discuss.

Students' estimates ranged from 10 to 28. I listed their estimates on the board as students reported.
　"What was the smallest estimate made?" I asked.
　"Ten," a chorus of students said.
　"What is next smallest?" I asked.
　"Fifteen." "Twelve." "It's twelve."
　I continued in this way, rewriting their estimates into a list on the board from least to greatest, writing each estimate that they gave only once.

10
12
15
17
20
21
25
26
27
28

A note about language: Students aren't all familiar with the word *estimate*, but using it in this context introduces it in a way that helps them learn what it means. In some classes, I've asked students to explain what an estimate is.

Distribute the containers, one to a group, and ask for a group estimate.

I then explained to the class, "I'm going to give each group a container that's filled with beans. All of the containers are the same size, and they're all filled with the same kind of bean. When I give your group a container, don't open it. Look from the outside and, as a group, agree on an estimate of how many beans there are inside. Your group has to agree on just one estimate." I distributed the containers to the groups.

　Within five minutes, all but two groups had agreed on an estimate. One of those remaining two groups was close to coming to a group decision, but the other group was far from the goal and didn't appear to be making progress. I told them they had just one minute more to agree on an estimate.

　Because this was the first estimating experience for the students, I wasn't surprised at the difficulty this group was having agreeing. I planned to take the time and have groups describe the processes they used for coming to consensus. I would use their descriptions to focus the class on different ways that groups can make decisions.

The first group that reported had made an estimate of twenty-eight. "Did you all agree on this number at first?" I asked.

"All of us but Emilio," Lei replied.

"What happened that made you agree, Emilio?" I asked.

"They talked me into it," Emilio answered.

"Did they do something or explain something to convince you?" I probed.

"They just talked me into it," Emilio explained.

Without opening the container, the group has to agree on an estimate of how many beans are inside.

I recorded *28* on the board and asked for another group's estimate.

Reem reported next for her group. "We were stuck on two answers, either forty or fifty," she said. "Then we decided to agree on forty-nine." I wrote *49* on the board.

The third group reported an estimate of thirty-seven. When I asked them how they had come to agreement on that estimate, Daniel confessed, "When you said we only had one more minute, it was easier to agree." I wrote *37*.

The fourth group that reported was the one that was having the most difficulty coming to a consensus. They had narrowed their estimate down to two choices. Bakari reported, "We think it is either twenty-nine or fifty." I wrote both *29* and *50* on the board and went to the last group.

Lei reported that her group's estimate was thirty. "Can you explain how your group agreed on that estimate?" I asked.

The students in the group looked at one another. All were silent. Finally, Shen spoke. "We just did," he said, shrugging. It's not always easy for students to verbalize their processes and this response didn't surprise me. I wrote *30* on the board.

In the meantime, the group that hadn't reached agreement had continued to work, even though they were supposed to be listening to the others report. Miho raised her hand. "We think it's twenty-nine," she said.

"Do you want me to erase the 50?" I asked.

"Yes," Miho responded.

"Is that OK with your whole group?" I asked. The other students in the group responded by nodding or orally giving their assent. I erased the 50.

Reorganize the group estimates sequentially and discuss.

"Let's list your group estimates in order from least to greatest," I said. I had students help and wrote the new list of five numbers next to the original list of ten estimates.

First estimates	Second estimates
10	28
12	29
15	30
17	37
20	49
21	
25	
26	
27	
28	

"What's different about these two lists?" I asked.

"There's less in the new list," Natalia said.

"Why do you think that's so?" I asked.

"Because the second time we could give only one guess for a group," Rebecca answered.

Swaraj raised his hand. "The new estimates are higher," he said.

"Why do you think that is?" I asked.

Swaraj shrugged, but Daniel had a thought. "When we got a closer look," he said, "we could see more." There were no other comments offered.

Instruct each group to organize their beans so they can be counted easily.

"Each group is going to count the beans in the container you have," I told students, "but I want you to do the counting in a special way. Open your container, carefully pour out the beans, and then arrange them in some way so that someone else could quickly count how many there are."

The students did this quickly. Two groups put the beans into piles of five—one group had six piles with one extra bean and the other group had six piles with two extra beans. One group made three groups of ten, with two extra beans. Another group made three neat rows with ten in each and had four extras beans. The group that had had difficulty coming to a consensus was struggling to share their beans so that each of them had the same amount. Each student finally wound up with five beans, and there was one extra bean, which they left in the middle of the table. I recorded the groups' counts on the board: 31, 31, 32, 34, 34.

Swaraj raised his hand. "Too bad no one got thirty-three," he said. His own need for order would have been satisfied if the gap didn't exist in the counts.

I said, "The small clear containers I used were all the same size and I filled them all full." I then asked, "Why do you think groups came up with different numbers when you counted?"

The students had several thoughts about this. "Maybe you didn't shake them down." "The beans aren't all the same size." "You didn't fill them all the same."

I then related their experience with the beans to place value. "When you arranged your beans, some of you made groups of ten and some of you made groups of five. Making the same size groups is helpful for keeping track of large numbers of things. The number system we use is based on grouping by tens."

Have groups reorganize their beans using small paper cups and a mat labeled *Tens* and *Ones*.

I then gave several small paper cups to each group, the kind used for medicine in hospitals. I also gave each group a 9-by-12-inch sheet of construction paper folded in half on the short side, with the left half labeled *Tens* and the right half labeled *Ones* (you may also use **REPRODUCIBLE C** for this).

I gave the directions to the class. "Using the beans from your container, fill as many cups as you can, putting exactly ten beans in each cup. Place the full cups on the left side, the Tens side, and place any extra beans on the right side, the Ones side."

The students did this quickly.

Sketch each group's results on the board. Have students read their count in two ways.

The groups reported how many tens and how many ones they had. For each, I drew a sketch on the board of the construction paper, labeling the left side *Tens* and the right side *Ones*. I recorded their information. I had the students read what I had recorded from each group in two ways, as three tens and four ones, for example, and also as thirty-four.

Although it might have been valuable for students to have seen how many beans the groups had altogether by combining their tens and ones, and grouping tens into a larger cup to introduce hundreds, I decided that the students had had enough for that day and collected the materials.

FURTHER EXPLORATIONS FOR OTHER DAYS

Ask students to group objects into tens and ones in the context of other activities.

Many opportunities arise in the class for grouping objects into tens and ones, often incidentally in the context of other activities. It's beneficial to take advantage of such opportunities so students come to see our place-value system of organization as a way of making sense of numbers.

For example, to count the books in the class library, a group of second graders put the books into piles of ten each. To find out how many field-trip permission slips had been returned, a committee of students organized them into groups of ten and counted how many groups and extras there were. Students responsible for putting out the cups for juice during snack time lined them up in rows of ten, with an additional row for the extra cups, so we could more easily see how many cups there were.

Ask students to graph their responses, then group into tens.

Graphing experiences are also useful for grouping objects into tens and ones. For example, in preparation for a field trip to the local children's museum, second graders reported whether they had visited the museum before by marking an X on a graph. When counting the Xs, it helped to circle ten of the Xs in the second row to see that there were one ten and seven extras.

Have you visited the children's museum before?
Mark an X.
YES   X X X X X X X
NO   X X X X X X X X X X X X X X X X X

From repeated experiences over time, students' understanding of place value will grow.

5

Cows and Chickens and Other Such Problems

Building Number Sense

Taught in Grades K–2

Problem-solving experiences that are designed to build number sense encourage students to organize and stretch their thinking. Here are instructional suggestions to use with students in kindergarten through grade 2. The descriptions illustrate how the same problem can be used in different grades and how problems can be extended.

OVERVIEW

Bonnie Tank engaged first graders with solving how many feet and tails there were with four cows and three chickens and then adapted the problem for second graders. Bonnie also presented another problem-solving experience to first graders, this time involving wheels on bicycles and tricycles. Leslie Salkeld adapted the problems to use with her kindergarten students.

In these classes, students worked with partners or groups to solve the problems. From discussing problems with classmates and presenting their reasoning processes, students gain valuable language experience. In addition, they have the opportunity to hear and learn from others' approaches to thinking.

MATERIALS

- paper, $8\frac{1}{2}$ inches by 11 inches, 1 sheet for each pair of students
- sticky notes, a large supply
- chart paper, 1 sheet
- 0–99 chart (**REPRODUCIBLE U***)
- counters or small objects for counting, a large supply (optional)

COWS AND CHICKENS An Experience with First Graders

Describe the farmer's problem.

"I'm going to tell you a story," I told the class of first graders to begin the lesson. "Listen carefully, because there's a problem for you to think about in this story."

I presented the situation to the students. "I took a ride in the country last weekend and drove past many farms," I told the class. "At one farm, I noticed a farmer standing near the road, looking up at a hill in the distance. He looked very worried. I stopped my car and got out.

"'Is something wrong?' I asked the farmer.

"'Yes,' he answered, 'I have a problem that I need to solve. I have one field up on that hill there.' He pointed at the hill. 'There are four cows and three chickens in the field. I know that because I put them there. Also, there's a fence around the field. What I'm wondering is how many feet and tails the cows and chickens have altogether. I'm trying to figure that out without climbing up the hill to the field to count.'

"I told the farmer that I knew a class of students who were learning about solving problems, and I thought the class could figure this out. I'm going to give you a chance to solve the farmer's problem."

Write the facts and the question on the board. Review the story.

I wrote some of the information on the board. This gave me a chance to review the story.

> There are 4 cows.
> There are 3 chickens.
> How many feet and tails are there altogether?

Explain how partners are to work with each other to solve the problem.

I explained to students how I wanted them to work. "You won't work alone on this problem," I told students. "You'll each work with a partner. You and your partner will have one sheet of paper for both of you to use together." The students seemed excited about this.

I continued, "Here's what you and your partner are to do. First you need to tell each other what the problem is so that you're sure you both understand it. Then, before starting to write anything on your one sheet of paper, you need to talk about what you will put on the paper and how you will share doing the work."

Tell students to use pictures, numbers, or words, and to record one answer.

I then talked about what it was students should be writing. "What you put on the paper should help you solve the problem. It can be a drawing, numbers, or anything that you think will help you. Also, you can use tiles or counters if you'd like." I paused and asked if they had any questions so far. There were none, so I continued. "You both must agree on one answer—you can't have two answers for the problem."

Give the final instruction: You and your partner will explain to the class how you solved the problem.

"When you think you have an answer, practice explaining to each other what you did so you can share it with the whole class. When you're both pleased with your solution and your explanations, bring your paper up to the front and sit on the rug. If you're waiting for others to come to the rug, use the time to practice your explanations some more."

Have students help you review the instructions.

Because students were seated in groups of four, it was easy for students to pair up with students seated next to them. One child, Melissa, had no partner. Melissa was one of the most capable students in the class. I went to her and told her that I thought she would be able to do the problem alone.

"I'll listen to your explanations," I told her.

"Good," Melissa declared, "I know you'll understand what I'm saying."

I reviewed the directions once more before students began solving the problem, asking students to explain what they were to do first, and next, and so on. The students then went to work.

Circulate, observe, and offer help as needed.

Just as instructed, students began by talking about the problem. As I circulated, I marveled at how most of the students plunged into explaining the problem and talking about how they would share the work in a variety of ways. "Each cow has four feet and one tail. Right?" "She said there were four cows and three chickens." "We have to find out how many feet." "Yeah, and how many tails." "You draw the cows, and I'll draw the chickens." "Let's each write our names on the paper first." "Oooh, there are lots of feet." "Let's do tails first."

I noticed that Muhran and Lorene seemed to be having difficulty getting started. "How about starting by telling the story to each other?" I suggested to them. They nodded.

"Who would like to tell the story first?" I asked, and I waited. Finally, Lorene said she would.

"OK," I said, "your job, Muhran, is to listen carefully to make sure you agree. Then you take your turn and tell the story to Lorene." I left them as they began.

I had to focus two other pairs of students in the same way. The rest of the students, however, had no trouble getting started. The level of interaction was high. Students were expressing themselves in many different ways and were listening to each other with great intensity. Understanding a problem is the first step toward solving it. Having the opportunity to verbalize that understanding can help this process, and I witnessed the benefits of this as students interacted.

> "Understanding a problem is the first step toward solving it."

As pairs worked, making drawings and writing numbers on their papers, I circulated and observed. Also, I asked questions of some when I noticed they hadn't dealt with all the information in the problem or to focus them on explaining what particular numbers on their papers meant.

Tina and Eduardo were wrestling with the problem of agreeing on a number for their solution. They had spread out crayons in a very orderly way on their table to represent the feet and tails. Each had counted the crayons. And though they could easily describe what each crayon represented and were clearly pleased with themselves, they couldn't agree on one answer. Eduardo thought the answer was 30, while Tina thought it was 29.

"What could you do to be sure?" I asked them.

"I'll count the crayons again," Tina offered. This time she counted 28.

After a moment, Eduardo said in a very determined way, "Let's count them again and push them." They did that together in a methodical and orderly way, with Eduardo pushing each crayon over as they counted it. This process convinced them that 29 was the correct answer.

Eduardo and Tina spread out crayons in an orderly way to represent the feet and tails.

Other students also used objects to solve the problem. Others counted on their fingers. Many drew pictures of cows and chickens. Some of the drawings were quite elaborate—cows with udders and chickens with beaks and feathers, many with exaggerated tails. A few of the students attempted to write an addition problem.

Melissa, who was working alone, chose to solve the problem by writing numbers and adding them. She explained her thinking to me. She first figured out the cows' feet by adding 4 + 4 and getting 8, then 8 + 4 for another cow, finally 12 + 4 for the fourth cow. Then she wrote 4 + 16 to get 20, which told her how many feet and tails the cows had in all. Then she started on the chickens. She added 3 to the 20 (for the chickens' tails, she explained) and got 23. Then she added on 6 for the chickens' feet, but she did this last computation incorrectly, adding 6 to 20 instead of to the 23. Her final answer was 26, which was off by 3 (see the student work below). When I questioned her about the error at the end, Melissa was unable, or unwilling, to rethink it. She had had enough.

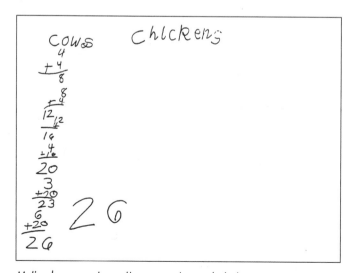

Melissa's paper shows the error she made in her answer.

When most of the pairs had gathered on the rug, I checked with the others. All but Michael were getting ready to come up. Michael, however, was reluctant to join the group, even though his partner, Joanne, had already seated herself on the rug. When I checked with Michael, he said, "But we haven't explained yet. I kept telling Joanne we had to explain, but she just kept on coloring the cows and chickens." I went to the rug and sent Joanne back so they could complete the task (see student work below).

Have students share with the class how they like working with a partner.

When everyone was settled on the rug, I asked the students, "How did you like working with a partner?" Expressing their thoughts was difficult for the students.

"I liked it," Josefa said, but when I asked her if she could tell us what she liked about it, she couldn't explain.

Philip said, "Working with a partner makes it faster."

Zoe said, "You have someone to help you draw."

"I don't like it," Rui said. Then he mumbled, "I like boys better." He was Annie's partner. I asked him if Annie had been helpful as a partner, and Rui begrudgingly nodded yes.

Collect students' answers, then have partners describe to the class how they found them.

I then asked the students to report the answers they had gotten for the farmer's problem. Their solutions ranged from 20 to 34. Five pairs of students had the correct answer, 29.

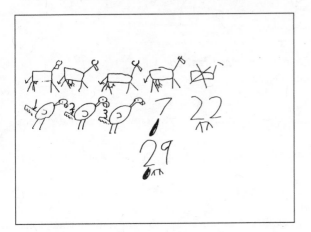

Students solve the problem in different ways—and arrive at different answers.

Then each pair stood up, showed their paper, and explained what they had done. They did this with varying degrees of ease and efficiency. Eduardo and Tina, still excited about their crayon layout, both talked at once and could barely get it all out quickly enough. There was a problem hearing some students who spoke very softly, whose hesitancy somehow made it difficult for them to project. Still, students enjoyed the sharing. Having more of these kinds of opportunities will increase their confidence.

No pair of students asked if their answer was the right one. It seemed that they were all satisfied with their results, even with the discrepancies reported. One student asked if I was taking their papers to the farmer, which seemed important to him.

COWS AND CHICKENS AGAIN An Experience with Second Graders

Increase the number of cows and chickens and have students write their explanations.

Later, when I visited a second-grade class to present the same problem, I made two adjustments to the lesson I had done with first graders. I upped the ante a bit, so students were asked to figure out how many feet and tails there were for five cows and four chickens. Also, after the students had reported their solutions, I had them write explanations of how they solved the problem. They also worked with partners.

The second graders differed from the first graders in that they were slower to get started. Many did not initially draw pictures but came to it when they weren't making headway with just numbers. Several groups of students got counters to use.

In the class discussion, each pair of students showed their papers, and explained what they had done. Students had reached four different solutions—28, 29, 33, and 37. Most had gotten the correct answer of 37, although they had arrived at that answer in different ways.

Second graders solve the problem of how many feet and tails there are for five cows and four chickens.

Thiago and Liam presented their solution. They had written *5, 8, 8, 8, 8* in a vertical row and then added them. "What do those eights stand for?" I asked.

Neither of the boys could explain, so I gave a prompt. "Do they have to do with a cow and chicken together?" I asked.

That jogged Thiago's memory. "Oh, yeah," he said, "for one cow and one chicken, there are eight feet and tails all together. One cow didn't have a partner."

When writing their descriptions, although I hadn't explicitly said they were to write to the farmer, some wrote Dear Farmer letters. Students requested help with spelling words, and I wrote the words they asked about on the board as a reference for others as well. Some of students' written responses follow.

Thiago and Liam

Dear farmer. A cow has 4 legs and 1 tail so that makes 5 each so that makes 25 and a chicken has 2 legs and 1 tail so that makes 37.

[Their writing did not reflect what they had numerically recorded on their paper.]

Otis and David

Dear farmer we are sorry you had this problem. This is how you solve it. 28 + 9 = 37. That is how you solve it. So you can solve it next time. You can draw them and count them.

[They were more compassionate than specific.]

Aaron and Elijah

Add the cows legs up 4 by 4 and 5 tails. Add the chicken legs 2 by 2 and 4 tails.

Rochelle and Corrine

You should count the legs in your mind. Then you should put the numbers on a piece of paper. Then put the tails on the piece of paper and count all of them together.

Asmara and Hugo

Dear farmer Get a paper and draw lines and count them and then add them up.

Miho and Tom

You get paper and you draw 5 cows and 4 chickens. You count the feet and tails. You add the tails and feet and you get your answer. Your farmers friends.

[They signed their paper.]

You get paper and you draw
5 cows and 4 chickens. You
count the feet and tails
You add the tails and feet
and you get your answer.
Your farmers friends
Miho
Tom

Heather and Angie

You can get a piece of paper and add the feet and the tails together and count the cows feet and tails and the chickens feets and tails together. Then every other year you count if they have babies.

[Heather and Angie had a long-range view.]

You can get a piece of paper and
add the feet and the tails together and
count the cows feet and tails
and the chickens feets and tails together.
Then every other year you count
if they have babise.
From Heather, Angie

Reem and Ivory
You should go to the field and count the feet and the legs or you should count the feet and legs all together.
[They offered the farmer two choices!]

TRICYCLES AND BICYLES An Experience with First Graders

Tell the story of the man who invented a special kind of tire.

On another day, I presented a problem to the first graders who had solved the problem about cows and chickens, giving them a second opportunity to work together to solve a problem, to record it in some way, and again to present to their classmates what they had done.

"There was a man who was feeling very proud," I told the students. "He was feeling proud for three reasons. First, he had just invented a special kind of tire that fit any size wheel on bicycles and tricycles. Second, he was proud because he had a factory in which he made these tires."

Otis interrupted the story with a question. "What's a factory?" he asked. I had several students explain what they knew to Otis. "It's a place where they make things." "It's where cars come from." Otis was soon satisfied.

Present the problem. Write the information on the board.

I continued with the story. "A third reason the man was proud was that he had just received his first order. The order said: 'Please send tires for three bicycles and four tricycles.' Now he had a problem to solve," I said. "How many tires should he send?" I wrote on the board, reading aloud:

3 bicycles
4 tricycles
How many tires?

Explain again how partners are to work with each other to solve the problem.

I told students that I would like them to try to solve this problem. I talked with them about how many wheels there were on bicycles and tricycles to make sure they all knew. As with the problem about cows and chickens, I organized them into pairs. I told students that they were to tell each other the story to make sure they both understood it, then work together to find a solution and record it on one sheet of paper, and finally practice explaining their solution so they are ready to share it with the class.

Circulate, observe, and offer help as needed.

All but two pairs of students arrived at the correct solution of eighteen tires. However, pairs of students worked in different ways.

Josefa and Jennifer used counters, organizing them into groups of three for the tricycles and groups of two for the bicycles. They counted them to get their answer. Then they drew pictures of the counters on their paper and wrote *18* to show their solution.

Mohammad and Jessica divided the task. Mohammad worked on the bicycles, carefully drawing them. He got so involved that he drew four of them, but then crossed out one. Jessica drew only the wheels for the tricycles, putting them in four neat boxes. They then counted twelve wheels for the tricycles and six wheels for bicycles. Jessica wrote *6 + 12*. She then called me over and said, "I can't do twelve and six." But then she jumped up and got interlocking cubes, and Mohammad and she worked together, using red cubes for bicycle wheels and white cubes for tricycle wheels.

Tina and Eduardo used a different system of teamwork. Eduardo drew the bicycles and tricycles, and Tina filled in the spokes on the wheels. After they counted the tires together, Tina wrote *18* in the center of the paper.

Liam and Yovan solved the problem by drawing just wheels on their paper.

The two pairs who didn't find the correct answer drew all the needed bicycles and tricycles. Lisa and Derek had gotten so involved coloring their drawings, even including a road with a dotted line down the center, that they seemed to have no energy left for the numbers. Randy and Annie wrote *4 + 3 = 7* as their solution.

COUNTING FEET An Experience with Kindergartners

Assemble the materials.

Leslie Salkeld taught students who needed an extra year to mature and additional experiences to prepare them for first grade. She had read the descriptions of the problems Bonnie presented and wanted to enagage her students in a similar problem-solving lesson. However, she wanted to present a situation that related more closely to her students' direct experiences. For these experiences, Leslie assembled counters, sticky notes, chart paper, and a 0–99 (**REPRODUCIBLE U**) chart to post.

Introduce the problem: *How many feet are under the table?*

Leslie presented the problem to a group of six students she gathered around a table. She did this during reading time, so the others were engaged in reading independently. "How many feet do you think there are under the table right now?" she asked. "Don't peek just yet. Let's see how we could figure that out together."

Elicit students' ideas. Try each one.

Jamal volunteered that there were 12. He explained, "I just counted everyone's eyes because we have the same number of eyes as feet." Other students had different ideas for figuring out the problem, and the group tried each of the suggestions. They went around the group and counted by ones, with each student saying two numbers in succession. They counted by twos together. Each student then took two blocks, and the group counted them altogether. Finally, they looked underneath the table to find out for sure.

Students are figuring out how many feet are under the table.

Have students post the number of people who live in their house on a class graph.

After repeating this experience with other groups over the next few days, Leslie created a class graph with her students during math time. She gave students each a sticky note and asked them to write their name on it. Then she posted a sheet of chart paper and wrote at the top: *How many people live in your house?*

She said, "Figure how many people live in your house. Be sure to count yourself as well. Write the number on your sticky note."

After the students had all completed this, Leslie listed the numbers from 1 to 10 on the chart paper and then called students up, one by one, to post their sticky note next to the number that told how many lived in their house. She talked with the class about what the information on the graph showed—who had the fewest number of people in the house, who had the most, how many children lived in a house that had four people, and so on.

Organize students into groups with the same number living in their house. Present a problem for groups to solve: *How many feet are under the table when families eat together?* Record on a 0–99 chart.

Next, using the information reported on the graph, Leslie organized students into groups, putting together those who had the same number of people living in their houses. This way all of the students at each table should get the same answer on the problem she was going to pose. The problem was to figure out how many feet would be under the table if everyone in their family ate together. Groups reported their results, and one child from each group colored in the group's answer on a 0–99 chart Leslie had posted.

Ask what the colored-in numbers on the 0–99 chart mean.

A few days later, Leslie extended the activity further. To review what they had done so far, she called students' attention to the 0–99 chart. She said, "Three people live in my house—my husband, my son Craig, and me. What number would I color in?" It was not difficult for students to discuss this and come up with the answer of 6.

Leslie then asked who could explain what the numbers that were colored in told. Several students explained, in their own words, that these numbers told how many feet there were altogether for all the people who lived in the house.

Introduce a new idea: *How many feet altogether if you have a pet?*

Then Leslie introduced a new idea. "Coloring in the number six doesn't tell the whole story of who lives in my house," she said. "We also have a cat and a dog."

Leslie demonstrated several different ways she could figure out how many feet there are altogether in her house, including her pets. She drew pictures on the board and had students count the feet with her. She used interlocking cubes, making trains of two for her, her husband, and Craig, and trains of four for the cat and dog. She figured aloud for the students, "Four and four are eight, and that takes care of the cat and the dog. Then I have to add two for me, two for my husband, and two for my son. So that's eight plus two are ten, plus two are twelve, plus two more are fourteen." Leslie colored in the number 14 on the 0–99 chart.

Leslie then gave the students an assignment. "Figure out again how many feet are in your house altogether," she said, "but this time include pets if you have any. Record your answer and how you found it." The students went to work and continued working on the problem the next day.

Have students record their answers on the 0–99 chart and share how they found them.

The mathematical potential of the problem continued to grow. When they had all finished, the students reported how they had solved the problem, then they colored their answers on the 0–99 chart. One student colored in the number 11, and that was the only number that was not in a column of even numbers. It provided the opportunity for a discussion about odd and even numbers.

Some students arrived at the same number, but for different reasons. For example, one student also reported 14, as did Leslie, but explained that four people, one parakeet, and one dog lived in his house. This led to another kind of problem—who could be living in a house for any of the numbers colored in?

The work on feet continued for quite a while.

FURTHER EXPLORATIONS FOR OTHER DAYS

Present a problem about raccoons: *How many dry feet?*

During the time when the class was studying about various animals, I introduced the following problem: "Four raccoons went down to the lake for a drink," I said. "Two got their front feet wet. One got its front and back feet wet. One didn't get any feet wet. How many dry feet were there?"

Present a problem about boots: *How many boots?*

Another day, I presented this situation: "Some students went out to play in the snow. When they came in, they put their boots by the door to dry. There were twelve boots. How many students put their boots by the door?"

Present a problem: *How many chopsticks do we need for our class?*

When the class was learning about eating with chopsticks, I presented students with another problem: "Suppose we were going to have Asian food and I was going to bring chopsticks for everyone to use. How many chopsticks would I need to bring?" Getting started on this problem required that we figure out how many students there were altogether. We talked about ways to do this, finally counting off to get to 27. "Will you be eating with us?" Rachel wanted to know. "Yes," I said, and the students got to work.

Note: For a lesson where the chopstick problem led to a further exploration of multiplication, see *Things That Come in Groups: Introducing Multiplication with Real-World Contexts*, page 153.

FINAL THOUGHTS

When presenting problem-solving experiences like these, it's helpful to use a consistent format for organization in the classroom: first present the problem, then organize students into pairs or groups, and finally lead a class discussion for students to share their solutions. Over time, students' abilities to work together, find solutions, and present explanations will improve.

CONVERSATIONS WITH MARILYN

What Do I Think Makes a "Good" Math Lesson?

THINKING ABOUT LESSONS THAT SUPPORT STUDENTS' LEARNING

www.mathsolutions.com/welcometomathclass4

> "If I'm doing all the talking, I'm doing all the learning. I have to shift this so I maximize the time each kid gets to talk. That means I shut up."

> 'Yours is not to question why. Just invert and multiply.' That's what I experienced as a student. As a teacher, I ask instead, 'How do you make sense of this? How do you think about this?' And my job is to hear students, acknowledge students, and then pull the mathematics out so we can all move forward."

> "If a child can be successful in a class without having to think and reason, that's not a good lesson. Now, how do we get to the good lesson? There are so many ways. So, could it be a whole class lesson? Sure. Could it be a lesson when they're just working in pairs? Sure. Could it be a lesson where they're working in small groups? Yes. Individually? Yes. All these are perhaps different reasons for different lessons, but most importantly, are the students doing the thinking and reasoning?"

Overview

I've often been asked by teachers, as has my Math Solutions colleague Patty Clark, about what really makes a "good" math lesson. In this conversation, I share my thoughts on what I think are essential qualities of effective math lessons.

Making Connections

There's no one way to teach a lesson. I've taught the lessons in *Welcome to Math Class* multiple times to different classes, often at different grade levels. I tweak my plans, paying attention to the particular needs of the students I'm teaching. For example, when you read the *Cows and Chickens* lesson, you'll see how it was used with first graders and then second graders. Then, you'll learn about how another colleague revised it to meet the needs of her kindergarten children. I've told older students the "answer" of how many feet and tails there were and asked them to figure out how many cows and chickens there might be. The ideas presented in this conversation play an important role when I plan and prepare for lessons, keeping the essential qualities of "good" lessons in mind. I encourage you to do the same.

6
Explorations with Four Toothpicks

Reasoning about Shapes and Their Attributes

Taught in Grades 2–5

In these explorations, students are involved in a hands-on experience that helps develop their spatial reasoning skills as they examine shapes and their attributes. Students investigate geometric patterns, sort and classify them, solve problems, and learn to play a strategic game. This sequence of toothpick activities also helps students learn about rotational and mirror symmetry.

OVERVIEW

I introduced these activities to third graders over four class periods, beginning with a lesson in which students searched for all the ways possible to arrange four toothpicks. Then I used their arrangements for follow-up activities. Not only did students' facility with visualizing spatially increase, but also their involvement with the activities continued long past the four class lessons I devoted to them.

MATERIALS

*REPRODUCIBLES
are available
in a downloadable,
printable format.
See page xii
for directions
about how to
access them.

- flat toothpicks, a large supply
- white glue, a large supply
- shallow paper cups for the glue
- construction paper, cut into 6-by-9-inch pieces, a different color for each group, 24 of each color
- *Toothpick Exploration* Recording Sheet (**REPRODUCIBLE D***), 1 for each group
- index cards, 5 inches by 8 inches, 4 for each group
- rubber band, 1 for each group
- scissors, a large supply
- chart paper, 1 sheet

TOOTHPICK ACTIVITY 1 Preparation

Assemble the materials.

I assembled the materials needed for the first activity—a supply of flat toothpicks, white glue, shallow paper cups for the glue, and construction paper cut into 6-by-9-inch pieces. I used a different color of construction paper for each group, and I cut twenty-four pieces of each color.

TOOTHPICK ACTIVITY 1 Introduce Patterns with Four Toothpicks

Ask, "How can we arrange four toothpicks so that each toothpick touches the end of another, making either a straight line or a square corner?"

I gathered students on the rug to introduce the first activity. "We're going to try and find all the different ways to arrange four toothpicks following two rules," I explained. "The first rule is that each toothpick must touch the end of at least one other toothpick, and the other rule is that toothpicks must be placed so they either make straight lines or so that they make square corners."

I poured some glue into one of the paper cups and asked, "Who can describe a way to arrange four toothpicks that fits the rules?"

Display an arrangement suggested by a student and glue it to construction paper.

Several students raised their hands. I called on Ann. "You can make a square," she said. I did so with four toothpicks, explaining that the toothpicks touched ends and made square corners. I demonstrated for the students how to dip the ends of the toothpicks into the glue and place them on a sheet of the construction paper.

"When the glue dries, the toothpicks will be glued to the paper," I said. Then I asked, "Can anyone think of another way to arrange four toothpicks?"

"You can make an F," Aiguo suggested next. I glued four toothpicks to a sheet of construction paper as he directed, first placing two toothpicks end to end in a straight line, then adding two, making square corners to form an F.

Other students also offered suggestions, but I didn't do any more gluing because I felt they understood how to glue toothpicks to papers.

Explain what "different" shapes mean.

I wasn't sure that students understood what I meant by "different" shapes. To explain, I drew an *F* on a sheet of paper and showed it upside down to students.

"This shape is the same as the one Aiguo suggested," I said. "Who can explain why?"

Several students had explanations. "It's upside down." "It's turned around." "It's still an F."

Then I drew a shape on another sheet of paper, this one a mirror image of an F. "This one is also the same as the F," I said. "Why do you think that's so?"

While some of the students were able to see that it was a backward F, others were perplexed. To help them understand, I turned the paper with the F drawn on it over and held it up to the window. The students could then see it was the same as the mirror image I had drawn. "If you flip a shape and then it matches another, they're considered the same," I explained. "You can always check a shape to be sure by drawing it and holding it up to the window."

Circulate, observe, and offer help as needed.

The students then got to work. This was one of those activities that seemed just right for students. The problem intrigued them. They enjoyed being able to work with their hands. They were challenged without being frustrated. They took care when gluing and were pleased with the toothpick patterns they were creating. As they worked, they discussed the similarities and differences among the shapes they made.

This group tackles the challenge of finding the different arrangements of four toothpicks.

After about half an hour, Grace, Hector, Min, and Paloma called me over. "We think we've found them all," Paloma reported for the group. "We keep trying and trying, and we keep getting the same shapes." I told them, "If you make a drawing of the shapes you've found, I'll check it against the ones I've found."

It was nearly the end of math time, and the other groups were still working. I designated a file tray for students to put their work so they could retrieve it tomorrow.

TOOTHPICK ACTIVITY 2 Preparation

Prepare a dot-paper recording sheet, one per each group of students.

That night, I prepared a sheet onto which the students could transfer their toothpick patterns. Though Grace's group had made a clear and accurate drawing of each of their shapes, I didn't think all the students would be able to do so.

To make the recording sheet, I ruled a sheet of paper into sixteen rectangles, each 2 inches by $2\frac{1}{2}$ inches. In each rectangle, I drew a 4-by-5 array of dots. This array would accommodate every possible pattern of four toothpicks. I made enough copies so that each group could have one, plus extras. (This is also available as **REPRODUCIBLE D**.) I also brought four 5-by-8-inch index cards to class for each group.

TOOTHPICK ACTIVITY 2 Making a Deck of Cards

Show the class how to record each toothpick pattern on the dot paper.

Before students got back to work the next day, I called them to the rug to show them how to make a deck of cards from their toothpick patterns. I showed them the recording sheet Grace's group had made and the dot-paper sheet I had designed. "Draw each pattern you find in one of these rectangles," I said. I drew a few to demonstrate.

Model cutting the dot paper into sixteen pieces and the index cards into fourths, then gluing them together to make a deck of cards.

"Then cut each index card into four parts," I said, demonstrating folding and then cutting the cards. "Cut your dot paper apart and glue each pattern to one of the quarters of the index cards. When you've done that, you'll have a deck of cards of all your patterns. Decorate the back of each card—do them all the same—so you can identify them as your group's deck. Then put a rubber band around your deck and set it in the basket." Again, this was a successful and enjoyable activity for students.

Have one group post its construction paper patterns to create a reference for the class.

Near the end of the class period, I asked Renata, Salim, Mira, and Ann, who were first to finish making their deck, to post the toothpick patterns they had glued on construction paper. They had found the same sixteen as the other group and I had. Their patterns provided a reference against which other groups could check their work. It was fascinating to watch groups check their patterns to see which matched those posted, which were mirror images or rotations, and which patterns they were missing. The interaction among the students was exciting to observe.

Before the next math class, check each deck of cards. Let groups know if there is an error.

I took the students' decks home that night to check them. There were errors in several of the decks, and I attached a note to each of them. For one, I wrote: *You have an extra card—two shapes are the same.* For another, I wrote: *You're missing the shape that looks like a staircase, and two others are the same.* For two groups, I wrote: *You have doubles of two shapes, and you're missing two.*

Number the posted construction paper patterns and have groups do the same with their deck of cards.

Before returning the cards for corrections, however, I gave another task for all the groups. I numbered the patterns posted and asked that the groups number their cards in the same way. The sequence of the numbers had no significance other than identifying the patterns and giving us an easy way to reference them in discussions.

"That way," I explained, "when we identify card number 7, for example, we'll all be talking about the same pattern." Not only was this a convenience for the next activity, it also posed another problem for the students. Matching their patterns to those posted required that they exercise their spatial abilities.

As groups began numbering their cards, I circulated and explained the notes to the groups that had errors or incomplete decks.

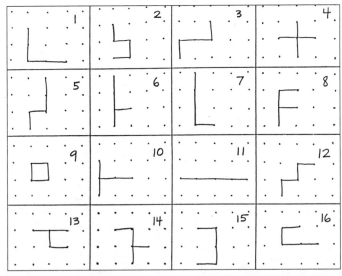

There are sixteen different ways to arrange four toothpicks placed end to end either in a straight line or at square corners. (The numbers are assigned arbitrarily to identify the shapes.)

TOOTHPICK ACTIVITY 3 The *Put-in-Order* Problem

Introduce the problem: *Arrange the cards in a line so that each pattern can be changed to the next one by moving only one toothpick.*

After all groups had made correct decks of cards, I posed the *Put-in-Order* problem. I asked the groups to arrange their cards in a line so that each pattern could be changed to the next one by moving just one toothpick.

"For example, look at the T pattern," I said, referring to the patterns posted. "What other pattern could I make by moving just one toothpick of the T?"

Several students had suggestions. "You can make the cross." "You can make number 7, the chair." "You can make the C." "You can make number 10."

Some had suggestions for how other patterns could be changed by following the rule of moving just one toothpick. "You can change number 6 to number 8," Aiguo said.

"Number 12 can be changed to number 13," Erika said.

> # Put-in-Order
> We put the cards in order changing one tooth
> pick every time. At the end we got stuck we had
> 11 and we had to change it to 9 so we put 11 in with
> 13 and 2. It worked this is the order we put them
> in. 1-16-7-3 15-14-4-13- 9-2-12-5 10-8-6-11.

Marina, Kendra, and Bryce describe how they solved the problem of arranging the cards so each can be changed to the next one by moving just one toothpick.

Restate the problem, adding two instructions: *Record how your group solved the problem and write the order of your cards on the class chart.*

I then restated the problem and added an additional direction. I said, "You are to make a group record of the order of your cards, and then explain how you solved the problem."

I posted a sheet of chart paper and titled it *The Put-in-Order Problem*. "There's one additional job," I added. "When you're finished, also record the order of your cards on the chart. After all groups solve the problem, we'll look for patterns in your solutions."

Circulate, observe, and offer help as needed.

Some groups were confused by the problem and had difficulty getting started. I helped Tara, Andreas, Erika, and Tiare. I gathered their cards, which were scattered on their table, and asked Andreas to choose one at random and place it face up. I said, "Each of you make that pattern with toothpicks and put the rest of the toothpicks back in the bowl." I waited as the four of them followed my directions. They were all successful.

"Now you'll take turns," I then said and explained, "Tara, you start. Move just one of the toothpicks to make a new pattern. Andreas, Erika, and Tiare, follow with your own toothpicks what Tara does."

Tara moved one toothpick, and the others did the same. "Now, Tara," I said, "find the card with your new pattern on it and place that next to the one Andreas chose." Tara did that, and their sequence was started.

"Now it's Tiare's turn," I said. "Tiare, move one toothpick from the pattern that Tara made to make a new pattern. Everyone else should make the same move." They did so.

"Now, Tiare," I continued, "find the matching card and place it in line."

I continued for Erika's turn. Then, satisfied that they had a way to work and were focused, I left them to continue.

Tara, Andreas, Erika, and Tiare need help getting started on the *Put-in-Order* problem.

Most of the groups had difficulty getting started. Their frustration resulted in less concentration and more silliness in the classroom than had been exhibited at any time during the past two days. I worked with three other groups as I had with Tara, Andreas, Erika, and Tiare.

Perhaps it would have been better to give the entire class more direction for how to approach the problem before they began work. I typically prefer to avoid prescribing one particular approach to a problem. I'd rather students find their own way. In this case, however, the direction seemed helpful, even necessary, for some groups, allowing them to focus on the problem at hand. The decision of how much direction to provide differs from situation to situation and it's always a judgment call for teachers when we teach. The logistical choices we make are often instrumental in helping a lesson go smoothly and, with experience, I'm able to facilitate more effectively.

"The decision of how much direction to provide differs from situation to situation and it's always a judgment call for teachers when we teach."

Offer a hint when groups have extra cards at the end.

All groups wound up with extra cards at the end, unable to make those patterns by moving just one toothpick from the last pattern in the line. I suggested that they look for opportunities where they could insert a card into their lineup, and that helped refocus their energy. By the end of the class period, all groups had solved the problem of using all of their toothpick patterns.

Discuss the information displayed on the *Put-in-Order* chart.

The students were fascinated by the results reported on the chart. There was little similarity among the solutions.

"Let's look at what each group put after card number 1," I said. Five different patterns followed it.

"Are there any other patterns that are possible to make from card number 1 by moving just one toothpick?" I asked, referring to the set of patterns still posted.

The students' concentration and visual ability were remarkable to me. Students were eager to suggest patterns they thought would work. For each one suggested, I would ask them how they changed it. Some were able to describe which toothpick they would move and how they would move it, while others needed to come up and show what they would do. As students reported, I recorded the numbers of the patterns they found.

Yuan discovered another relationship. "Look," he said excitedly, "numbers 1, 3, and 5 all work together."

"What do you mean by that?" I asked.

"See," Yuan explained, "you can move one toothpick and change 1 to 3, and 1 to 5, and 3 to 5, and they all work backward too." This started the students looking for other combinations of three patterns that worked together like this.

Salim discovered a triple that wouldn't work. "I found a funny one," he said. "Number 1 can be changed to 4 or 8, but 4 and 8 can't be changed to each other." The class checked that this was so. Salim's discovery sparked interest in searching for other combinations of patterns with the characteristic he had found. The discussion continued for about twenty minutes. It was one of those wonderful occasions when every student had something to contribute to a class discussion.

> "The discussion continued for about twenty minutes. It was one of those wonderful occasions when every student had something to contribute to a class discussion."

Have groups share how they solved the problem.

Groups then reported what they had recorded about the problem.

Ann, Renata, Salim, and Amber
We had a problem putting the T and the straight line in line so it would work until Ms. Burns came. It was tricky, but interesting.

Grace, Hector, Min, and Paloma
The two ones that were the hardest were 5 and 15. 5 and 15 were hard because they were the last two. They were hard to find a place for and when we did find a place for 5 and 15 we had to move several.

Tim, Aiguo, Alana, and Michelle
[This group encountered a problem with their deck of cards that I had missed when I had checked it. They reported the problem and how they solved it.]
Our group had a problem. We found out that we had two Fs. We found that out because Alana made the T, but when we looked for the card, we couldn't find the T, but we found two Fs. Then we looked at the board and we looked for the T and when we found it, we looked for the number and it was number 10. Then we looked for our number 10, and it was a F, so we erased it and changed it to a T.

TOOTHPICK ACTIVITY 4 Playing the *Toothpick Game*

Give directions for a game that uses one deck of cards and only four toothpicks.

The next day, I taught the students how to play the *Toothpick Game* with their patterns. Each group needed its deck of cards and just four toothpicks. I presented the game so that, although there would be a winner, they played cooperatively.

I explained how to play. "First your group chooses any card and makes that pattern with four toothpicks. Shuffle that card back into the pack and deal all the cards so each player has four." I modeled this with Gabe, Nick, Shaney, and Mairead.

"For groups with three students," I explained, "don't shuffle the beginning pattern card back into the deck. Instead, leave it face up on the table. Then deal the remaining cards." I modeled this with Marina, Kendra, and Bryce.

I posed a question, "How many cards will Marina, Kendra, and Bryce each have?" This wasn't obvious. The students counted and reported they each had five.

"To play," I continued, "place your cards face up in front of you so all cards are visible to each other. The goal is to be the first to play all your cards. Take turns. On your turn, you may discard one card, as long as the pattern on that card can be made by changing the position of just one toothpick on the pattern on the table." I stopped and did a sample to demonstrate this, using the four toothpicks to verify that I had made the change correctly.

Then I continued with a few more instructions. "Help one another with moves and discuss the patterns," I said. "If you can't play and everyone else in your group agrees, you say, 'I pass.' Whoever goes out first scores a point. Then start another game. Most of the time, someone wins. Sometimes there's a stalemate, and you have to agree as a group that a stalemate has happened. Then there's not a winner and no one scores a point for that round."

While groups play the game, circulate, observe, and offer help as needed.

Not only was the game interesting for the students to play, it encouraged them to continue examining the geometric configurations and their flips and rotations. The students continued to play at free time for the rest of the week. Some made decks of cards to take home so they could play with their families. It was a successful experience for all of the students.

Toothpick Game

In the toothpick game, if I have good cards like L, +, I, F, ☐, T, |, or h, I try to save them till last. If I didn't save cards that change into a lot of other cards, I'd get stuck. I have an unlikely chance of winning if I get +.

Toothpick Game
You don't want the + card because you can only change it to ⊢. You want to have cards that can change to lots of things. For example F ⊢ ⊤ Γ ⅃.

My stratigy is to always put the hardest ones to change down. I learned to keep trying and to do the hardest cards to change.

Toothpick Game
My strategy was to win the game!!

There were three cards I did not want to get, number four wich is this one +, number eleven wich is this one | and number twelve with is this one ⌐. I did not want them because they are very hard to change into other paterns.

The cards that you want are number nine wich is this one, ☐ and number therteen wich is this one, H and number two wich is this one, ⅃. These cards made it easy for you to win.

From playing the Toothpick Game, students develop a variety of strategies.

7

The Four-Triangle Problem

Exploring Geometry— An Investigation for All

Taught in Grades K–6

This exploration is one of those rare and wonderful opportunities that's accessible and appropriate for students of all ages. Over the years, I've taught the lesson to students in all grades and also to teachers in professional learning situations. *The Four-Triangle Problem* provides experience with sorting and classifying shapes, helps students develop spatial reasoning abilities, and encourages flexible thinking. It provides students the opportunity to see and investigate shapes in relationship to each other. It's useful for introducing and reinforcing the vocabulary and geometric concepts of diagonal, square, triangle, rectangle, parallelogram, trapezoid, pentagon, and hexagon.

OVERVIEW

The lesson described in this section was taught by Bonnie Tank to first graders in one class period that lasted just over an hour. However, students continued to investigate the shapes they made for several weeks. With older students, I've stretched the problem-solving experience with the further explorations suggested at the end of the section. Possibilities for extensions of this activity seem endless and this offers just a beginning.

MATERIALS

- construction-paper squares in two colors, 3 inches by 3 inches, a large supply
- paper, 6 inches by 9 inches, a large supply
- scissors, a large supply
- gluesticks, a large supply

THE LESSON

Have each student cut a 3-inch square into two triangles, then re-create the square. Introduce vocabulary.

I began by giving each student a 3-inch square of construction paper and a pair of scissors. "In a moment, you're going to fold and cut your square into two pieces," I said. "But first watch carefully as I fold and cut my square because I want you to fold and cut yours exactly in the same way."

I demonstrated how to fold the square in half on the diagonal, open it, and cut along the diagonal to cut the square into two triangles. As I did this, I used the word *diagonal* so that students would become familiar with it in the context of the experience. I also talked about the two resulting shapes. Most of the students knew the shapes were called triangles. I wrote the words *square*, *diagonal*, and *triangle* on the board. I watched as students followed my directions, helping those who needed some support.

When all students had cut their square into two triangles, I asked, "Can you put your two triangles back together to make a square? Place them on your desk so I can see what you've done." Some of the students were able to do it instantly. Others had to fiddle with their triangles a bit before making a square, but all were eventually successful.

Tell students to create a new shape with their two triangles, introducing two rules.

"What I want you to do now," I said, "is to see if you can put your triangles together to make a different shape. But I want you to follow two rules. One is that you must place your triangles so that two edges are touching, and the other is that the two edges that touch have to be the same length." I showed them, using my triangles, what was allowed and what was not allowed.

"When you have a shape," I continued, "raise your hand so I can come and see what you've made."

Ask two students with different shapes to glue their shapes on a large sheet of paper and post.

The students got busy. Taliba found a shape first and raised her hand. She had put her two triangles together to make a parallelogram. I asked her to glue her parallelogram onto a sheet of 6-by-9-inch paper and post it on the board.

Erick put his two triangles together to make a larger triangle. I asked him to glue his triangle on paper and post it next to Taliba's parallelogram.

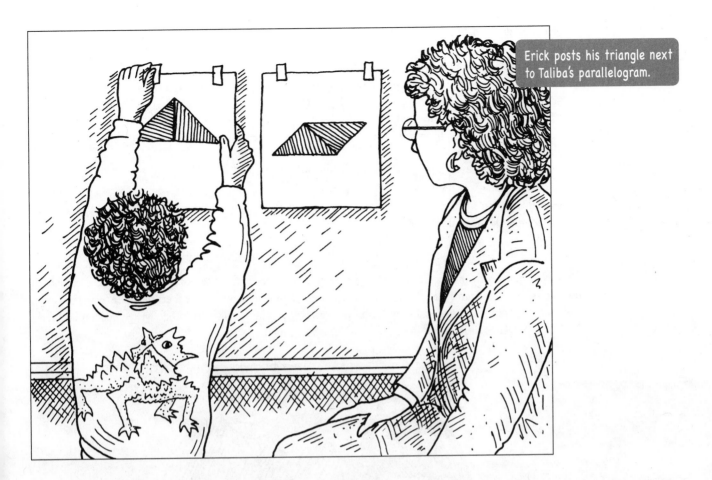

Erick posts his triangle next to Taliba's parallelogram.

Have students see if the shapes they made match the posted shapes.

I then called the class to attention. "Taliba and Erick posted the shapes they made. Did anyone else make a shape like the one Taliba posted?" Some of the students raised their hands. Seeing whether their shape was the same as Taliba's was challenging for some of the students, especially if their shape was oriented in a different way. I took Taliba's shape off the board and rotated it into several other positions to help other students check to see if their shape was the same.

"This shape has a name," I said. "It's called a parallelogram. Try to say *parallelogram* softly after me." I repeated the word several times for students. Then I wrote it on the board under the other words.

"Now look at the shape Erick made," I said. "Who knows the name for this shape?" Several students raised their hands and others called out that it was a triangle.

Review what the students have done so far.

I then reviewed with students what they had done so far by asking them to respond to a series of questions:

- "What shape did you each start with?"
- "Who remembers the name of the line you got when you folded your square?"
- "What did you have when you cut your square?"
- "What other shapes did we make from the two triangles?"

> **"**I then reviewed with students what they had done so far by asking them to respond to a series of questions.**"**

Describe the task: *With a partner, use four triangles cut from two different-colored squares to make new shapes with sides of the same length touching.*

I explained what they were going to do next. "Now I'm going to have you work with a partner," I said. "You'll each have one square to start with. One of you will have a green square and your partner will have a purple square. First, you each cut your square in half on the diagonal, just as you did before. What pieces will you each have?" Students all knew they would have two triangles.

"How many triangles will you and your partner have together?" I asked. Most of the students knew that they would have four.

"This time," I continued, "you and your partner will take all four of your triangles and put them together to make another shape. You'll have to follow the same rules that you did before. Who can tell what the rules are?"

"They have to touch," Zahra said.

"Yes, that's right, sides have to touch," I said, "but the other rule tells you something else to remember about the sides that touch."

Richmond raised his hand. "The sides have to be even," he said.

Ari had another way to say that. "They have to fit exactly," he said.

I restated the rules for them. "When you put your triangles together, the sides must touch, and the sides that touch must be the same length."

Tell students that when they create a shape that follows the rules, they are to glue it on paper.

I then continued with the directions. "When you have a shape that you're both satisfied with," I explained, "raise your hands so I can check that it follows the rules. Then you'll take a large sheet of paper from the supply table and glue your shape on it the way Taliba and Erick did. When you've done that, write your names on the paper." I reviewed the directions once more, and the students then got busy.

Students work with partners to make different shapes from four triangles.

Circulate, observe, and offer help as needed.

All but two of the pairs of students arranged their triangles into a rectangle. One pair made a square from the four triangles. Another pair made a triangle.

Have students post their shapes, putting like shapes together to form a graph.

When all partners had completed the task, I had each pair of students come and post their shapes on the board. I had them post the shapes in three rows, one for the rectangles, one for the square, and one for the triangle, organizing students' shapes into a graph. There were nine rectangles, one square, and one triangle.

Discuss the graph, focusing on the differences among shapes in the same row.

I asked students questions, as I would about any graph, such as:

- "Which shape appears most often?"
- "How many rectangles are posted?"
- "How many triangles are there?"
- "How many squares?"
- "How many shapes are posted altogether?"
- "How many shapes posted are not rectangles?"

Delicia raised her hand. "The rectangles aren't all the same," she said.

"What do you mean?" I asked.

"See the one that's a green square next to a purple square?" Delicia explained. "The others are different." Delicia was commenting on the color arrangements of the four triangles.

"That's interesting for us to examine more closely," I said. "How many different kinds of rectangles are posted? Turn and talk about this with your partner, and then I'll ask what you think."

While the students discussed this subject between themselves, I checked what was posted. There were five color variations of rectangles, three with duplicates. I was curious to hear how the students would describe the differences. I called the class to attention.

"Delicia described one rectangle as a green square next to a purple square," I said. "How many like that do you see?" There were three of them, and the students pointed them out easily.

"Who can describe a different rectangle?" I asked.

I called on Aaron. "There's one with a green triangle in the middle and a purple triangle on each side."

"Can you find that one?" I asked the class. "Which one is it?"

"It's that one!" Hassan called out excitedly.

"Which one, Hassan?" I asked. "Is it the first one?" I pointed to the first rectangle in the row. "The second one? The third?" In this way, I reinforced the ordinal numbers, important for first graders to learn. The rectangle Aaron described was the fifth one in the row.

"Can someone describe a different rectangle?" I went on.

I had Derek answer. "There's one that goes green, purple, green, purple."

There were several responses. "Oh, yeah." "That's the one we were going to say." "Let's see, it's the fourth one." "There's another, the next to the last."

I continued this procedure for the other rectangles. The students were animated and stayed interested.

Finally, I said, "I'll bet there are other color arrangements of rectangles that could be made. In a moment, I'm going to give you and your partner more squares so you can investigate not only other ways to make rectangles, but also other color arrangements for the squares and the triangles that are also posted."

"Also," I continued, "I know another way you and your partner could have arranged your four triangles to make a different shape." I arranged two green and two purple triangles into a hexagon, a shape that was not a familiar one for the students. I glued the shape to a sheet of paper.

"Did I follow the rules about sides touching and the sides touching being the same length?" I asked. The students agreed that I did.

"If I were going to add my shape to our graph, where would I put it?" I asked.

Ebba responded, "You'd have to start another row." I agreed with her.

"What do you call it?" Richard asked.

"It looks like an arrow," Carmen said.

"Let's see how many sides it has," I said. I counted the sides, marking each with an X as I did so. We then counted the six Xs. "A shape with six sides is called a hexagon," I said, adding that name to the list on the board. I introduced the hexagon because I was going to have the students make additional shapes, and I wanted to suggest that other shapes also were possible.

EXTENDING THE LESSON

Have students, working in pairs, continue to find as many shapes as they can, including different color arrangements.

It was now half an hour into the lesson, I gave students directions for continuing to explore shapes with their partners.

"I'm interested in seeing how many other shapes you can find," I explained. "You may find new shapes, such as I did with the hexagon. Or you may find different color arrangements for shapes you've already made. Either sort of variation is okay as long as you follow the rules about matching sides."

I then reinforced that I wanted them to work together on this activity. "You and your partner are to work together," I said. "Each time you find a shape that you agree is different from what you've already made, glue it on a sheet of paper. Then get another green and another purple square, cut each into triangles, and try to find another shape to glue on paper. Keep the shapes you make in a pile. Are there any questions?" There were none, and the students were eager to get to work. I put a stack of green and purple squares at each table along with a stack of paper. The students got busy and worked for another 35 minutes.

Circulate, observe, and offer help as needed. Collect the shapes when work time is over.

Some of the pairs worked more quickly than others. Muhran and Derek made three new shapes, the fewest number of any pair. Muhran did most of the work, as the task was challenging for Derek. But Derek was able to contribute, mostly by printing Muhran's name and his carefully on each paper. Juan and Shara completed the greatest number of shapes, making ten.

Some of the students made shapes that were the same as others they had already made, not checking carefully through their pile. Still, there was a rich variety of shapes after the work time, which I collected for future sorting activities.

FURTHER EXPLORATIONS FOR OTHER DAYS

Distribute a stack of the shapes (that were glued to paper) to each group, then have students cut out the shapes and sort them into four piles—triangles, rectangles, squares, and others.

I collected all the students' shapes into one pile, including the ones I had previously posted. On another day, I divided the shapes so each group had a stack. "First, cut each of the shapes out of the paper they are glued to," I said. I cut out one shape to demonstrate. I wanted students to cut the shapes so they could more easily rotate and flip them in order to compare them to one another.

"When you've done that," I continued, "sort your stack into four piles. Make a pile of squares, a pile of rectangles, a pile of triangles, and a pile with all the other shapes."

Post one of the cutout rectangles. With the class, compare each other rectangle to it, posting only those that are different.

After collecting the sorted shapes, I said, "What I'd like us to do now is find all the different arrangements of rectangles that you made. Here's how we'll do this."

I took a rectangle from the pile and posted it. Then I held up another rectangle and asked, "Is it the same or is it different from the one I've already posted?" I rotated and flipped it so we could be sure we compared it correctly. The students agreed that it was different, so I posted it beside the first one.

I continued through the pile of rectangles, holding up each one for the students to examine and decide whether it was the same or different. I gave a reminder. "If I flip a rectangle or turn it upside down," I said, "and it looks the same as one that's already posted, then it doesn't count as a different arrangement."

The students were excited about this activity. Some began to shout out their thoughts. To calm them down, I asked that students indicate with thumbs up or thumbs down whether they thought the rectangle I was showing was different or not. That helped.

Discerning differences was easier for some students than for others. Some needed to touch the rectangles as they described the arrangement. "See, it goes green, purple, purple, green, just like that one," Zhong said, coming up and pointing to one of the arrangements. Other students started to think about possibilities that were missing from the chart. "We need a purple, green, purple, green, with the lines going the other way," Taliba said, using her hands to explain what she meant. We investigated all of the rectangles they had created.

As with the rectangles, have students determine the number of different arrangements of triangles they had made. Do the same for the squares.

The next day, I repeated this investigation for the triangles and squares they had made, posting them into a separate row for each. I then made a suggestion. "If you think of other arrangements of rectangles, triangles, or squares that aren't posted, make them. Then the class will check to see if they agree that they should be posted."

Ask the class to sort the remaining shapes according to the number of sides.

On another day, we sorted the rest of their shapes. The shapes left were four-sided shapes other than squares or rectangles, and some five- and six-sided shapes. As I had done before, I distributed some of these to each group. "Work together," I said, "and sort your shapes according to the number of sides they have." I demonstrated counting the sides of several shapes for the students, modeling for them how to keep track of the sides as they counted. I posted their shapes.

Have students continue to find new arrangements and new shapes.

By now, the entire board on the side of the room was filled with shapes made from the green and purple triangles. The display kept students' interest for a period of several weeks as they discovered new arrangements and new shapes. They continued to talk about the shapes, and often went over to look at something more closely or to point out something to a classmate. (You might present older classes, or individual students who are interested, with the problem of finding how many different shapes and color variations are possible to make from the four triangles.)

> "The students were excited about this activity. Some began to shout out their thoughts. To calm them down, I asked that students indicate with thumbs up or thumbs down whether they thought the rectangle I was showing was different or not. That helped."

CONVERSATIONS WITH MARILYN

Why Talk in Math Class?
THE VALUE OF CONVERSATION WHEN LEARNING MATH

www.mathsolutions.com/welcometomathclass5

> "I've shifted my whole teaching from being the giver of information to being the receiver of how students are thinking."

> "In my early experiences as a kid in school, you did your own work and you sort of cupped your hands so that nobody could see your work. And it was very, very isolating. So, I'm shifting. I believe that talking is a way to make sense of math for yourself, that the more kids have the opportunity to talk, the more they get to explain their thinking and the more they're going to learn."

> "I used to have kids working in groups of four, but then I thought, that's one kid talking out of four. Maybe if I put them in pairs and I have one kid talking out of two—if everybody's talking to a partner—then half the class is talking."

Overview

In this conversation I share with longtime Math Solutions colleague Patty Clark why talk is important in learning math, how to get students talking, and the importance of listening as part of talk. I also address the concern, "What do I do if I don't understand or can't make sense of what students are saying?"

Making Connections

Having students work cooperatively in groups and also talk with partners—using turn and talk or think–pair–share—has become an important element of my pedagogical repertoire. Throughout the lessons in *Welcome to Math Class*, you'll read examples of these routines. In *Explorations with Four Toothpicks*, for example, you'll read about how partner work was structured. Also, in *Multiplication with Rectangles*, you'll read about how both partner and small-group work was used to support learning.

8
Multiplication with Rectangles
Connecting Multiplication and Geometry

Taught in Grades 3–5

The fourth graders described here had spent a good deal of time studying multiplication. Most knew their multiplication tables fairly well, and most could multiply by a one-digit multiplier with and without re-grouping. They had learned that multiplication is related to addition. In response to being asked what multiplication can accomplish, one student said, "It's a way to do adding when you need to add the same thing over and over." Also, they had experience solving word problems for which multiplication was required.

In exploring *Multiplication with Rectangles*, students investigate multiplication from a different approach—through a geometric investigation of rectangular arrays. Having students look at multiplication from a geometric perspective contributes to their understanding.

OVERVIEW

When students are introduced to a new idea, it's helpful to relate that idea to other areas of mathematics, so that students can see how different areas of mathematics connect. None of the students in this class had discovered that the multiplication table they had been studying could be generated from a geometry investigation of rectangles. Also, none of them had explored visually the patterns of multiples on the multiplication table. Making these connections was not only enjoyable, but also contributed to their seeing the interrelatedness of the different areas of mathematics.

Multiplication with Rectangles spanned five days of instruction in the classroom and sparked some students to continue further. During all the activities presented, the students worked cooperatively in small groups. This sequence of lessons has become a staple for me when teaching multiplication and I've used it with students in grades 3 through 5.

MATERIALS

*REPRODUCIBLES
are available
in a downloadable,
printable format.
See page xii
for directions
about how to
access them.

- 1-inch-square tiles, at least 25 for each group
- $\frac{1}{2}$-inch-squared paper (**REPRODUCIBLE E***), a large supply
- business envelopes, 1 for each group
- *Exploring Multiplication with Rectangles* recording sheet (**REPRODUCIBLE F***), 1 for each group
- paper strips, 3 inches by 11 inches, at least 30
- multiplication tables, at least 11 for each group
- tape, 1 roll
- scissors, a large supply
- colored pencils or markers, a large supply

DAY 1 PREPARATION

Gather the materials.

For this part of the lesson, I gathered several materials: 1-inch-square tiles, paper ruled into $\frac{1}{2}$-inch squares (**REPRODUCIBLE E**), and scissors. The students in this class were seated in small groups—six groups of four students each and one group of three. I had enough tiles to give twenty-five to each group, and I had duplicated enough squared paper so that each group had four sheets. I put an extra stack of paper on the supply table. Students each had a pair of scissors.

DAY 1 Making the Rectangles

Direct students to arrange twelve tiles into a rectangle.

I began by introducing rectangular arrays. I explained, "There are twenty-five tiles at your table. I'd like you to work with partners for this first task. You'll each work with your shoulder partner." It was an established routine in the class that students worked either with the person they're sitting next to (their "shoulder" partner) or the person sitting opposite (their "across" partner). Becky's hand shot up. She was in the group of three students, and I told them they should work together as a group.

"It was an established routine in the class that students worked either with the person they're sitting next to (their "shoulder" partner) or the person sitting opposite (their "across" partner)."

For this part of the exploration, I had students work in pairs because I didn't have enough tiles for each student to have twelve, which they'd need for this activity. In retrospect, the support of partners was useful.

I continued, "You and your partner need twelve tiles. Together, decide how to arrange them into a rectangle. Don't use the tiles just to outline a rectangle, rather arrange them into the shape of a rectangle."

Pairs explored how to arrange twelve tiles in different shape rectangles.

Discuss the rectangles: *Are they the same or different?*

After a minute or so, everyone had accomplished the task. I drew their attention to the rectangles they had built. "Look at your group's rectangles. Raise your hands if both the rectangles are the same." About a third of the students raised their hands.

I continued, "Now raise your hands if the rectangles are different." Again, about a third of the students raised their hands.

"How come some of you didn't raise your hand for one or the other?" I asked.

Atticus raised his hand to respond, "I wasn't sure if ours was the same. It looks like the same shape, but theirs is sideways and uses different colors."

Several others nodded to indicate that they were confused about what I meant by rectangles that were the same and rectangles that were different. (Ah, giving clear directions is always a teaching challenge.) I asked Atticus a question, "I can't see your rectangle from where I am. How could you describe it to me so I would know what you've built? I'm not concerned about the colors, just the shape."

Atticus and Jason, his partner, answered together, "It has four tiles across one way and three tiles across the other."

"Does that description fit your rectangle?" I asked the two others in their group. They nodded yes.

"So, color doesn't matter?" Jason asked. I nodded.

Abby raised her hand. "Ours is different. It has six across and two down."

"Before we talk about your rectangle, Abby, let's talk a bit more about Atticus and Jason's rectangle. Who else in the class built a rectangle that is 4 by 3?" About half the students raised their hands.

Draw each possible rectangle in two different positions, writing *12* on each. Define "same" and "different."

I drew a 4-by-3 rectangle on the board. I drew it so it had four tiles across the bottom and was three tiles tall. I could have oriented it the other way and that would also be fine. I wrote *12* on it. "What does the 12 mean?" I asked.

"That's how many tiles we had to use," Sarah answered.

"What if I drew it this way?" I asked, drawing a rectangle with the same dimensions, but now positioning it so it was four tiles tall and three tiles across. "Are these two rectangles the same shape?"

Jayden answered, "Yes, but one's sideways."

"Yes," I said, "I drew them in different positions, but they have the same dimensions. Both are three squares by four squares, and we'll consider them the same 3-by-4 or 4-by-3 rectangles. So, I don't need to record both of them. One will do." I erased the second rectangle I had drawn.

I then returned to Abby. "Describe your rectangle again, Abby. What are its dimensions?" Introducing a word that may be new for some of the students, such as *dimensions*, is best done in the context of an activity, especially where the students have a physical model to refer to. Abby answered easily, "Ours is six across and two down."

I drew a 6-by-2 rectangle on the board and wrote *12* inside. "Is it OK to write a *12* inside this one also?" I asked. Nods confirmed their agreement. "How many of you built a rectangle with dimensions 6 by 2?" I asked. About half the students raised their hands.

"Did anyone build a rectangle with twelve tiles that has a different shape from either one I've drawn on the board?" I asked.

There were no volunteers, so I offered another possibility. "What about a long skinny rectangle?" I asked and then drew a 1-by-12 rectangle on the board. There were several "Oh, yeah," murmurs. I wrote *12* in that rectangle as well.

Have groups find all the ways to build rectangles with sixteen tiles, recording and cutting out each one.

"Let's try another number," I said. "This time, work together as a group instead of with partners. See if you can find all the ways to use sixteen tiles and build rectangles with different dimensions. Draw each rectangle you find on the grid paper, write *16* inside, and cut it out. If you finish that and others are still working, do the same for the number 7." I wrote the numbers *16* and *7* on the board.

Circulate, observe, and offer help as needed.

The groups got busy. It was interesting to watch and notice that finding the rectangles wasn't obvious to them. Generally, groups counted out the sixteen tiles and then started to arrange them. Most groups found the 8-by-2 and the long, skinny 16-by-1 rectangles and then went on to try 7.

One group of four raised their hands. "Does a 4-by-4 square count?" Elena asked.

"Yes," I answered, "a square is also a rectangle, but a special kind. What makes it special?"

Todd answered. "The sides are all the same."

"Then it counts?" Sasha asked, wanting to be sure.

"Yes, since a square is a special kind of rectangle, it also counts," I answered. I don't think Sasha believed or was comfortable with the idea that a square could also be a rectangle, and I suspected this was true for many of the other students as well. I had purposely chosen 16 because I planned to discuss this idea with the class.

As I left the group, I heard Elena turn to the group next to them and hiss, "See, I told you it would count."

Discuss the three possible rectangles for sixteen tiles.

I interrupted the students as soon as I noticed that all groups had cut out rectangles for 16 and two groups had done one for 7 as well. I called the students to attention and said, "I'll draw on the board what I see you've cut out for the number 16." I drew three rectangles: 1 by 16, 2 by 8, and 4 by 4. I explained to the entire class, as I had to the smaller group, that the square was included because squares were a special kind of rectangle. Also, I wrote *16* in each rectangle and asked students to check to make sure they had done so. Several had forgotten.

Manny raised his hand, "We did 7 too."

"What did you find?" I asked.

"We only found one, a 1 by 7," he replied. I drew this on the board and labeled it.

"Do you think there are others for 7?" I asked.

"Nope, we think that's it," Manny said confidently.

Present the task: *With your group, find all the different rectangles for each of the numbers 1 to 25.*

"I think you have the idea about how to find rectangles for different numbers," I said to the class. "Now I'll explain what your group task is. You are to work together to find all the different rectangles there are for each of the numbers from 1 to 25. Use the tiles to help. Draw each rectangle you find on the grid paper, write the number of tiles (squares) on it, and cut it out.

"You'll need to find some way to keep organized because you'll be cutting out lots of rectangles. Try to conserve paper by drawing rectangles close to each other. If you need extra paper, however, there's a stack on the supply table. Also, don't forget about the number 12. We already did that one and I drew the rectangles on the board, but you'll need to cut them out also. Any questions?"

Jayden raised his hand. "What if the paper isn't long enough to cut out a rectangle?"

"Does someone have an idea about what to do then?" I asked.

Harlow answered. "You could tape paper together."

"Would that help?" I asked Jayden. He nodded, and I added, "I'll put tape on the supply table as well. Don't take it to your group. Take what you need and leave it there so others can find it."

Have students restate the instructions before starting the task.

"Before we start," I said, "who can tell me what you need to be doing in your group?" I asked this to check that they understood the task and to have the opportunity to clarify any details. As each of several students explained, I encouraged the others to listen and to ask questions if they weren't sure what had been said.

I ended with an additional reminder, "Take a few minutes first to discuss how you'll get organized in your groups. Remember, I'll come and help whenever all of you in your group have the same question."

There were no other questions, and the class got to work.

Circulate, observe, and offer help as needed.

Groups organized themselves in different ways. Some assigned specific jobs so that one student, for example, drew the rectangles and another cut them out. Some groups divided into partners again, each pair taking different numbers. Some split up so individuals tackled different numbers. Some groups worked together. In general, students seemed to feel that there was a lot to doing this task, and they responded by settling down and getting busy.

As I circulated and observed, I gave suggestions and reminders to some of the groups. To a group that had a pile of unlabeled rectangles, "Don't forget to write the number of squares on each rectangle." To a group with each working on different numbers, "How are you keeping track of which ones you've finished? Can you find a way to check with each other to make sure you've found all the rectangles for each number?" To a group that had a mess of paper on their desks and on the floor, "I see some of your rectangles on the floor. I think you should take a minute to get organized. Throw away the scraps, collect your rectangles, and then get back to work."

One group called me over to tell me what they had discovered. Manny explained, "The odd numbers only have one rectangle each." This is an incorrect assumption that students often make. My way of responding was to point out a contraction.

"Which ones have you done already?" I asked.

They showed me the rectangles they had cut out for 1, 3, 5, 7, 9, and 11. Deryn added another to the pile that she had just cut out, a 1-by-13 rectangle.

"You've come to a hasty conclusion," I told them. "Watch how I can arrange nine tiles into a 3-by-3 square." I did this, and they groaned.

I made one more comment before leaving the group, "I agree that some odd numbers can be done in only one way, but look carefully before you give up on a number."

Prepare for the next day.

When it was near the time for math class to end and for students to go to lunch, I put an envelope at each table and interrupted the groups. "It's almost time to stop now," I said. "I'd like you to put your names on your envelope and put all the rectangles you've cut out inside it. Put all the extra paper, including parts of pieces that are still big enough to use for more rectangles, on the supply table. The tiles go in the box on the supply table, and put your envelope on the table too. Tomorrow, when it's time for math, get your envelope, some tiles, and paper and continue your work."

DAY 2 Continuing the Work and Beginning to Summarize

Have the group that completes the work first post their rectangles on the board.

The group with Atticus, Nadia, Jason, and Harlow finished first the next day. I gave them the job of taping their rectangles on the board so we could use them for a class discussion. I numbered across the board from 1 to 25 and asked them to tape each rectangle under the correct number.

As a few other groups finished, I asked them to organize their rectangles by number and to compare what they had found with what was being posted to see if they were missing any or if any were missing from the board. The squares were missed by several groups, as was the 3-by-7 rectangle. Some negotiations went on at this time, and groups worked to fill in what they were missing.

A group that finished early posts their rectangles for the class.

Have students use the prepared recording sheet to investigate patterns.

I had created a recording sheet with questions related to the rectangles (see **REPRODUCIBLE F**). I planned to discuss these questions with the entire class when all groups had finished. Since some groups were taking longer to cut out the rectangles, I let those groups continue to work and gave copies of the recording sheet to groups as they were ready.

The questions on the recording sheet directed groups to investigate patterns:

1. Which rectangles have a side with two squares on them? Write the numbers from smallest to largest.
2. Which rectangles have a side with three squares on them? Write the numbers from smallest to largest.

3. Do the same for rectangles with four squares on a side.
4. Do the same for rectangles with five squares on a side.
5. Which numbers have rectangles that are squares? List them from smallest to largest. How many squares would there be in the next larger square you could make?
6. What is the smallest number that has two different rectangles? Three different rectangles? Four?
7. Which numbers have only one rectangle? List them from smallest to largest.

Prepare for the next day.

By the end of class, all but one group had finished cutting out rectangles. I left the rectangles posted on the board for the next day's lesson and directed students to clean up as before. For the group that hadn't yet finished, I arranged for them to have extra time before math class the next day.

DAY 3 Summarizing and Making the Multiplication Table

Lead a class discussion: *How did your group work? What patterns did you notice?*

I began the next day's lesson by gathering students close to the board so everyone could see the rectangles posted. Some sat on the floor, others brought up their chairs, and some perched on desktops. I find it easier to focus the class for discussions when the students are together at the front of the room.

First, I asked them to report how they had worked on the task in their groups. Though I didn't spend much time on this, I feel it's valuable for groups to share their methods of working. Learning how to organize to work cooperatively improves when students pay regular attention to the processes.

Then I went through each of the questions on the worksheet, listing the answers on the board, discussing the patterns, and introducing new vocabulary when appropriate. For the rectangles that had a side with two squares on them, for example, Sarah called out the numbers and I wrote them: 2, 4, 6, 8, 10, 12, 14, 16, 18, 20, 22, 24.

"They skip every other one," Harlow said, noticing the pattern on the numbers from 1 to 25.

"Who could continue the numbers in this pattern?" I asked.

Deryn volunteered and continued to recite the twos. I stopped her at 40.

"These numbers are called the multiples of two," I explained, "because each can be written as two times something. For instance, 2 is 2 times 1 and 4 is 2 times 2. What about 6? 8?" I continued this pattern, in order, up to 16.

We explored the multiples of 3, 4, and 5 in the same way.

Then we looked at the squares and listed these numbers: 1, 4, 9, 16, 25. Students had not initially included the 1 by 1, though agreed that it should be included when I pointed it out to them. "These numbers have a pretty obvious name," I said. "They're called *square numbers*." I then explained that the smallest square number is 1 by 1, or 1; next is 2 by 2, or 4; next is 3 by 3, or 9; and so on. I asked, "What's the next square number after 25?"

Elena raised her hand and gave the answer 36. I asked her to explain how she had gotten that. "Because 25 is 5 times 5, and next comes 6 times 6, which is 36." I asked students what came next, and as they told me, I continued listing the square numbers to 100—*1, 4, 9, 16, 25, 36, 49, 64, 81, 100.*

Next, we looked for the smallest numbers with two, three, and four different rectangles. They were 4, 12, and 24. "Is there a number that has five rectangles?" Atticus asked. I told the class that I knew there was at least one and that I'd leave that problem for those who were interested.

We then listed the numbers that had only one rectangle: *1, 2, 3, 5, 7, 11, 13, 17, 19, 23.* I gave the class the mathematical name for these numbers. "Just as the numbers with squares have a name, these numbers have a name also. They're called *prime numbers*, except that the number 1 isn't included as a prime number."

> "I feel it's valuable for groups to share their methods of working. Learning how to organize to work cooperatively improves when students pay regular attention to the processes."

"Why not?" Jason asked.

"One is different from all the other numbers on the list in a particular way," I explained. "Each of the others can be written as a multiplication equation with two different factors—2 equals 2 times 1, 3 equals 3 times 1, 5 equals 5 times 1, and so on. But 1 has only one factor, the number 1 equals 1 times 1. The mathematical definition of prime numbers is that they have exactly two factors."

"That's dumb," Sasha said.

"Not necessarily dumb," I said, "but perhaps picky. Lots of things in life are arbitrary like this, such as putting the fork on the left side of the plate or always celebrating Thanksgiving on a Thursday. Arbitrary decisions can help us keep things orderly."

Demonstrate how to transfer the rectangles numerically to a chart.

I then left that discussion and introduced a way to transfer their rectangles numerically to a chart. I kept students at the front of the room for this so they could see more easily as I modeled what I wanted them to do.

"Here's what you'll do next," I began. "I'll demonstrate on the board; then you'll each do this individually. You'll each need your own clean sheet of grid paper, but you'll share your group's rectangles."

I taped a sheet of $\frac{1}{2}$-inch grid paper (**REPRODUCIBLE E**) on the board for my demonstration and took down the three rectangles for the number 12. I took the 4-by-3 rectangle first and placed it on my grid paper in the upper left-hand corner. Then I lifted the lower right-hand corner of the rectangle, explaining what I was doing, and in the square under that corner, wrote the number *12*.

I removed the rectangle and explained why I had done this, "If I drew a rectangle around the 12, I would outline the 3-by-4 rectangle I used to locate the 12." The students were watching carefully.

I continued, "Now I'll use the same rectangle, but I'll rotate it into the other position." I placed the rectangle in the corner again, and again lifted the lower right-hand corner, writing *12* in the square underneath.

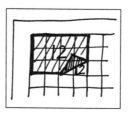

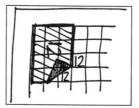

I did the same for the 2-by-6 and the 1-by-12 rectangles, writing *12* in four additional squares. Then I demonstrated the process again, this time using the two rectangles for the number 9, the 1-by-9 and 3-by-3. I chose 9 so I could show that for the squares, such as 3 by 3, rotating it doesn't matter since the lower right-hand corner will be over the same square either way.

Circulate, observe, and offer help as needed.

I then had students return to their seats and follow this process for each of their rectangles that would fit on their grid paper. I gave them the rest of the class period to finish and told them we would discuss what they had done the next day.

Ask the class to share what they see on their grid paper.

It wasn't obvious at first to the students that they were constructing part of the multiplication table through this activity. As they worked, some noticed and others did not. However, once we looked at their work and extended the patterns, it became clear to students that this was the multiplication table they were familiar with, that the numbers they were writing were products.

1	2	3	4	5	6	7	8	9	10	11	12	13	14	15	16
2	4	6	8	10	12	14	16	18	20	22	24				
3	6	9	12	15	18	21	24								
4	8	12	16	20	24										
5	10	15	20	25											
6	12	18	24												
7	14	21													
8	16	24													
9	18														
10	20														
11	22														
12	24														
13															
14															

The cutout rectangles are used to produce part of the multiplication table.

It was exciting to watch this happen, in part because the students were so enthusiastic. So often students learn math without understanding the basis for what they are learning. This connection of the numbers in the multiplication table to the rectangles was an eye-opener for many of them.

We discussed the numerical patterns in what they had done. We looked at rows with patterns that were familiar to them—the twos, fives, and tens. I modeled for them how we could continue those rows as far as the sheet allowed. Then we did the same for the 2, 5, and 10 columns.

We then tried the threes. Some knew the multiples. I modeled skip-counting by 3.

Have students extend their tables to 12, then write and post the patterns they see.

I left the students to complete their multiplication tables so at least a 12-by-12 array of numbers was filled in.

"When you have filled in your tables, "I also explained, "I want you to look for patterns. I'd like you to describe the patterns you find on strips of paper." I had cut some paper into 3-by-11-inch strips. "If you need a wider strip, cut one from another sheet of paper. Then we can post them and compare."

The students found a variety of patterns.

Everything in the 11's column is double digit.

On our multiplication table, for the 10s x n just add a zero to that number and you have the answer.

On our table, if you multiply the number at the top of a column by a number at the left of a row, the product will be where the row and column intersect.

On the even numbered rows or columns, all of the products are an even number.

On the odd numbered columns and rows, the products are odd, even, odd, even, odd, even.

On our multiplication table for the nines, the product will add up to nine.

On the 12 column, for 1 x 12, 2 x 12, 3 x 12, 4 x 12, the answer will have a 1, 2, 3, or 4 in it.

On the fives if you start at the bottom of the column on the last number of the number it goes like 0, 5, 0, 5, 0, 5, etc.

If you look at the square numbers on our table, the number just above and just to the left are the same.

In the 6 column or row, if you add the digits in the product you get the pattern 6, 3, 9, 6, 3, 9 . . .

On our table, the difference between our square numbers increased by two each time.

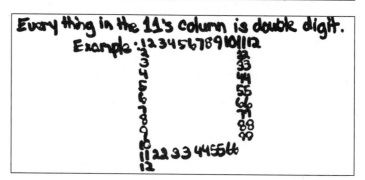

Students describe patterns from the multiplication table.

Prepare for the next day.

For the next day's activity, I duplicated multiplication tables, enough so there were eleven for each group. I planned to have students examine the visual patterns on the multiplication table by coloring what I would introduce as *Times-Table Plaids*.

Model creating a "multiples of 6" *Times-Table Plaid.*

I began the lesson by explaining to students what they were to do. I said, "I'm going to show you another way to investigate patterns on the multiplication table. I call these *Times-Table Plaids*. I'll demonstrate with the multiples of 6. First, I need to make a list of the multiples of 6. Read them to me from the 6 row or column on your multiplication table." As students read the multiples, I wrote the multiples down the side of one of the multiplication tables I had duplicated. The list went to 72.

"What is the largest number on the 12-by-12 table?" I asked.

Students answered, "One hundred forty-four."

"We need to continue the list of multiples to get as close to 144 as we can. We can add 6 to 72 to get the next number. What is 72 plus 6?"

After a moment, Sarah gave the answer, "Seventy-eight."

I asked, "If we continue adding 6, do you think we'll land on 144? Is 144 a multiple of 6?"

Most of the students had no idea. Jason thought so, but wasn't sure about his explanation. "I think so, because 144 is in the twelves column and so is 6."

We continued the list. Jason was pleased to find that he was correct, that 144 is a multiple of 6.

"Once you have your list of multiples made," I continued, "color in all of those multiples on the multiplication table." I demonstrated, starting with 6, coloring in the four different squares in which it appears. When we agreed there were no other sixes to color, I put a check mark next to the 6 in my list of multiples to indicate that I had colored them all. Then I did the same for 12, coloring in the six squares in which it was written and checking it off.

"You can continue in this way with the rest of the multiples," I said, "or you may find a pattern emerging as you color and use it to decide which squares need to be colored in. Any questions so far?" There were no questions, so I continued.

Give the task: *As a group, complete eleven charts.*

I explained, "As a group, you'll complete eleven charts—for the multiples of 2, 3, 4, 5, 6, 7, 8, 9, 10, 11, and 12. Decide who will do which numbers, but be sure that you each do different ones. Look for patterns that emerge as you color. We'll post a set and talk about them later as a class."

Have groups, as they finish, tape one of their charts on the board.

When the class got to work, I wrote the numbers from 2 to 12 on the board, spacing the numbers so a colored-in chart could be posted beneath each. As students finished charts, I asked them to tape them to the board. Soon a colored-in chart for each multiple was posted.

1	2	3	4	5	6	7	8	9	10	11	12
2	4	6	8	10	12	14	16	18	20	22	24
3	6	9	12	15	18	21	24	27	30	33	36
4	8	12	16	20	24	28	32	36	40	44	48
5	10	15	20	25	30	35	40	45	50	55	60
6	12	18	24	30	36	42	48	54	60	66	72
7	14	21	28	35	42	49	56	63	70	77	84
8	16	24	32	40	48	56	64	72	80	88	96
9	18	27	36	45	54	63	72	81	90	99	108
10	20	30	40	50	60	70	80	90	100	110	120
11	22	33	44	55	66	77	88	99	110	121	132
12	24	36	48	60	72	84	96	108	120	132	144

Patterns emerge in shaded multiples of numbers.

Ask the class what they noticed about the Times-Table Plaids.

We had about fifteen minutes at the end of class for discussion. "What did you notice?" I asked.

Sasha raised her hand. "The twos surprised me," she said. "I thought it would look like a checkerboard, but it was in stripes."

Manny's hand was raised. "Some just have stripes, but some have stuff inside the stripes." Others had noticed that also.

"Which of the numbers have just stripes?" I asked.

We picked them out together—2, 3, 5, 7, and 11. "Who remembers the special name for these numbers?" I asked.

Several students raised their hands. "They're prime," Atticus said.

I then said, "We colored in multiples of only two square numbers, 4 and 9. Do you notice anything about them?" They noticed that the fours pattern had a pattern of one square inside each larger square of stripes and the nines pattern had a pattern of four squares in it.

The students talked about other things they had noticed. Though they saw patterns, it was challenging for them to describe in words what they saw. This is not uncommon. They'll improve with practice verbalizing what they notice.

I kept the posted tables for a bulletin board display on which I also had students post the patterns they had written the day before.

> "The students talked about other things they had noticed. Though they saw patterns, it was challenging for them to describe in words what they saw. This is not uncommon. They'll improve with practice verbalizing what they notice."

 ## FINAL THOUGHTS

The students enjoyed the explorations. Though such an experience will not result in their memorization of multiplication facts, students develop a familiarity with multiples, deepen their understanding of the concept of multiplication, and have the opportunity to see relationships between numbers and geometry. Also, by constructing the multiplication table from their cutout rectangles, they have the opportunity to see that the numbers come from a geometric interpretation of multiplication, an important and valuable connection. The week was well spent.

9

Pattern Blocks, Hinged Mirrors, and More

Understanding and Measuring Angles

Taught in Grades 4–6

When studying about angles, students initially learn that angles are the shapes of corners and describe them with words like *pointy*, *wide*, and *square*. Later, they explore the properties of angles, relate angles to other geometric figures, and learn how to measure them. These explorations model ways to provide students with hands-on experiences for learning about angles using pattern blocks, mirrors, folding and tearing paper shapes, and protractors.

OVERVIEW

Understanding angles and how to measure them is typically taught in fourth grade. I've based the instruction I've provided to fourth graders on the following description of how Cathy Humphreys engaged her middle school students over six days of instruction. The results, both with the middle school students and the fourth graders, were definitely an "angles without tears" approach. I also learned that the experiences had the extra benefit for fourth graders of providing them much needed practice with division calculations. For a description of my instruction with fourth graders, read my blog post: "Teaching about Angles—A Hands-On Approach" (www.marilynburnsmathblog.com/teaching-about-angles—a-hand-on-approach/).

Students learning to use protractors to measure angles often get confused by the two scales of numbers and commonly ask, "Which number do I use?" When students' understanding of angles is fragile, they can lose sight of the meaning of the measures. In these lessons, the protractor was introduced after students had a series of concrete experiences with angles. The students first used hinged mirrors to measure the angles of pattern blocks. They then used the mirrors to construct angles of different sizes and fold and tear paper to explore other angles. Only after these experiences were the students given protractors. Working in pairs, they figured out for themselves how to use the protractor to measure angles and write directions for its use.

MATERIALS

- hinged mirrors, 2 inches by 3 inches, 1 pair for each pair of students
- paper, 12 inches by 18 inches, a large supply
- pattern blocks, a large supply
- Dot and Line (**REPRODUCIBLE G***), 1 for each group
- equilateral triangle, about 4 inches on a side, cut out of construction paper, 1 for teacher demonstration
- construction paper, 9 inches by 12 inches, 1 sheet for each student
- scissors, a large supply
- gluesticks, a large supply
- protractors, 1 for each student

DAY 1   Measuring Pattern Block Angles with Hinged Mirrors

Ask students what they know about angles.

"We're going to be studying about angles," I said to begin the class. "To start, I'm interested in finding out what you already know about angles."

"They're like the corners of things," Mateo said. "They have something to do with triangles and rectangles."

"They're lines like the hands on a clock," Lasya offered.

"They have degrees," Erica said.

Patty raised her hand. "Isn't an angle, like, not straight up and down? You know, slanted?" I asked Patty to draw on the board what she meant so everyone could see it. She drew an acute angle with one horizontal leg.

"I know about right angles," Russell said. "They're like Ls." I drew one on the board to illustrate Russell's idea.

"You know when you're on a skateboard and you turn all the way around?" Yumiko asked. "Isn't that like 360 degrees?"

"Yes," I answered.

"You do 180s, too," Herman said. This resulted in some comments about skateboard techniques. I drew the class back to attention.

I then asked, "Does anyone know anything else about angles or have another question to ask?"

"Does a right angle have 90 degrees?" Jennie asked.

"Yes," I answered. Several students were nodding in agreement. "Can anyone explain why a right angle has 90 degrees?"

Patty remembered learning about that. "I think it has to do with what Yumiko said about 360 degrees and dividing it up." Though others knew that a right angle measured 90 degrees, no one else had any idea about why.

The students brought a variety of ideas to this discussion. Most seemed to have the general understanding that an angle is the shape of a corner. Fewer, however, seemed to know about measuring the size of an angle.

Explain that the size of an angle is related to a complete rotation of a circle having 360 degrees.

I then shared with the class what I had planned for the next few days. "You're going to be exploring angles in several different ways this week," I said. "Today I'll show you how to measure all the different-size angles of the pattern blocks using a pair of hinged mirrors. For this activity, you'll be using the information that a rotation of 360 degrees makes a complete circle, as Yumiko said." If Yumiko hadn't come forth with the example, I would have told the students that there are 360 degrees in one complete rotation, a standard mathematical convention that students need to learn.

Demonstrate how to use the hinged mirrors to measure the angles of the orange square pattern block.

I gathered students around one group's table to show them how to use the hinged mirrors to measure the angles of the pattern blocks. The class had enough previous experience with pattern blocks that they didn't need time to explore them. (If not, I would have planned for time for them to explore the materials so that they could focus on the lesson I planned.) They were familiar with the shapes and colors.

The class gathers together to learn how to use hinged mirrors.

I placed a corner of an orange square into the corner of a pair of hinged mirrors and closed the sides so that they were touching the sides of the square and the square was firmly nestled. I had students do the same with three other pairs of mirrors on the table so that more of the class could see.

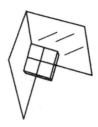

Ask students what they see as they look into the mirrors.

"What do you see when you look into the hinged mirrors?" I asked.

Gabriela was positioned so she had a clear view. She said, "There are four squares, three in the mirrors and the one on the table." There was much interest among the students to explore with the mirrors. Gabriela arranged four squares to show what she saw.

Explain why the corner of the orange square, a right angle, is 90 degrees.

"As Yumiko said," I continued, "it takes 360 degrees to make a complete circle. Putting the square in the mirrors shows that it takes the corners of four squares to fill a complete rotation. So, one square corner is one-fourth of 360 degrees." Some of the students understood this immediately while others looked perplexed.

I restated, "Because it takes four squares, I have to divide 360 by four. How much is that?" Some students figured quickly that it was 90 degrees.

"So, a square corner, called a *right angle*, equals 90 degrees," I said. "It's called a right angle."

"Why is it called a *right angle*?" Russell asked.

"I don't know," I said. "That might be a topic of interest for someone to research. I've never thought about it." (I later researched and learned that it relates to the Latin terminology of *angulus rectus*.)

"Maybe it's a left angle if it goes like a backward L," Jennie said.

"No," I said, "a square corner is a right angle no matter what position it's in." I brought the students' attention back to the pattern blocks.

"Notice that all four angles of the squares are the same size," I said. "They're congruent. Some of the pattern blocks have all congruent angles and some don't."

Some students called out what they noticed. "They're all the same on the green triangle." "On the yellow block, too." "They're different on the blue blocks." I had the students seated at the table take one of each of the six pattern blocks and sort them into two groups—those with all congruent angles and those with different-size angles.

Model measuring the angles of the blue rhombus with the mirrors. Use mathematical language whenever possible.

I next used the blue rhombus to model how to explore the angles on pattern blocks that have angles of more than one size. "You can place the blue block in the hinged mirrors two different ways," I said. "The vertex you put in the corner of the mirrors determines the reflection you see."

"What's *vertex*?" Jennie asked.

"It's another word for the corner of a polygon or the point of an angle," I said. I made a note to myself to use the word as often as possible so students would become familiar with its use.

There were pleased reactions when students saw the pattern made by putting the smaller angle into the mirrors. "Ooh, that's pretty." "It's like a star." "You can see six blocks." Kristin, also seated at the table, built what she saw.

"Since it takes six blocks to complete a rotation," I said, "we have to divide 360 by 6 to figure out how many degrees in each angle. Each of those angles is one-sixth of 360 degrees." A few students quickly did the division in their heads.

"But then you need to figure out the size of the other size angle as well. To do this, position the block with the wide corner nestled in the hinged mirrors," I said. I did this with a blue pattern block.

"Go back to your seats now," I then said, "and I'll give you specific directions about what you're to do."

Present the task: *With a partner, figure out and record how many degrees there are in each angle of each pattern block shape.*

When students were seated, I asked them to figure out the number of degrees in each angle of the blocks. "Use the hinged mirrors as I showed you," I said. "Build what you see and then draw it." I showed on the board what students should draw for the square. I then said, "It's pretty easy to draw the squares, but you may find it easier, with other pattern blocks, to trace them instead of making a sketch." I've learned that this suggestion is helpful to many students.

I continued, "Then draw a circle to show the complete rotation and figure out how much the angle measures. To write degrees, you can use the mathematical symbol of a little circle." I showed them how to do this.

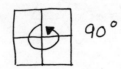

Share with students what materials they will need.

To prepare, I had distributed the contents of five buckets of pattern blocks into eight zip-top plastic bags. Also, I had used strapping tape and hinged small plastic mirrors (about 2 inches by 3 inches), so there was a pair of hinged mirrors for every two students. I put all of the materials on the supply table. I gave the class directions about the materials. "You and your partner will each need pattern blocks, a pair of hinged mirrors, and a sheet of 12-by-18-inch paper for recording," I said.

"Send someone to get supplies for both pairs at your table," I said. "Because you've never explored with the hinged mirrors before, take some time to do so. But be sure to start on the assignment by five after the hour." That gave students about seven minutes for exploring. I've learned that students need time to satisfy their curiosity about new material. Setting a time limit honors that need while reminding them of their task.

> "I've learned that students need time to satisfy their curiosity about new material. Setting a time limit honors that need while reminding them of their task."

Circulate, observe, and offer help as needed.

Once students began working on the task, some confusion surfaced. I helped several pairs who hadn't been able to see very well during the demonstration. A few other pairs could figure how many blocks it took to make 360 degrees but couldn't remember what to do then. Gradually, the groups figured out what to do, and the room settled into the hum of purposeful work. The students' interest was high.

The tan rhombus posed a problem for students. Placing the small angle in the hinged mirrors produces a star cluster of 12 blocks. This delighted students, and most were able to figure that the angle measured 30 degrees. However, placing the larger angle in the hinged mirrors produces a reflection that's frustrating because it can't be built. Students had to find other ways to figure out the angle's size.

Kristy and Erika discovered that the larger angle of the tan rhombus was equal to two angles of the green triangle plus the smaller angle of the tan rhombus. They added 120 degrees and 30 degrees to get 150 degrees and wrote: *Two of the triangles and one tan rhombus fit in the angle.*

Kailani and Mia proved that the angle measured 150 degrees by seeing that the angle was the same size as the 30-degree angle and the larger 120-degree angle of the red trapezoid combined.

Muteteli and Kelly showed how combining an angle from the orange square (90 degrees), two angles from green triangles (60 degrees each), and the larger angle of the tan rhombus (150 degrees) added to 360 degrees (see the last drawing in their work that follows).

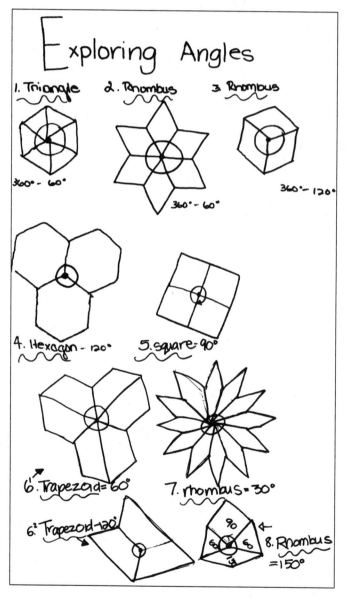

Muteteli and Kelly noticed they had omitted the larger angle of the trapezoid and included it at the bottom of their paper.

The hinged mirrors aren't absolutely essential for this activity. It's possible to use just the blocks and see how many of each angle are needed to complete a 360-degree rotation. However, using the mirrors with the blocks is not only aesthetically pleasing and exciting for the students, it prepares them for the next day's activity.

Give the homework assignment.

I gave students a homework assignment for that night. "Fold one corner of a sheet of paper so that you've halved the right angle." I said. I modeled this for the class. "Trace the angle on a sheet of paper and record the number of degrees in it. Then fold the angle in half again, trace, and record the degrees. Continue until you can't fold the angle any more. Tomorrow, bring the paper you folded along with your recording sheet."

DAYS 2 AND 3 Creating "Weird" Angles with Mirrors, a Dot, and a Line

Have groups discuss the homework assignment.

I began class by having students, in their small groups, compare the angles they traced for homework. I circulated and checked who had completed the assignment.

When I called the class to attention, I had one group report the sizes of the angles they had traced. They had angles of 45 degrees, $22\frac{1}{2}$ degrees, and $11\frac{1}{4}$ degrees. I recorded these angles on the board using the mathematical symbol for degrees.

$45\frac{1}{2}°$
$22\frac{1}{2}°$
$11\frac{1}{4}°$

The rest of the class indicated they had the same answers.

I noticed when I checked students' assignments that they had folded angles from different-size sheets of paper. I pointed this out to the class. "Although you used different-size papers," I said, "you all recorded the same-size angles."

This led to a discussion about the sizes of angles. Patty's statement summarized the conversation. She said, "It's how pointy that counts, not how long."

Draw intersecting perpendicular lines. Have students determine the number of degrees in each angle and share their reasoning.

Next, I drew intersecting perpendicular lines on the board.

"Can anyone tell me how many degrees there are in each of these angles?" I asked. Most of the students raised their hands. I called on Russell.

"It's 90 degrees," he said.

"How do you know that?" I asked him.

"Because I learned that an L shape is 90 degrees," he said.

Mateo raised his hand. "I imagined a circle," he said.

"How did that help you?" I asked. Mateo shrugged his shoulders. Some students have difficulty expressing their ideas. Lasya helped out.

"A circle has 360 degrees, so you can divide by four," she said.

Rochelle gave a different explanation. "Anytime you see a line going straight up and down, and another one going straight across," she said, "you know that it's 90 degrees."

I redrew the lines, still keeping them perpendicular to each other, but rotated them so that it looked as if I had drawn an X. "Are they still 90 degrees?" I asked. For a moment, the class was silent, and then students began to talk. "They're just on a slant." "But it doesn't look right." "Their size wasn't changed, just the tilt." "Oh, yeah, it's still the same."

Add two more lines that bisect each of the angles. Again, ask students to determine the number of degrees in each angle and share their reasoning.

I added two more lines to my figure, bisecting each of the angles.

"What about the size of these angles?" I asked. "Talk this over in your groups." I gave them a moment to do this, then called on Bijou.

"It's 45 degrees," she said. "We divided 8 into 360."

"It's the same as one of the angles on our homework," Dani said.

"This is just like the pattern blocks," Ron said, a bit impatiently.

Explain how to measure an angle using a dot and a line and a pair of hinged mirrors.

I then explained the exploration that students were to do next. "Today you'll investigate angles of other sizes," I began. "You'll use the hinged mirrors, pattern blocks, and a sheet of paper like this on which I've drawn a dot and a line." I showed a sample to the class (see **REPRODUCIBLE G**).

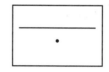

"First I'll give you some time to explore what the hinged mirrors produce on the paper with the dot and the line," I continued. "Place the hinged mirrors so the dot is inside and near the vertex of the angle. Also, make sure the mirrors cross the line." I showed them what I meant.

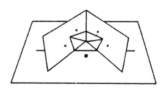

"The size of the angle the mirrors make determines whether you see three dots, four dots, five dots, or more," I said. "Also, the shapes made by the reflections of the lines change. Look at the angle of the hinged mirrors for different numbers of dots and different shapes and see what you can discover."

Give students a few minutes to discover what happens as they move the mirrors, creating different numbers of dots.

The students were intrigued with what they saw. Sam, who rarely is interested in class, got involved with making the angle of the hinged mirrors smaller and smaller. "I see twenty dots!" he said. Gabriela and Lamia also got interested. They claimed they saw twenty-four dots. Soon there was an informal contest. Shirin and Patty counted thirty-six dots. "That's a 10-degree angle," Shirin announced.

Introduce the idea of "weird" angles and model how to create them.

After a few minutes, I called the class back to attention and explained what they now were to do. "The next activity is called *Weird Angles*," I said. "You use hinged mirrors, pattern blocks, the dot and the line, and folded paper to create six 'weird' angles. Construct each angle by tracing and then describe how you made it."

I modeled an example for them. "If I position the mirrors so I see five dots and trace inside the mirrors to draw an angle," I said, "I can figure its size by dividing five into 360 degrees." I did this for the class.

"Then if I put the 45-degree angle from the folded paper adjacent to it and trace," I continued, "I've made an angle that is 72 degrees plus 45 degrees, so it measures 119 degrees. That's one way to construct an angle using the hinged mirrors and folded paper."

The class seemed interested but unsure. I added, "I could also use one of the pattern blocks with either the 72-degree angle or the folded angle to make a different-size angle." I modeled this for the class as well.

"Don't construct any of the angles you've already found," I said. I wrote on the board:

Do not construct 30°, 60°, 90°, 120°, 150°, 45°, $22\frac{1}{2}°$, or $11\frac{1}{4}°$.

"Also," I continued, "although you can help each other and talk about what you're doing, each of you should individually draw angles on your own paper."

Circulate, observe, and offer help as needed.

There was a fair amount of insecurity and confusion among the students when they got to work. I've come to expect this when students tackle something for the first time. Many students raised their hands for help, and I was busy troubleshooting. Just before the end of the period, I asked who was still having difficulty. Ten students raised their hands. I wrote a list of their names.

The next day I had the students who weren't having difficulty get back to work and gathered the ten students on my list. I showed them again what they were to do. All but two were able to get to work. I worked some more with the remaining two, and finally they were on their way.

One of the difficulties that arose was with angles greater than 180 degrees. Students weren't accustomed to these, and some were unsure if they "really counted."

The class went smoothly. It was a good idea to call the activity *Weird Angles*. The students seemed to get confidence and energy from creating something they thought was unusual and mathematically important. Students' papers showed they used a variety of methods to construct angles.

> "There was a fair amount of insecurity and confusion among the students when they got to work. I've come to expect this when students tackle something for the first time."

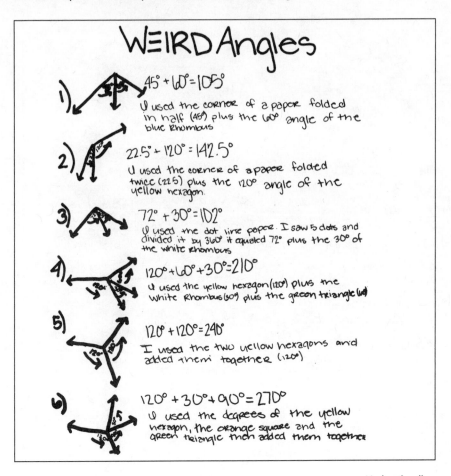

WΞIRD Angles

1) 45° + 60° = 105°
U used the corner of a paper folded in half (45°) plus the 60° angle of the blue Rhombus

2) 22.5° + 120° = 142.5°
U used the corner of a paper folded twice (22.5) plus the 120° angle of the yellow hexagon.

3) 72° + 30° = 102°
U used the dot line paper. I saw 5 dots and divided it by 360° it equaled 72° plus the 30° of the white Rhombus

4) 120° + 60° + 30° = 210°
U used the yellow hexagon (120°) plus the white Rhombus (30°) plus the green triangle (60°)

5) 120° + 120° = 240°
I used the two yellow hexagons and added them together (120°)

6) 120° + 30° + 90° = 270°
U used the degrees of the yellow hexagon, the orange square and the green triangle then added them together

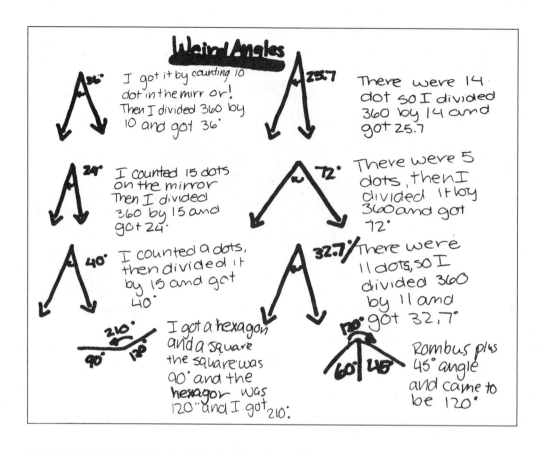

Weird Angles

36° — I got it by counting 10 dot in the mirror! Then I divided 360 by 10 and got 36°

25.7 — There were 14 dot so I divided 360 by 14 and got 25.7

24° — I counted 15 dots on the mirror Then I divided 360 by 15 and got 24°

72° — There were 5 dots, then I divided it by 360 and got 72°

40° — I counted 9 dots, then divided it by 15 and got 40°

32.7 — There were 11 dots, so I divided 360 by 11 and got 32.7°

210° 90° 120° — I got a hexagon and a square the square was 90° and the hexagon was 120° and I got 210°

120° 60° 45° — Rombus plus 45° angle and came to be 120°

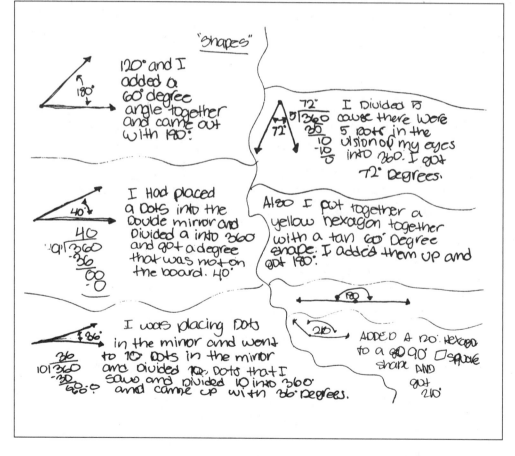

"shapes"

180° — 120° and I added a 60° degree angle together and came out with 180°

72° 72° — $5\overline{)360}$ — I Divided 5 couse there were 5 roots in the vision of my eyes into 360. I got 72° Degrees.

40° — $9\overline{)360}$ — I Had placed 9 Dots into the Double mirror and Divided 9 into 360 and got a degree that was not on the board. 40°

Also I put together a yellow hexagon together with a tan 60° Degree shape. I added them up and got 180°

180

210

ADDED A 120° Hexagon to a 90° square shape AND got 210°

36° — $10\overline{)360}$ — I was placing Dots in the mirror and went to 10 Dots in the mirror and divided the Dots that I saw and divided 10 into 360 and came up with 36° Degrees.

Weird Angles

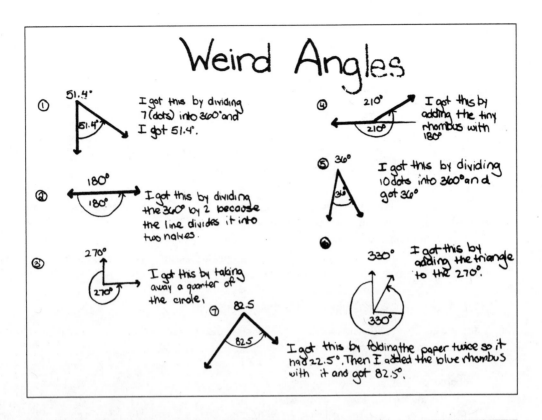

① 51.4° 51.4° I got this by dividing 7 (dots) into 360° and I got 51.4°.

② 180° 180° I got this by dividing the 360° by 2 because the line divides it into two halves.

③ 270° 270° I got this by taking away a quarter of the circle.

④ 210° 210° I got this by adding the tiny rhombus with 180°

⑤ 36° 36° I got this by dividing 10 dots into 360° and got 36°

⑥ 330° 330° I got this by adding the triangle to the 270°.

⑦ 82.5 82.5 I got this by folding the paper twice so it had 22.5°. Then I added the blue rhombus with it and got 82.5°.

Weird Angles

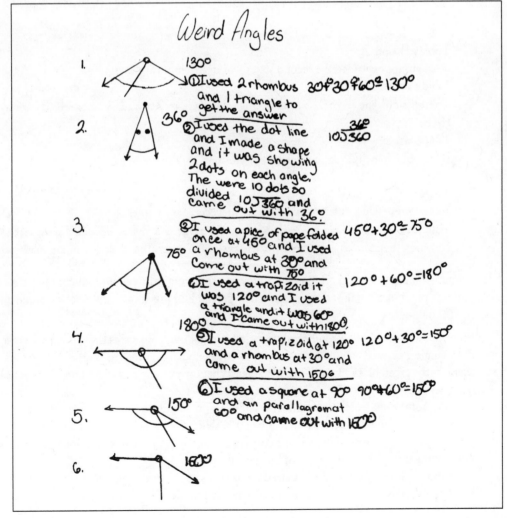

1. 130° ① I used 2 rhombus and 1 triangle to get the answer 30°+30°+60°=130°

2. 36° ② I used the dot line and I made a shape and it was showing 2 dots on each angle. The were 10 dots so divided 10⟌360 and came out with 36°
$\dfrac{36}{10⟌360}$

3. 75° ③ I used a piece of pape folded once at 45° and I used a rhombus at 30° and come out with 75° 45°+30°=75°

180° ④ I used a trapizoid it was 120° and I used a triangle and it was 60° and I came out with 180°. 120°+60°=180°

4. ⑤ I used a trapizoid at 120° and a rhombus at 30° and come out with 150° 120°+30°=150°

5. 150° ⑥ I used a square at 90° and an parallagromat 60° and came out with 150° 90°+60°=150°

6. 150°

Write two statements on the board. Ask students to discuss them in their group and describe in writing how to prove one or both of them.

To begin the next day, I wrote the following two statements on the board:

1. The sum of the degrees of the three interior angles of a green block is 180°.
2. A straight line, or straight angle, measures 180°.

"Mathematicians believe these two statements to be true," I said. "Discuss them in your groups and describe in writing how you might prove one or both of them."

"What does *interior* mean?" Cuong asked.

I explained, "It means 'inside.' The interior angles are the angles inside the shape." I drew a few shapes on the board to illustrate. This seemed to satisfy Cuong.

Have students share their thinking in a class discussion.

After the groups had discussion time, I led a class discussion for them to report their thinking. There was agreement among the groups on how to verify the first statement.

Table 3
The reasoning that Table 3 wrote was typical:
Each angle is measured to be 60°. The triangle has three angles. If you times 60 by 3 you get 180°.

Tables 4 and 2
Most groups explained the second statement in either of two ways:
Table 4 wrote:
The straight line is 180° because a whole circle is 360°. If you divide 360° by 2 you will get 180°.
Table 2 wrote:
If you put two 90° angles together, you get 180°.

Table 1
Table 1 presented a different explanation, however. They wrote:
You have a triangle. If you cut the top, the sides will fall down and form a 180° angle.
However, they weren't able to convince many of the others that their reasoning made sense.

Demonstrate how tearing off the corners of an equilateral triangle and placing them so that the vertices meet at a point and the sides touch proves that the sum of the interior angles of the triangle is 180 degrees.

I then showed the class an equilateral triangle I had cut out from a sheet of construction paper. Each side of the triangle measured about 4 inches, so it was large enough for everyone in the class to see. "This is the same shape as the green block," I said, "but it's larger. What can you say about the sum of the interior angles of this triangle?"

Most of the students were confident that the sum would be 180 degrees, as it was for the angles of the green block. "I know a concrete way to prove it," I said. I cut out the triangle and tore off each of the corners.

I explained, "The reason I tore off corners rather than cut them is so I don't get confused about which point of the torn piece is the vertex of the triangle."

I drew a dot on the board and placed the vertices of all three angles on it with their sides touching. They lined up to make a straight line. The students seemed impressed.

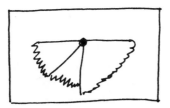

"How does this prove the sum of the interior angles of a triangle is 180 degrees?" I asked.

Several students had responses. "They make a straight line." "They're half a circle." "It's a straight angle."

"What do you think about differently shaped triangles?" I asked. "Suppose I draw a long, skinny triangle. What do you think the sum of the interior angles will be?" No one seemed willing to predict.

Give the task: *With your group, investigate the sum of the interior angles of differently shaped triangles.*

"As a group," I said, "investigate the sum of the interior angles of other triangles. To do this, each of you should draw a triangle on construction paper, cut it out, tear off the corners, and paste them touching a dot as I showed. Paste all your triangles on one sheet of paper. Then look at your results and together write at least one statement that summarizes what you notice."

Circulate, observe, and offer help as needed.

The groups got to work. Watching the students work reminded me how much students enjoy working with their hands. The summary statements they produced were similar:

All the triangle corners add up to 180° when put together.
After you cut out the corners of the triangle and glue them they equal 180°.
Whatever sizes of triangles you put together they will always measure up to 180°.

Kristin and Muteteli verify that the sum of the angles of triangles is 180°.

As groups finish, have students start the same investigation for quadrilaterals and complete it for homework.

As groups finished, I asked them to try the same investigation for quadrilaterals. I told them they were to do this individually. "Each of you needs to do the experiment with four quadrilaterals of different shapes," I instructed. "Make a sketch of each quadrilateral before you tear the corners. After you've pasted down the corners, write a statement that describes what you noticed." The students' homework assignment was to complete the quadrilateral investigation. I've found that giving students the chance to get started in class on a homework assignment helps to clarify the directions.

DAY 5 Investigating the Sum of the Interior Angles of Other Polygons

Have students share their summary statements from last night's homework.

"Who would like to read the summary statement you wrote for last night's homework?" I asked the class to begin the lesson.

Tiffany reported first. "I thought they would equal 180 degrees because the triangles did," she said. "But I was proved wrong."

"No matter what angles there are," Leon read, "it always comes out to 360 degrees." Many of the others agreed.

"I noticed that on all the shapes I made a circle going around," Sunnee read.

"That's what I wrote," Kailani said. Others indicated that they had written something similar.

"I think it's very weird how all corners meet and make a 360-degree angle," Lori read.

Explain the task: *With your group, investigate the sum of the interior angles of other polygons.*

I then wrote:

> Sum of Interior Angles of Polygons
> Triangle (3 sides) = 180°
> Quadrilateral (4 sides) = 360°

"This is what you know so far," I said. "As a group, investigate the sum of interior angles of other polygons. I suggest you start with the yellow hexagon from the pattern blocks since you've already figured the degrees in its angles. Then see if you can use your information to predict the total number of degrees for other polygons. Look for patterns and report what you find."

Circulate, observe, and offer help as needed.

Some groups had difficulty with this activity. Tearing corners wasn't effective because the sum of degrees of the angles of polygons with more than four sides is greater than 360 degrees. Also, using hinged mirrors only helped with some angles. Some students focused on drawing angles that they already knew to find the sums. Others worked from the pattern of the total degrees for triangles, quadrilaterals, and hexagons.

Table 6 made a chart and wrote a conclusion:

3	180	7	900
4	360	8	1080
5	540	9	1260
6	720	10	1440

They wrote: You keep adding 180° and you get the answers.

Table 2 wrote:

The sum of the three angles of a triangle equils 180°. There are 3 sides in a triangle. The sum of the four angles of a quadralateral equils 360°. There are 4 sides. The pattern is for each additional side there is another triangle.

5 sides   3
6 sides   4
7 sides   5
8 sides   6
9 sides   7
10 sides   8

Therefore a decagon with 10 sides would have 8 triangles inside or 8 × 180° which equils 1440°.

DAY 6   Experimenting with a Protractor

Introduce the protractor by asking who has used one.

"How many have used a protractor before?" I asked to begin class. I held up a protractor for students to see. Some students raised their hands, but many commented that they hadn't or weren't sure about how to use one.

"Tearing corners off triangles and pasting them down told you the sum of the degrees in all the angles," I said. "But it doesn't tell you how many degrees in any one angle. Also, when you were looking for patterns in the sum of interior angles of polygons, I noticed that some of you were frustrated because you had no way to measure some of the angles." Several groups nodded in agreement.

Distribute a protractor to each student. Task the class with examining the protractors and talking in their groups about how to use them.

"Help is here," I said. "The protractor is a useful tool for both measuring angles and drawing angles of specific sizes. In a moment, I'll give you each a protractor. In your groups, examine the protractors and talk about how to use one. It may be helpful to use a right angle as a reference since you already know it's 90 degrees."

I distributed protractors, one for each student. The groups immediately began talking about what to do with them. Some were drawing angles and trying to measure them.

Have the class share what they noticed.

After a few minutes, I called the class to attention and had them share what they noticed.

"You put the hole on the point," Russell said.

"Yes," I said, "the hole should match with the vertex of the angle."

"The lines of the angle have to be long enough," Gabriela said.

"Is it OK to make them longer?" Kristin asked.

"What do you think?" I asked the class.

Ricardo answered. "It's not how long the lines are," he said, "it's how they open, like the mouth of a shark."

"There are two rows of numbers that are different," Lamia said.

"Except the 90 is the same on both," Michelle added.

Give the task: *With a partner, write directions for how to use the protractor.*

I then said, "Your job is to work with the person next to you and write directions for how to use the protractor. Your directions should tell how to measure angles and also how to draw angles of different sizes. You can include drawings if it will help make your directions clear." I drew an angle on the board and labeled the vertex and rays.

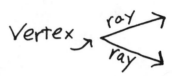

"These words might be useful for you," I said. I also wrote *protractor* and *angle* on the board for students to reference.

"What other words about angles might you use?" I asked. I listed all the words that students volunteered: *acute, right, obtuse, straight, degrees.*

Circulate, observe, and offer help as needed.

On this assignment, students expressed their thinking in different ways.

Lasya and Lamia
First, you make an angle. Then you place the bottom line of the angle on the line of the protractor. Then you put the dot on the vertex of the angle. Then you find out what degree the angle is. If you can't figure it out, you do this. First you find out if your angle is obtuse or acute. If it's obtuse you use the top line, if it's acute you use the bottom line. Then you get the arrow and take it up to the number and the number that the line hits is the degree of your angle.

Cuong and Yumiko
One rule you must always remember is you must always have the bulls eye on the straight line at the bottom. If the angle goes to the right you must read the bottom numbers. But if it goes to the left you must read the top numbers.

Ron M. and Ron S.
You place the vertex of the angle you are measuring in the middle of the hole. The hole is on the bottom of the protractor. When measuring, let's say that it is 69 degrees. On the protractor it does not say 69°. Only 50, 60, & 70. What you do is measure and count by the lines on top of the protractor.

Will and Patricio
[This pair designed their work as a pamphlet. They titled it "The Protractor Manual."]
There are 2 things a Protrator does for you. It 1. measures angles and 2. It makes new angles. To measure an angle you put the rough side of the protractor down then put the vertex of the angle in the little hole in the middle, (shown on page 2) and if the angle is acute you use the numbers on the bottom on the right but if it is acute but it is pointing to the left you use the left side and the top (shown on page 2) to make angles you use the bottom part of the Protractor (shown on Page 2) to make any angle you disire.

Directions

There are 2 things a Protrator does for you it 1. measures angles and 2. It makes new angles. To measure an angle you put the rough side of the protractor down then put the vertex of the angle in the little hole in the middle, (shown on page 2) and if the angle is acute you use the numbers on the botton on the right but if it is acute but it is pointing to the left you use the left side and the top. (shown on page 2) To make angles you use the bottom part of the Protractor (shown on Page 2) to make any angle you disire.

①

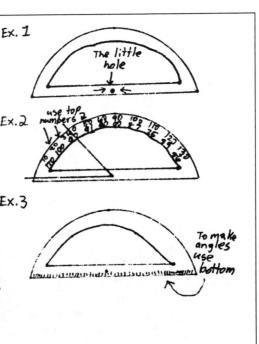

Ex. 1

The little hole

Ex. 2

use top numbers

Ex. 3

To make angles use bottom

②

Protractor Directions

A. The directions for measuring angles is to put the little circle on the vertex of the angle and to line up one of the rays to the line next to the little circle.

. To read the numbers you know what a right angle is (90°) if the angle is like this you know you are suppost to read the bigger number because its obtuse. If the angle is you're suppost to read the smaller number because its less than 90°.

B. The directions for making an angle is to first, draw the bottom line and make the vertex where ever you want it, then you match up the vertex with the small dot, circle and then match it up with the degree you want. After you make a dot on the degree you want, take the bottom of the protractor and make the line from the small circle, dot to the angle, dot.

1. _____ 2. _____ 3. _____ 4. 40°

Xtra

rays

rays

vertex

Writing directions for using a protractor makes learning about protractors a problem-solving experience.
(continued)

step 1 - measuring

place the protractor on your paper where the angle is. where you see the vertex put it in the center circle. to find the degrees use the numbers closest to the half circle and there you have it, a measured angle.

step 2 - drawing

after you place the protractor on the paper, place a dot in the center circle. from the dot draw a straight line to your right. then look at the degrees closest to the half circle. draw a straight line from the vertex to the degrees. then (hopefully) you drew an angle.

(continued)

Writing directions for using a protractor makes learning about protractors a problem-solving experience.

Have students exchange papers and try to follow each other's directions.

As they finished, students exchanged papers and tried other pairs' directions. Reading the work of their classmates gives them experience with different viewpoints.

This assignment made figuring out how to use a protractor a problem-solving challenge. Working in pairs to write directions resulted in a great deal of discussion about how to measure angles. I think the results were as successful, or even more so, than they would have been had I given the class directions on how to use a protractor and assigned angles to measure. Also, this approach was certainly more interesting and engaging for students.

🧠 FINAL THOUGHTS

Watching students work during these activities was convincing testimony about the benefit of concrete materials. Not only did students thoroughly enjoy exploring with the pattern blocks and mirrors; folding and tearing paper; and using protractors, it seemed that the more active their hands were, the more active their minds were. Discussions were animated, and all students were engaged. Classes were a pleasure to watch.

As stated early in the chapter, students had enough previous experience with pattern blocks so that they didn't need time for general exploration with the blocks before focusing on the angle activities. However, I allotted time for students to explore with the hinged mirrors.

I've learned from experience the importance of providing time for students to satisfy their curiosity with new material. This time is more than worthwhile—it's essential. It helps lessons go more smoothly and also honors students' needs to become acquainted with a new learning tool.

The emphasis of the angle activities was on students actively exploring angles and making sense of how to use a protractor. The students were in control of their learning. They were the creators of their understanding rather than receivers of explanations from a textbook or me. Approaching mathematics in this way contributes to helping students see that thinking for themselves is an important aspect of their math learning.

> **"** Students were in control of their learning. They were the creators of their understanding rather than receivers of explanations from a textbook or me. **"**

CONVERSATIONS WITH MARILYN

· ·

Questions, Answers, and Errors

THINKING ABOUT ANSWERS AND ERRORS AS OPPORTUNITIES FOR QUESTIONS

www.mathsolutions.com/welcometomathclass6

> **"**I was really lucky to have an undergraduate advisor who shaped my whole teaching career. He said something that has stuck with me forever: When a student gives you the wrong answer to a problem, the student's probably giving you the right answer to a different question.**"**

> **"**Right answers can mask confusion; wrong answers can hide understanding.**"**

> **"**If you're going to ask a question, no matter the question, the follow-up should be, can you explain that? How did you figure it out? Why do you think that? How do you know? How did you decide?**"**

Overview

In this conversation with my longtime Math Solutions colleague Patty Clark, we talk about the importance of listening for more than the answer, the value of mistakes, thoughts on correcting students, what makes a good question, the definition of OBIDI, and more.

Making Connections

One of the challenges I've faced in my teaching practice is how to encourage students to take risks when sharing their thinking. An important element of my classroom instruction now is to reinforce, over and over again and on a regular basis, that we all make mistakes and that mistakes are opportunities for learning. While I think that correct answers are important, how students think must also play an important role during classroom lessons. In *Welcome to Math Class*, you'll read about how I did this in many of the lessons. For an example, in the lesson *Pentominoes Explorations*, you'll see how I kept groups engaged when they thought (and I didn't) that they had solved the problem of finding all of the possible pentominoes.

10

Pentominoes Explorations

Investigating and Classifying Shapes

Taught in Grades 4–6

This incredibly rich exploration works well with students in grades 4 and up. It gives students the opportunity to see connections among geometric concepts and helps them develop spatial relationships. In addition, the activity necessitates students' deciding when they have found all possible pentominoes, thus requiring that they apply logical reasoning to a spatial task.

OVERVIEW

This problem-solving exploration provides students a common base of experience for studying several geometric ideas. Students used 1-inch-square tiles to search for all the possible ways to arrange five squares into shapes called pentominoes. The concept of congruence became key as students tried to find all the different pentominoes. In order to compare the figures they created, students explored geometric transformations, including translations (slides), rotations (turns), and reflections (flips). In a follow-up activity of investigating which of their pentominoes will fold into boxes, students related their two-dimensional experience to three-dimensional shapes. Also, as they sorted their pentomino shapes, students explored the concepts of perimeter and mirror symmetry.

MATERIALS

■ 1-inch-square tiles, 20 for each group

■ 1-inch-squared paper (**REPRODUCIBLE H***), 2 sheets for each group

■ centimeter-squared paper (**REPRODUCIBLE B***), 1 sheet for each student

■ #10 envelopes, 1 for each group

■ scissors, a large supply

*REPRODUCIBLES are available in a downloadable, printable format. See page xii for directions about how to access them.

INTRODUCING

Organize students into small groups and distribute the materials they need.

The students in this class were accustomed to working in small cooperative groups. Their individual desks are grouped into clusters of four, with groups of three or five as needed to accommodate all the students. The students were told yesterday that I would teach today's math lesson and that it would be a problem-solving activity to launch a unit on geometry.

When I arrived, the thirty-one students were seated in eight groups, seven groups of four and one group of three. I distributed materials to each group—twenty 1-inch square tiles, enough for each student to have five, and two sheets of 1-inch-squared paper (**REPRODUCIBLE H**).

Share with students that they will be looking for specific shapes called pentominoes that are each made from five squares.

I then began the lesson by telling the class that in this problem-solving activity, they would search for different shapes that could be made from five squares, using the tiles I had distributed. "These shapes made from five squares are called pentominoes," I explained, writing the word *pentominoes* on the board. "There are three ideas you will need to understand in doing this activity."

Explain that in a pentomino, at least one whole side of each square must touch a whole side of another square.

"First of all," I continued, "there's a rule you'll need to follow when making pentomino shapes. When you arrange the squares into shapes, at least one whole side of each square must touch a whole side of another." I drew the following examples on the board and labeled them:

This is OK:

This is not OK:

Demonstrate how to determine if two shapes are the same or different. Define *congruent*.

I continued, "Then you will have to decide if the shapes you create are the same or different. That's where the squared paper will come in handy. Here are two legal shapes." I drew them on the board:

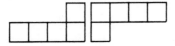

I cut both shapes from a sheet of the squared paper and showed how to compare them. I explained as I demonstrated, "I can move these, flipping one and turning it like this so it fits exactly on the other. Even though they look different the way I drew them on the board, they can be positioned to match each other exactly. Because of this, they're considered to be the same shape. Does anyone know the word that describes two figures that are exactly the same size and the same shape?"

A few volunteered responses: "Matching." "Equal." "Congruent." "Exact."

"The mathematical term for figures with the same size and shape is *congruent*," I told them, and wrote the word on the board. I explained once again, "In our exploration today, if two cutout shapes can be placed one on top of the other so they match exactly, they're called congruent and count as only one shape."

Discuss the derivation of the words *domino, tromino, tetromino,* and *pentomino*.

I discussed the derivation of the word *pentomino*. I drew a picture of a domino on the board with five dots on one side and two on the other. I could tell from the buzz that students recognized the shape. I explained, "A domino is made from two squares. The pentominoes you will explore are five-square versions. What do you think a three-square version might be called?"

After several predictions, I wrote the word *tromino* on the board. I also wrote the word *tetromino*, telling students that this is what four-square shapes are called.

Ask, "What shapes can be made from three squares?"

After this introduction, I posed a problem to the class that's similar to but less complex than the pentomino exploration I would ask them to begin shortly. "Suppose we were trying to find all the different arrangements of three squares, all the different trominoes. What shapes could we make?"

Hyun volunteered immediately, "They could be in a straight row." I drew that possibility on the board.

Diego said, "You could make an L." I drew that also.

"I've got one," Todd said, but when he looked up from his desk and noticed what I had already drawn on the board, he corrected himself, "Oh, no, you've already got that L."

"I've got a different L," Sharbat offered. But Mei, one of her group members, told her that it would look the same if she just turned it upside down. Sharbat looked up at the drawing on the board and back at the shape at her desk a few times and finally rotated the shape on her desk to convince herself that the two Ls were indeed the same. Merely looking hadn't been enough.

"Cutting them out of paper will give you a way to prove whether two shapes are congruent," I reminded them.

I felt that the class understood what had been presented so far and decided to get them started on their problem. (If I had thought they were at all shaky, I would have had them search for the different tetrominoes, the shapes from four squares.)

Present the problem: *With your group, find all the possible ways to arrange five squares into pentominoes and cut the shapes out of squared paper.*

I then presented the problem to be solved. "In your groups, find all the possible ways to arrange five squares into pentominoes. Cut each of them out of the squared paper provided. As a group, you should make one set of all the different pentominoes, accounting for all the possible arrangements. Are there any questions?"

"How many shapes are we supposed to find?" Sandor asked. I, and the class, have learned to expect Sandor to ask that kind of clarifying question.

"That's part of the problem for your group to solve, to find all the pentominoes and to convince yourselves that you've found all the possible arrangements there are. Let me know when you think you've done that and I'll come and discuss what your group has done."

There were no other questions.

EXPLORING

Circulate, observe, and offer help as needed.

As students got to work exploring the problem, the noise level rose in the room, but it was the productive kind of noise that was purposeful. The students seemed focused and interested in the problem. With this class, as in others, whenever students have the opportunity to handle materials, they seem to get interested more easily than when solving abstract, paper-and-pencil problems.

Working with a group helps when looking for all the pentominoes.

I circulated as students worked. I checked on Sharbat to make sure she was moving along with the others and decided that she was doing fine. During this exploring time, I stay out of students' group interactions as much as possible. I listen casually to their comments, noticing how individual students are working. I note ideas I overhear that will be useful for later discussion. I'm ready to offer assistance when all group members raise their hands, as they've learned to do when they need help, or when I feel a group is totally bogged down.

After almost twenty minutes, a group called me over. "We think we've found them all," they announced. "How many do you have?" I asked.

They did a quick count of their cutout shapes. "Nine. No, ten."

As I was looking to see if I could find any duplicate shapes that they hadn't noticed, a nearby group that had overheard them chimed in, "We have eleven." I told the second group that I'd be there in a moment and refocused on the first group. I saw two of their shapes that were congruent. "Examine your shapes again," I told the group. "I see two that are congruent and are really the same. See if you can find those, and then see if you can discover any new ones." I purposely used the language of "congruent" to model and reinforce its use.

The group seemed a little discouraged, but Eamon got them back on track. "I see them," he said, picking up the two congruent shapes. Eamon is usually motivated to continue a search and can be counted on to keep a group probing. It didn't surprise me that the group with Eamon in it was the first to call me over.

I moved to the second group. "We found another," they told me. "Now we have twelve, and we think we have them all." I looked over their shapes and noticed two in their arrangements that were the same. "I see two that are congruent," I told them, moving away. I heard Tamara comment, "Let's find those and then look some more. There can't be just eleven. There are never eleven of anything."

Another group signaled for me by raising their hands. It's often at this stage in a problem-solving activity that the class gets a bit hectic. This group had found eight shapes and seemed satisfied. "The group with Eamon in it has found nine, and the group with Tamara has found eleven," I told them. "Keep looking." They groaned a bit, but got back to work.

One more group was ready. They had found twelve, all different, and felt calmly secure and satisfied. "We think we found them all," they announced.

"Tell me why you think that," I responded.

Sandor explained. "We know there's only one with all five in a row. Then we looked for shapes with four in a row. Then with three. There were lots of those. Then two. We threw out the doubles." This explanation is typical of Sandor, who usually provides leadership in thinking.

"Do we have them all?" Sara asked, not having Sandor's confidence and needing to know.

"Yes," I answered them, "but don't announce this to the others. Let's give them some more time to search."

To keep this group involved, I gave a suggestion for another investigation with their pieces. "Here's a puzzle to solve," I said. "See if you can get your twelve pieces to fit together into one large rectangle. How many squares are there in all with your twelve pieces?"

They thought a bit. Diego jotted down *12 × 5* on a piece of scrap paper and came up with 60. "So," I continued, "a large rectangle will use all sixty squares. What dimensions might it have?"

"Ten by six," Sara answered quickly. "Will that work?" she asked, again needing to know.

"I'm not sure," I responded honestly, "but I've fit them into a 5-by-12 rectangle and into a 3-by-20 rectangle. I don't know how many different ways there are to do it. Maybe you can find out."

By this time two other groups had their hands raised. One was the group with Tamara in it. "We have twelve now," they said. I directed them to ask the group with Sandor and Sara in it to explain the puzzle activity to them. When I approached the other group, they waved me away, having gotten back to work. They had probably heard Tamara's group report that they had found twelve and were willing to look some more.

One more group raised their hands to announce that they were done. They had ten shapes, all different. "I've seen two other groups with those same ten shapes, and more," I told them. "See if you can find others."

"During exploring time, I stay out of students' group interactions as much as possible. I listen casually to their comments, noticing how individual students are working. I note ideas I overhear that will be useful for later discussion."

SUMMARIZING

Have groups share how they organized themselves to work.

After another few minutes, I decided to interrupt the entire class for a discussion. It took a while to get their attention and settle them down.

"Let's summarize this activity," I said when I had their attention. "Let's talk first about how you got organized as a group. I'd like you to hear from each other."

Sara started. "Sandor organized us. He wanted us to look for shapes in a system. We did it his way."

"Did you understand his system?" I asked.

"Not really at first," Sara answered, "but then as we got into it, I kind of caught on and was able to find some shapes."

"How about another group?" I asked.

Mei responded. "We just all started working, and when someone found a shape, they told the rest, and we looked to see if it was a new one or not. Then they cut it out."

"We did it the same way," Mike offered, "but Simona did all the cutting out."

"Why did you decide to do that?" I asked.

Simona answered. "We really didn't decide. I just did it." The other students giggled.

"Did it work well for you?" I pursued.

The group looked at each other and nodded. "I think so," Mike said. "I liked it," Simona said. Simona likes being organized and often offers to do the kinds of chores that keep things orderly.

"Are there any other ways groups organized that were different?" I continued. I waited a bit. No other groups had an idea to report.

Have groups talk about finding the pentominoes.

> "I waited, having learned that students need the time to think that a few moments of silence can provide."

"What about the problem of finding the pentominoes? Was it hard, easy, enjoyable, unpleasant? How did you feel about searching for all the shapes? Do you think your group solved the problem?" No comments were immediately offered. I waited, having learned that students need the time to think that a few moments of silence can provide.

Finally, Mei raised her hand. "It started off being easy, but then it got hard to find more." Some murmurs of assent went through the class.

"What did you do when it got hard?" I asked.

Mei responded, "Oh, we just kept looking. I found that when I just kept moving the tiles around, I would find a new shape. Then we had to check all the ones we had."

Riley agreed. "It was real hard once we got ten. We knew there were more because you had said that Eamon's group had eleven."

"What did you do then?" I asked.

"We went and looked at his group's shapes," Riley confessed. Giggles again from the class.

"How did you tell which ones you didn't have?" I asked.

"That wasn't easy," Riley said. "It was hard to figure that out. We had to bring our pieces over."

"Where was I when all this was going on?" I asked, wondering how I had missed it. The class laughed.

Catalina, also in Riley's group, offered an explanation. "Oh, you were talking to Sandor's group. You were real busy."

Ask a group who found all the pentominoes to post them. Have every student draw the shapes on grid paper.

"Are there really twelve shapes?" Sharbat asked.

"Yes," I replied. "How about one group that has found them all post theirs so the other groups can see which ones they're missing. I want each group to have a complete set for tomorrow's activity. Also, I will give each of you a sheet of centimeter-squared paper (**REPRODUCIBLE B**) on which you should sketch all twelve shapes for an individual record. You'll need that for tomorrow as well. There are lots of other geometry ideas I want you to investigate using your pentomino pieces. Who will post the pieces?"

Eamon posts his group's pentominoes for the class.

Eamon volunteered to do so, and I gave him a box of push pins so he could pin his group's pentominoes in a corner of the bulletin board. I put out a stack of centimeter-squared paper (**REPRODUCIBLE B**) for students to use to make their individual recordings and suggested that one person from each group come get enough for the entire group. I had Simona pass out a small envelope to each group for the pentomino pieces. "Take some time now to make your own recordings and to clean up the scraps of paper," I instructed. "Label the envelope for your pentomino pieces with your group name. I'll keep the envelopes for tomorrow. If you have time and are interested in a puzzle, check with Diego's group to learn one you can do with your pentomino pieces."

The class got busy again, finishing up and organizing. I felt good about this lesson. The students worked well together and were approaching these kinds of problem situations more eagerly than they had when the year began. It was a good sign that they were able to suspend their need for the answer of how many pentominoes there were. I believed that good attitudes toward solving problems were being developed in the class.

FURTHER EXPLORATIONS FOR OTHER DAYS

Ask students to sort the pentominoes into two groups—those that fold up into a box and those that don't.

As students were finishing up, I discussed with the students' teacher how I'd like to structure additional lessons. I wanted the groups to sort their shapes into two sets, those that would and those that would not fold into boxes. That way students would experience relating two-dimensional shapes to a three-dimensional one, a cube with one face missing.

I planned to introduce this activity by starting with the shape that looks like the Red Cross symbol:

I'd ask students to visualize how they could fold up the sides of this shape so that it would be a box without a lid. Students then would predict which side they thought would be the bottom of the box, opposite the open side, and mark their prediction with an X on the appropriate square on their group's pentomino. Then I would model for them how to fold the pentomino shape to check their prediction.

For each of the other pentominoes, students would individually inspect the pentominoes on their individual record sheets to predict whether or not each would fold into a box. They then would compare predictions with their group members. They would discuss which squares should be marked with an X to indicate the bottom of the boxes. Finally, they would test their predictions, using their group's cutout pentomino shapes. Some students find these types of activities difficult, and this sort of experience can help them strengthen their spatial skills and build their confidence in doing so.

Ask students to determine which pentominoes have mirror symmetry, which have more than one line of symmetry, and which have the same perimeter.

To engage the students in thinking about symmetry, students could fold each of the pieces to decide which have mirror symmetry and which do not and also find which have more than one line of symmetry. Students could also sort the shapes by their perimeters, providing a concrete experience with the notion that shapes with the same area do not necessarily have the same perimeter.

Have students make a pentomino puzzle.

For another follow-up activity, each student makes a set of pentomino pieces from sturdy paper. Everyone also needs a 5-by-12 grid for a game board, with squares matching the size of the squares used for the pentominoes. As an individual puzzle, each student tries to fit all twelve pieces onto the board, the puzzle some groups had already begun to explore. As a two-person game, players take turns placing pieces on the board, with the object being to play the last possible piece so that it's not possible for the opponent to place another. These games could go home as family gifts to help students communicate what sorts of things they were doing in their math class.

Have students create pentominoes from school milk containers.

School milk cartons are useful for a further follow-up activity, for which students need to save enough school milk cartons so each student can have several. The cartons should be rinsed well to avoid them smelling sour, and the tops should be cut off, making them topless boxes. For this exploration students try cutting the milk cartons so they will lie flat in the different pentomino shapes they have chosen.

11
A Place-Value Menu

Supporting Understanding of Place Value

Taught in Grades 1–2

Over the years that I've supported classroom math instruction, teachers have consistently asked me three questions: What do I do with students who finish assignments more quickly? How can I free up time to work with students who need extra help? How can I differentiate experiences to support all learners? I've found that using math menus is a pedagogical strategy that helps answer these questions. Here I present how a menu can be used to support place-value instruction.

OVERVIEW

Bonnie Tank used a menu in a second-grade class to engage the students in a collection of experiences that focused on place value. She organized the classroom so there were seven learning stations at which students worked, one for each menu activity. The students worked in pairs to complete the menu activities. Although they had to complete all the activities, they were able to choose the order in which they did them. Directions for all of the menu activities are included in the Reproducibles section.

When I've used this place-value menu with other classes, I haven't set up stations in the classroom, but instead listed the activities on a sheet of chart paper and kept the supplies in a central location. Then students get the materials they need and work wherever they'd like. Both organizations work well.

While it's time-consuming to get the menu organized (take a deep breath after you look at the list of materials needed), once you've organized it, you'll have planned for several weeks of instruction. If you're interested in more information about using menus, read my blog post: "Using Math Menus: Some Nuts and Bolts" (www .marilynburnsmathblog.com/using-math-menus-some-nuts-bolts/). Also, to learn about your students, either before or after you engage them in these activities, read my blog post: "Place Value: How to Assess Students' Understanding" (www.marilynburnsmathblog.com/place-value-how-to-assess-students-understanding/).

Place-Value Menu: The Ten Activities

Five-Tower Game	0–99 Patterns
Digit Place	Fill the Cube
Stars	Handfuls
Pinch a Ten	Fill the Boxes
Make a Shape	Number Puzzle

MATERIALS

- shape signs, a different one for each station, 7 to begin and 3 for later
- tubs for directions, plastic sleeves, and materials, 7 to begin and 3 for later
- directions (**REPRODUCIBLES I–R***), 1 copy of each for each tub
- plastic sleeves and cardboard for each sheet of directions
- recording booklets (construction paper, 9-by-12-inch paper, lined paper, and markers), 1 for each student (see page 117)
- materials as needed for each of the ten activities (see **REPRODUCIBLES I–R***)

*REPRODUCIBLES are available in a downloadable, printable format. See page xii for directions about how to access them.

GETTING ORGANIZED

Organize the classroom for the menu.

In this classroom, learning stations were a cluster of four or six desks or an available table, and each was designated by a shape sign suspended above it from the ceiling. (Or you can draw the shapes on 5-by-8-inch index cards, then fold them in half and prop them on the desks or table.) When you add additional menu activities, you'll need to establish new learning stations.

I placed the materials for each activity in rubber dish tubs labeled to match the station labels. Also, in the tubs I put the directions for the activity, mounted on cardboard and in a sturdy plastic sleeve. The tubs were stored on bookshelves easily accessible to students so that when it was time for work on the menu, assigned monitors would carry the tubs to their stations, set up the materials, and place the tubs back on the bookshelf at the end of math time.

Make a recording booklet for each student.

Along with preparing the activity directions and collecting the materials, I made a recording booklet for each student, folding 12-by-18-inch construction paper for covers and inserting seven sheets of 9-by-12-inch paper, one for each of the activities on the menu so far. I also included a sheet of lined paper on which students were to make a list of the menu activities, copying them from the list I had prepared and posted. In front of each task, students were to draw the symbol used for the station where that task would be put—a triangle, square, circle, heart, or other shape. The students pasted their list in the inside cover of their booklets. When they completed an activity, they would color in the symbol they had drawn. This helped each student keep track of what they had completed and also made it easy for me to glance into the students' booklets to get a sense of their progress.

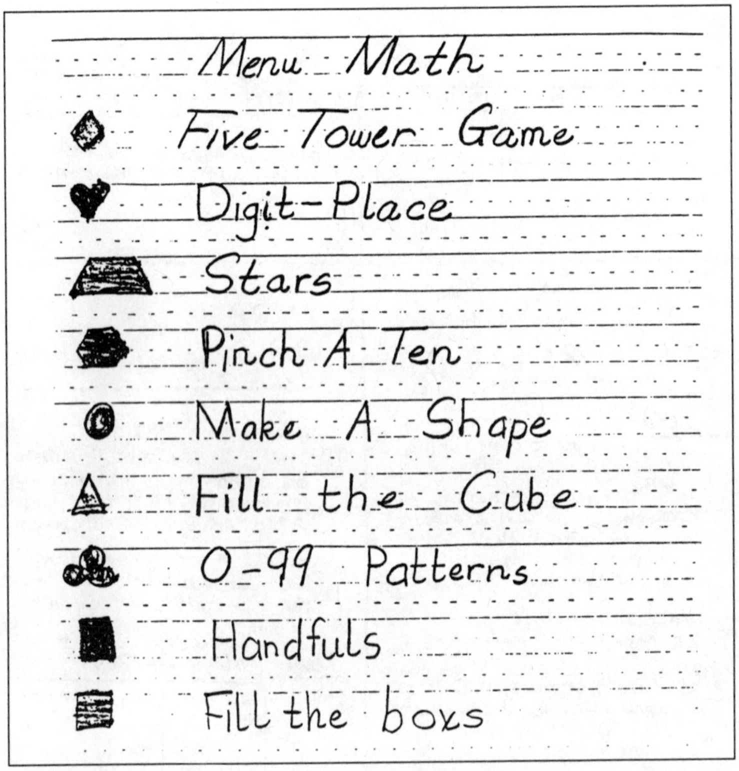

Menu Math
◆ *Five Tower Game*
♥ *Digit-Place*
▲ *Stars*
⬟ *Pinch A Ten*
◉ *Make A Shape*
△ *Fill the Cube*
🐞 *0-99 Patterns*
▮ *Handfuls*
▤ *Fill the boxs*

The students make a list of the menu activities, paste it in the inside cover of their recording booklets, and color in the symbol for each as they finish. This student had completed the initial seven activities and had added two more to the list.

Familiarize yourself with the menu activities.

When introducing the menu activities, I gave students specific directions for what I expected—how the monitors should set out the materials, how the students were to do each activity, and how they were to record their results. To prepare students for the activity called *Stars*, students needed to draw stars and time one minute. I modeled doing this with the whole class. For the games on the menu—the *Digit Place* and *Five-Tower Game*—I played sample games with the class and modeled how they should record in their recording booklets.

I presented and discussed each menu task carefully. Although this was time-consuming, it was valuable for minimizing the clarifications that most likely would be needed later.

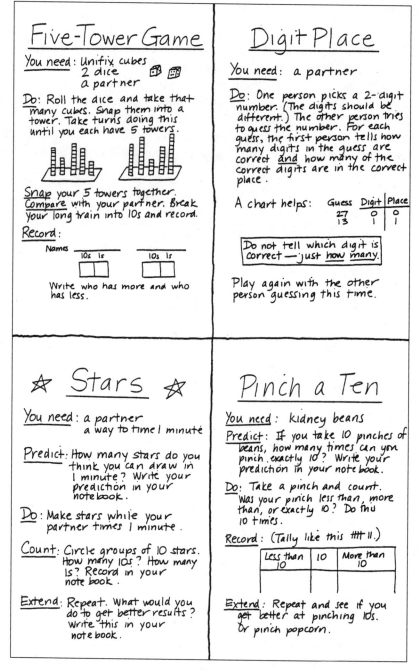

Five-Tower Game

You need: Unifix cubes
2 dice
a partner

Do: Roll the dice and take that many cubes. Snap them into a tower. Take turns doing this until you each have 5 towers.

Snap your 5 towers together. Compare with your partner. Break your long train into 10s and record.

Record:

Names

10s	1s		10s	1s

Write who has more and who has less.

Digit Place

You need: a partner

Do: One person picks a 2-digit number. (The digits should be different.) The other person tries to guess the number. For each guess, the first person tells how many digits in the guess are correct and how many of the correct digits are in the correct place.

A chart helps:

Guess	Digit	Place
27	0	0
13	1	1

Do not tell which digit is correct—just how many.

Play again with the other person guessing this time.

☆ Stars ☆

You need: a partner
a way to time 1 minute

Predict: How many stars do you think you can draw in 1 minute? Write your prediction in your notebook.

Do: Make stars while your partner times 1 minute.

Count: Circle groups of 10 stars. How many 10s? How many 1s? Record in your notebook.

Extend: Repeat. What would you do to get better results? Write this in your notebook.

Pinch a Ten

You need: kidney beans

Predict: If you take 10 pinches of beans, how many times can you pinch exactly 10? Write your prediction in your notebook.

Do: Take a pinch and count. Was your pinch less than, more than, or exactly 10? Do this 10 times.

Record: (Tally like this ‖‖ II.)

Less than 10	10	More than 10

Extend: Repeat and see if you get better at pinching 10s. Or pinch popcorn.

An example of the directions for some of the place-value menu activities (for all of the directions, see REPRODUCIBLES I–R).

Plan how to introduce the menu—part on one day, and the rest on the second day.

To introduce the menu, I planned to spend one class period teaching students how to play the game *Digit Place*, and then introducing a few of the other activities. On the second day, I would review the game and play it again with the class. Then I would introduce the remaining activities and give students the rest of the period to begin work.

I decided on this plan for several reasons. First, I felt it was best to avoid giving directions for all of the activities at one time. From previous experience with classes, I felt that teaching the rules for *Digit Place* on one day and then reinforcing the rules the next day would be helpful. Also, I've come to learn that the initial work time on a menu can have logistic difficulties, and allowing just half a period would give me adequate time to identify difficulties and note clarifications I needed to make.

Introduce vocabulary needed to play the game *Digit Place*.

To teach *Digit Place*, I had students gather on the rug. I find that gathering students on the rug helps remove them from distractions at their desks. Also, because students are sitting more closely together, it's easier for me to monitor their attention and participation.

"I'm going to teach you a game," I said when the students were settled. "It's a guessing game. I'll pick a number, and you'll try to guess what it is. The number I pick will have two digits in it. You'll make guesses by telling me a two-digit number. Then I will tell you how many of the digits in your number are correct and how many of those are in the correct place."

I asked, "Who can give an example of a two-digit number?" Several students offered examples. "Fifty." "Seventeen." "Eighty-four." I wrote each number on the board. In my experience, there are always some students who aren't familiar with the term *digit*. Introducing it in this way—using it and eliciting responses from other students—helps others build understanding. I find it's best to introduce new vocabulary by using it rather than by giving a definition.

When I called on Khalid, he suggested, "Ninety-nine." I wrote it on the board.

"I'm glad you suggested that number, Khalid," I said. "That reminds me of an important rule for this game. You cannot use a double-digit number, one with both digits the same. So aside from ninety-nine, what other numbers can't be used?"

The students called out others. "Fifty-five." "Thirty-three." And so on. If Khalid hadn't made this suggestion, I would have presented the rule because it's important to playing the game. Also, I wrote *99*, *55*, and *33* on the board and then crossed them out to help students who benefit from seeing numbers with two digits the same, not just hearing about them.

Now I decided to press for a definition of *digit*. "What does *digit* mean?" I asked, interested in hearing their ideas.

"It means number," Ramona answered. Other students nodded in agreement.

"Two digits means two numbers," Felix added.

I clarified, "There are ten digits in our math system—one, two, three, four, five, six, seven, eight, nine, and zero." I used my fingers as I said the numbers to show there are ten of them. "Numbers are made up of one or more digits. So, a number like 368 has three digits in it. But, in our game, we're only going to use two-digit numbers."

Explain how the game *Digit Place* is played.

I then explained how to play *Digit Place*. "Suppose the number I picked was seventeen. In a real game, I wouldn't tell you this, but I did this time just for practice." I wrote *17* on the board and circled it. I also drew a line to make two columns, writing *digit* at the top of the left-hand column and *place* at the top of the right-hand column.

"Now suppose that someone guesses seventy-four," I continued. "I would tell you that seventy-four has one correct digit, but no correct place." I modeled for the class how to record the guess of 74, then wrote 1 under *digit* to indicate that one of the digits in 74 is correct, and then wrote 0 under *place* to indicate that neither of the digits is in the correct place.

> "Even when students have the same idea, it's beneficial to give as many as possible the chance to explain their thinking. This gives more students the experience of expressing their ideas and gives everyone a variety of responses to hear."

digit	place
74	1 0

"Who can explain why I said seventy-four has one correct digit?" I asked. Several students raised their hands, and I gave all who volunteered the chance to explain. Verbalizing their thoughts is important. Even when students have the same idea, it's beneficial to give as many as possible the chance to explain their thinking. This gives more students the experience of expressing their ideas and gives everyone a variety of responses to hear. Very often students' wording differs for the same idea.

"Who can explain why I wrote *0* in the place column?" I asked. Again, several students offered explanations.

> "I find it's best to introduce new vocabulary by using it rather than by giving a definition."

Play a round of the game _Digit Place_ with the class.

I then played a real game of _Digit Place_ with students. I chose the number 42, wrote it on a slip of paper, and put the paper in my pocket. This was to model for students that they were to write their number down when they played the game with one another. Writing the number avoids the problem of students forgetting it in the midst of the guessing.

Heather made the first guess, "Sixteen." I started a new chart and wrote _0_ in both columns.

"What do you know now?" I asked.

"There's no one or six in your number," Emanual answered.

Natsu made the second guess, "Eighty-four." I wrote a _1_ in the digit column and a _0_ in the place column.

"What do you know now?" I asked again. This time, I asked students to turn and talk with their shoulder partner before I called on someone to report. The turn-and-talk routine gives all students the chance to think and try out their ideas, and also avoids having the same students volunteering. I called them back to attention and called on Reem.

"There's either an eight or a four in your number," he said.

"You don't know which one, but you know it's not in the right place," Natsu added.

I continued, recording students' guesses and giving clues. After I gave clues for each guess, I asked students to talk in pairs, and then I called on students to tell what they now knew. The students guessed my number on their eighth try.

digit	place	
16	0	0
84	1	0
79	0	0
8	0	0
47	1	1
43	1	1
41	1	1
42	2	2

The students enjoyed the game and were anxious to play again. I told them they would have the chance to play with their partners on the menu.

Introduce two more activities on the menu.

I spent the rest of the math time introducing two more menu activities, _Five-Tower Game_ and _Pinch a Ten_. This gave me the opportunity to demonstrate activities that required materials, and I explained the system of keeping the materials in the correct tubs. I chose a monitor for each of the activities and had the monitors practice getting the tubs, placing them at the appropriate stations, and then replacing them to the bookshelf.

When playing *Digit Place*, students use the clues to help them figure out the number.

digit		place
16	0	0
84	1	0
79	0	0
89	0	0
47	1	1
4	1	1

DAY 2 Introducing the Four Remaining Activities

Describe the four remaining activities. Choose the monitors responsible for each station's materials. Organize students into partners.

The next day, I introduced the four remaining activities. At this time, I didn't introduce the extra activities I had planned. Seven different choices seemed enough for students at this time. I chose the monitors for these learning stations. Next, I had all seven monitors take the tubs to the stations and set up the materials. Then I organized students into partners. The class had previous experience with this system and the setup went quickly and efficiently.

Remind students to work with their partners and to begin with any activity they like.

Once the materials were in place, I reminded the students about some of the operating principles necessary. "Remember, you and your partner are to work together. You can choose any task you like to begin, and you can do the tasks in whatever order you'd like."

Ask, "What will you do if a station is full?"

I then presented students with a potential problem. "What will you do if the station where you were planning to go is full, with students in all the available chairs?" I asked.

The students offered several different responses. "You have to choose another." "You wait until there's a space." "But in the meantime, you go somewhere else." For the seven activities, there were more than forty places, enough places so students would be likely to get their choices. When I introduced the extra activities, there would be even more options.

Have pairs of students decide where to start the menu and then begin to work.

I then asked each pair to talk and decide together where they thought they'd like to go first. As partners raised their hands and reported the activity they chose, I dismissed them to go and begin work. Students filtered throughout the room and began working.

Circulate, observe, and offer help as needed.

Students approached their work enthusiastically and with purpose. They were careful about how they followed directions and how they recorded in their booklets. However, several rough edges were evident during this beginning work period.

On three of the tasks—*Stars*, *Pinch a Ten*, and *Fill the Cube*—students were asked to record predictions, then to do the activity, and then to compare their predictions to their actual counts. I noticed that a few of the students were disturbed wby the discrepancy between their predictions and the actual counts and were busily erasing to make changes in their booklets. I made a note to discuss this with the class at the beginning of the next period.

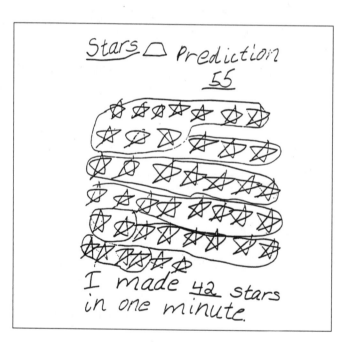

For the task of Stars, students make a prediction, do the activity, and record their actual count.

I noticed that students were confused by the directions for *Make a Shape*. I decided that I would discuss the directions with the students again and have them help me reword the directions, so they more clearly explained what to do.

Only two students elected to play *Digit Place* in this first work time. I didn't know if that was because the other students weren't comfortable with the game or if they were curious about the other tasks. I made a note to play another game with the class.

Digit-Place

	Digit	Place
45	0	0
78	0	0
42	0	0
29	0	0
31	1	0
34	0	0
14	1	1
15	1	1
19	1	1
10	2	2

Work from the two students who chose the game Digit Place from the menu. Note that their guesses of 15 and 19 are not necessary, since the first and fourth clues indicate that neither 5 nor 9 is possible.

Even with these challenges, the interaction between students was exciting to watch. One pair of students was coloring in the pattern of the even numbers on the 0–99 chart. Khalid noticed quickly that the even numbers went in stripes and was coloring down the columns. "My pattern looks like a purple zebra," he said. His partner, Stacy, however, had her own approach. She was coloring in the numbers in order—2, 4, 6, 8, 10, 12, and so on. Though she kept glancing over at Khalid's paper, she methodically continued as she had begun. It wasn't until Stacy had colored in almost three-fourths of her sheet that she felt secure enough to change her method and color in the numbers by columns.

Both students, however, had left 0 uncolored, and I talked with them about that, pointing out both that 0 fit the pattern of the stripes and that every other number that ended in 0 was even. I also showed them how all the even numbers could be written as the sum of two of the same addends, which included 0 since it could be written as 0 + 0. Khalid seemed to be comfortable with this, but Stacy wasn't convinced.

When working on *Fill the Cube*, students had to predict how many popcorn kernels it would take to fill a Unifix cube, and then how many lentils it would take. After making her guess for popcorn, Ilia commented to her partner, "It looks like it takes two lentils to make a piece of popcorn." She went back to thinking about how to use that information in her prediction for lentils.

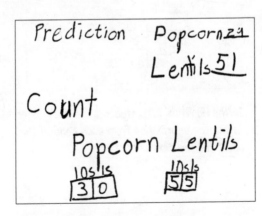

In Fill the Cube, students put kernels of popcorn and lentils into groups of ten to count how many of each fill a Unifix cube.

DAYS 3 AND 4 Working on the Menu

Before starting work on the menu, discuss what you noticed the day before.

Before students went back to work the next day, I gathered them together. I had them participate in the re-wording of the directions for *Make a Shape.* I discussed why it was OK that there were differences between predictions and counts. I played another game of *Digit Place* with the class.

Work continued more smoothly each day. I continued to circulate, observe, and offer help as needed.

DAYS 5 THROUGH 14 Completing the Menu

Day 5: Introduce two of the additional, but not required, activities—Handfuls and Fill the Boxes.

On Day 5, I began math period by introducing *Handfuls* and *Fill the Boxes,* two of the additional choices. They added a bit of new interest for the students. Ramona, however, was unimpressed. "Fill, fill, fill," she said, "all we ever do is fill." Hers did not seem to be a majority position, however. Work on the menu continued for the next three days.

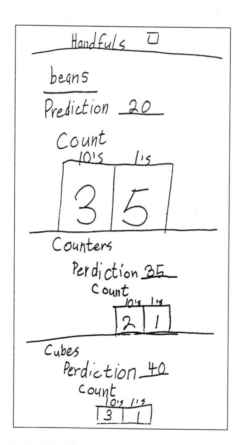

In the Handfuls task, students are encouraged to use the information from each handful they count for the next prediction.

Day 8: Introduce the *Number Puzzle* activity.

On Day 8, I explained the *Number Puzzle* activity to students, the last activity I had prepared for this menu. "As with the two other new activities," I told the students, "this activity isn't required. It's something extra that you can do if you'd like when you have completed all the other activities."

Following the directions propped at the *Number Puzzle* station, Danny and Akiko test whether thirty-two tiles will cover their shape.

Have students read each other's booklets and offer suggestions.

All in all, students worked for about two weeks on this menu. During that time, they stayed involved with the activities. When they completed their work, partners had the responsibility of reading each other's recording booklets and suggesting changes or corrections that could be made to improve their work. In this way, they had a chance to revisit all the tasks before the unit was over.

CONVERSATIONS WITH MARILYN

....

What's a Math Menu?

THE VALUE OF USING MENU—A COMPONENT OF MATH WORKSHOP—IN TEACHING AND LEARNING MATH

www.mathsolutions.com/welcometomathclass7

> "There are three questions I've been asked by teachers over and over again. One is, 'What do you do when some kids finish more quickly than others?' The second is, 'I want to find time as a teacher to work with a small group. How do I manage that in the classroom?' And the third is, 'How can I give kids things to do so that students with the least experience are as engaged as kids who are ready for a greater challenge?' I call these questions the big three. My answer is, 'math menus.'"

Overview

In this conversation with my longtime Math Solutions colleague Patty Clark, I discuss what math menus are, what are their benefits, what makes a successful math menu, how to get ideas for menus, and more. I also share insights about some of my favorite menus.

Making Connections

Using math menus is a low-tech classroom management solution for addressing "the big three" questions I talk about in this conversation. In my math class, math menus are lists of options on chart paper. They offer games, problems to solve, explorations for partners, and more. They can be something new for students to try or extensions of what they've experienced during class. When I'm constructing a menu, I often revisit my book *About Teaching Mathematics*, where I've included many ideas that come from menu choices I've given students. If you've never used menus, I urge you to try.

12
Raisin Math

Estimating, Dividing, and More

Taught in Grades 2–4

Students benefit from numerical experiences that emphasize thinking, reasoning, and solving problems. This investigation, another of my longtime favorites, involves students in several ways with small snack boxes of raisins. Students compute, estimate, consider statistical ideas, use measurements of volume and weight, and make proportional comparisons. The emphasis is on the thinking students bring to the problems and, throughout, students are asked to explain their reasoning as they report their ideas and solutions. It's valuable for students to confront numbers in a firsthand investigation, where the numbers are less tidy than traditional paper-and-pencil practice and where they're encouraged to estimate and make decisions when it isn't always possible to be exact.

OVERVIEW

Here I describe the lesson, *Raisin Math*, as I taught it to third graders. I've since taught the same lesson to second graders, sometimes engaging the entire class with the small boxes of raisins and then putting the investigation with the larger box on the menu as a choice activity. Also, I've used the investigation with fourth graders, spending additional time on sharing the raisins in the larger box to support their learning about division.

The lesson as I described it here spanned one long class period of about an hour and a half. The students' attention didn't lag. However, it was a great deal to cram into one session. At the end of the chapter, I present an alternate plan for presenting the lesson over two days.

MATERIALS

- $\frac{1}{2}$-ounce boxes of raisins, one for each student plus 1 extra
- $1\frac{1}{2}$-ounce boxes of raisins, one for each group
- lined paper, $8\frac{1}{2}$ inches by 11 inches, a large supply
- unlined paper, $8\frac{1}{2}$ inches by 11 inches, 1 sheet for each student

BEGINNING THE LESSON

Prepare for the lesson.

In preparation for the lesson, I bought $\frac{1}{2}$-ounce boxes (the smallest size) of raisins, one for each student plus one extra box. I also bought larger, $1\frac{1}{2}$-ounce boxes of raisins, one box for each group of three or four students.

Show the small boxes of raisins to the class. Explain that they will be able to eat the raisins after they use them to do several math activities with their group.

"Who likes raisins?" I asked the class. All but a few raised a hand. I showed the small boxes I had brought and shared with students that they'd each get to eat a box of raisins a bit later, if they wanted. "But first," I said, "we're going to do some math with the raisins. I have several different explorations for you to try, working together in your groups. For some of the activities, I'll ask you to report your group's thinking in writing." Although I planned to give students specific directions for each activity when we did it, I told them this much now to help prepare them for what I had planned.

Hold up one small box. Ask, "How many raisins do you think are in this box?"

I held up one small box and said, "Think for a moment about how many raisins might be in a box this size." Nicholas voiced a concern. "You can't know," he said, and explained, "because raisins are different sizes, so there could be a different number in one box than in another." However, Nicholas's comment didn't deter most of the others from guessing and there was a range of guesses—12, 20, 50, 17, 40, and 26. I gave all the students who were interested the opportunity to offer their opinion.

Explain that you will give each student a box of raisins and that they are to open the box, look at only the top layer, count how many raisins they can see, and share the result with their group.

"You'll have the chance in a short while to find out how many raisins are in the small box," I said. "Then we'll find out if Nicholas was right about the boxes containing different amounts. In just a moment I am going to give you each a box. Listen carefully to what I want you to do. You'll open the top of your box, but not touch any raisins or spill them out. Instead, I want you to count how many raisins you see just by looking in from the top. Then use that information to make an estimate about how many raisins you think are in the entire box." I then asked several students to repeat the directions I had just given. I find this gives a better chance that they all understand what I expect.

After several students revoiced what I had said, I gave one last direction before distributing the boxes, "Don't touch or munch on any raisins yet—you'll have the chance to do that in a while. Now, just open your box, quietly examine what you see, and make an estimate of how many raisins you think are in the box. Then, discuss your estimate with your group and decide on a group estimate of how many raisins are in a box."

MAKING GROUP ESTIMATES

Circulate, observe, and offer help as needed.

After students had opened their boxes and thought about the problem, they began to talk in their groups about a group estimate. It was difficult for some groups to agree on an estimate. Some students were invested in their own individual estimates and, as I circulated, I prodded gently to focus them on coming to a group decision.

As the groups were discussing, I interrupted the class to give two more directions. First, I asked them to write down their group estimate. Second, I asked them to choose someone in their group who would be the spokesperson to report their estimate to the class and explain their reasoning. (Sometimes when teaching this lesson, I assign a group writing task for explaining their estimate, with one student writing while the others give ideas. Other times, I ask students to write individually, which helps each of them focus. Here, I asked them to record only their estimate. All ways are fine, just different.)

Have groups report their estimates.

I began a class discussion. First Valeria explained for her group, "We each counted how many raisins were on our top layer. Then we multiplied by four. We picked twenty-four for our group estimate."

Trevor reported, "We think thirty raisins. When we looked in the box, we saw about six raisins, and we thought about five rows."

Two groups used informal averaging techniques to come to their estimates. Becky reported for her group, "Our group estimates twenty-six because Asmara wanted twenty-five and Emilie and I wanted twenty-seven. So we took the in-between number and decided on twenty-six."

The other group's individual estimates were more disparate. They agreed on a group estimate of thirty-one but explained their own estimates individually.

Nicholas
I say twenty-two because I counted eleven on top and timed it by two.

Kito
I think forty-two because I counted seven levels and six on each level.

Lucy
[Explaining her estimate of 27.]
I counted twelve on top and figured there were fifteen on the bottom.

Nina
[Explaining both her estimate and the group's decision.]
I say twenty-eight because I counted eleven on top and figured there was little more than fifteen on the bottom. Because forty-two was our high and twenty-two was our low, we picked thirty-one because it's sort of in the middle.

COUNTING AND SHARING THE RAISINS

Give students directions for counting the raisins in their own boxes.

I explained, "Now you'll count the raisins in your box. I'm going to give you each a sheet of paper. Carefully spill your raisins onto your paper to count them. When you do this, arrange the raisins on your paper so that I can easily see how many you have. When you've all done this, I'll record on the board how many raisins you each have."

List the numbers from 25 to 45 on the board. Tally each count that is reported, occasionally verifying the count.

While students were counting their raisins, I listed the numbers from 25 to 45 on the board. I planned to use tally marks to record their individual counts and then see what conclusions they could draw from the information.

Students arranged their raisins in different ways. I called on Marisol to report first. She announced, "I have thirty-eight raisins."

I made a tally mark on the board next to the 38 and asked, "How did you group them?"

Marisol answered, "I did it in fives, but I had one group with only three."

"How many full groups of fives did you have?" I asked.

Marisol counted. "Seven groups."

"Let's see how Marisol got thirty-eight raisins," I said to the class. I held up seven fingers to keep track of the seven groups and together we counted by fives to 35. Then we added three more to get 38.

We continued around the room, each student reporting. I marked each count with a tally mark. We verified some, but not all, by skip counting as we did with Marisol.

Although grouping by fives was a common method, students also used other ways to arrange their raisins.

Hannah
She grouped by threes and reported, "I have eleven groups of three. That makes thirty-three raisins, but my guess was twenty-seven."

Nina
Nina arranged hers into three groups of 10 with 6 left over.

Ryan
He spread his raisins on his paper and numbered each one in no particular pattern, getting to 36.

Trevor
Trevor arranged his into two long lines, numbered them in order, and reported, "I grouped them by ones and got thirty-seven."

Hannah grouped her raisins by threes and reported, "I have eleven groups of three. That makes thirty-three raisins, but my guess was twenty-seven."

Hold up a small unopened box of raisins. Ask, "Which one number would be a good estimate for the number of raisins in this box?"

I directed students' attention to the information on the board. The counts in the students' boxes ranged from 26 to 42. Six boxes contained 39, which was the count that occurred most often.

I held up a box of raisins that hadn't been opened or counted. I raised a question, "Suppose you were to estimate how raisins are in this box. Based on the information on the board, what one number do you think would be a good estimate?"

At that moment, I noticed that Rodrigo was leaning over, practically off his chair, searching on the floor. When I asked him what the problem was, he told me had dropped a raisin. I responded, "Don't worry, Rodrigo. One raisin doesn't matter so much." This answer was clearly not satisfactory at all to Rodrigo. Not only did he continue to look for the missing raisin, several of the students seated near him also began to search the floor. These things happen. To avoid having the lesson totally disintegrate, I took a raisin from the extra box and gave it to Rodrigo. Only then were the others and he ready to attend again.

I stated the question again, "What number do you think would be a good estimate?" Students' answers varied, some offering intuitive explanations for using the mode, mean, and median.

Iveth

I'd choose thirty-nine because that came up most.

Brandon

[Brandon's thought was related to Iveth's but different.]
I'd choose thirty-eight because even though thirty-nine came up most, there were more guesses that were less than thirty-nine, so I'd guess a little lower.

Nina

I'd guess thirty-seven because that seems to be in the middle.

Some did not relate to the information reported. Carrie, for example, said, "I'd guess thirty-six because that's what I got."

I didn't pursue the idea of averaging more formally. I decided that students would benefit from other experiences that provided the opportunity to think intuitively about averages. It's from these kinds of informal and experiential experiences that students begin to develop understanding of concepts.

GROUP COMBINING AND SHARING

Give instructions for groups to combine their raisins and then share them equally.

I described their next task. I said, "There are three things your group needs to do now. First, figure out how many raisins your group has altogether. Second, share the raisins equally, so everyone in your group has the same number of raisins. Third, record the answers for both and explain, in writing, how you figured out your answers."

Sometimes I write the directions on the board as a reference, but at this time I opted instead for asking a few students to repeat the directions. That had worked earlier in the lesson and I think it's good to involve students as much as possible so that I'm not doing most of the talking in the class. After this, the groups got to work quickly.

Circulate, observe, and offer help as needed.

The groups' solutions and explanations varied.

Group B (Three Students)
One group approached the problem concretely:

We have 112 raisans.
[They showed their work for adding 39, 37, and 36.]
We decided to give the raisans one at a time. We each have $37 + \frac{1}{3}$ raisans.

Group C (Three Students)
Another group avoided the problem of the extra raisin.

We have 112 rainsins altogether.
[Brandon had the 39 raisins.]
We added 37, 36, 39. Each of us got 37 raisins. Brandon took two away and gave one too Rick. We gave the extra one to Mrs. Hunn.

Group G (Four Students)
This group wrote the following, inventing a procedure that is similar to a division algorithm without the symbolism:

We have 146 raisins altogether. We added all the numbers up. Everybody gets $36\frac{1}{2}$ each. We devided 100 into 4 parts. We each had 25. Then we took apart the 40. Then we had 35 each. After that we took apart the six. We had $36\frac{1}{2}$.

Group E (Three Students)
This group reported:

We have 105 raisins altogether. We counted them by fives. We divided them by fives. And we all had 35 each.

Group A (Four Students)

This group wrote:

We have 154 raisins altogether. We added it altogether. We passed it around. Sara & Carrie will give 9 to each person. Kelly will give 7 to each person. Kirsten will give 10 to each person. Each person got 35 raisins. They showed their work for arriving at 35 by adding 18, 7, and 10. They did the addition twice. First, they arranged the numbers so that the 7 was in the tens place, producing a sum of 98. They crossed that out and did it again, the second time producing a sum of 35. This is a wonderful example of students noticing an error because of the context of the problem—it didn't make sense for each person to get 98. The eventual answer, however, was still incorrect, leaving 14 raisins somehow unaccounted for.

At this time, I told the students that they could eat their raisins, if they'd like, but to save their boxes. Groups wrote about how they combined their raisins and shared them equally.

We have 146 raisins altogether. We added all the numbers up. Everybody gets $36\frac{1}{2}$ each. We devided 100 into 4 parts. We each had 25. Then we took apart the 40. Then we had 35 each. After that we took apart the six. We had $36\frac{1}{2}$

36
39
40
+39
‾‾‾‾
154

We have 154 raisins altogether. We added it altogether. We passed it around. Sara & Carrie will give 9 to each person. kelly will give 7 to each person. kirsten will give 10 to each person.

18   18
70   10
‾‾‾ ‾‾‾
98   35

Each person got 35 raisins.

We have 112 raisins altogether. We added 37, 36, 34. Each of us got 37 raisins. Brandon took two away and gave one too Rick. We gave the extra one to Mrs. Hunn.

We have 112 raisins.

39
37
36
‾‾‾
112

We decided to give the raisins one at a time. We each have $37\frac{1}{3}$ raisins.

EXTENDING TO THE LARGER BOX

Give each group a large box of raisins. Ask students to figure out and record how many raisins are in the box without counting each raisin.

Finally, I gave each group a larger box of raisins, the $1\frac{1}{2}$-ounce size, and asked that, without opening it, they try to figure out how many were in this larger box and again record their thinking. Their conclusions varied.

Group G

For a box this big [this group made an actual-size illustration of the $1\frac{1}{2}$-ounce raisin box] we agreed on 117 raisins in the box. We looked at the net wt. and it was $1\frac{1}{2}$ oz. And we also used the little box to measure.

Group C

From the group of three that had 112 raisins altogether:

105 raisins in the big box. We took three small boxes and put them on the big box and there were about 7 left over from the 112 out of all three.

Group A

We guess there is about 95 raisins in the big box. We sized three little boxes up with the big box. We added all the amounts of raisins in thee little boxes and it ended up to about 95 raisins in all. We guess there is about 95 raisins in the big box in all.

Group E

99 because it took two and a half little boxes to fill up the big box.

Students' conclusions were rough, but their discussions were animated and exciting to observe. Their methods included using the statistics already collected, comparing the sizes of the boxes, and a combination of the two. When using the statistics, some students referred to their own previous counts, while others used the record of class counts on the board. When comparing the sizes of the boxes, some groups made use of the $\frac{1}{2}$-ounce and $1\frac{1}{2}$-ounce information on the boxes, some physically compared the boxes, and some did both.

REFLECTING ON THE LESSON

I thought about how the lesson contributed to my instructional goals.

All in all, the raisin exploration provided a variety of benefits. Listening to students discuss and come to conclusions gave me insights into their thinking, their capabilities, and their differences, all useful for making decisions about future experiences to provide.

For example, the group that intuitively used the long division algorithm shared 146 by dividing the 100 first, then the 40, then the 6. What would they have done if the numbers hadn't been so "nice," if they had had to share, for example, 135 raisins? I could use this problem for a whole-class lesson.

Another group shared the raisins by giving each student five raisins at a time, while another group doled out the raisins by ones. What would those groups do if they faced a problem without the concrete materials, if they were asked, perhaps, to figure how much they would each get if they found a five-dollar bill that no one claimed and could share it? How would the first group handle this problem? This was another idea for a follow-up lesson.

My assessment of students' abilities is key to making instructional decisions. I rely on what I learn from the students. This activity reminds me how assessments of students' readiness can be made during learning situations when students are actively involved exploring problems and using their mathematics skills and understandings.

> "My assessment of students' abilities is key to making instructional decisions. I rely on what I learn from the students."

I thought about the benefits of this lesson for students.

The major benefit to students from this experience is that they were thinking, reasoning, and solving problems—the overarching goal of elementary math instruction. My lesson objective wasn't for students to master a particular skill, but rather to provide a learning opportunity in which they were engaged and their mathematical thinking could be stretched as they dealt with computing, estimating, statistical ideas, proportional reasoning, and comparing measurements of volume and weight, all in a problem-solving situation.

Who learned most from this experience? Perhaps Trevor. He reported: "My mom puts raisins in my lunch sack. She buys a big bag and fills the little boxes. She's been cheating me. I never get more than seventeen raisins when she fills it up. I'm going to tell her when I get home."

AN ALTERNATIVE TEACHING PLAN

Although the lesson was valuable, it was a great deal to squeeze into one day's instruction. When I taught the lesson again, I spent two days on the experience and didn't race students through quite so much. Here's an alternative two-day plan that I've used:

Day 1: Introducing and Exploring

1. Show a small box. Have students guess how many raisins it contains; then ask them to report their predictions.
2. Distribute the boxes. Students open the boxes, count what they see, and make an estimate. They then discuss their estimates in their groups, decide on a group estimate, and report their estimate in writing, explaining their reasoning.
3. Students count their raisins, arranging them on paper so it's easy to see how many there are. Record their counts on the board.
4. Based on the information recorded on the board, students decide on one number as an estimate for how many raisins are in another box. Have them record their prediction individually, explaining their reasoning. They should then discuss their thinking in their groups and, finally, report to the class.
5. Students figure out how many raisins their group has altogether and record the number, explaining how they determined it. They can eat their raisins, but have them save the little boxes for the next lesson. Also, save the information you recorded about their actual counts.

Day 2: Exploring

1. Give each group a $1\frac{1}{2}$-ounce box of raisins. Have them estimate how many raisins there are in it and explain in writing how they did this. Groups report to the class.
2. Have groups count the raisins in the box, then share them equally, again describing how they did this.

FINAL THOUGHTS

> "I find that teaching is enhanced when the impetus for instructional decisions evolves from students' ideas, acknowledging their thinking and embracing their interests."

Problem-solving experiences such as this help develop students' conceptual understanding of number and operations. Several times during the lesson, teaching opportunities arose to focus on the operations. For example, when I asked students to group their raisins so it would be easy to see how many there are, this provided the chance to discuss multiples. When I asked students to share their raisins equally in their groups, the different methods they reported could lead to a discussion of division. (One group in the class described chose a method that replicates what we normally do in the long division algorithm although they had not yet had formal instruction with it.) I find that teaching is enhanced when the impetus for instructional decisions evolves from students' ideas, acknowledging their thinking and embracing their interests.

13
Riddles with Color Tiles

Building Number Sense

Taught in Grades 3–6

*R*iddles with Color Tiles emphasizes logical reasoning and language skills while helping students develop number sense. I introduced these riddles at the beginning of the year to help students learn about my expectations for them to work with materials, collaborate with a partner, listen to their classmates, and practice sharing their thinking. Building on students' interest in riddles, I presented clues for students to decipher in order to determine which color tiles were in a bag.

OVERVIEW

The color tiles are one-inch-square tiles in four colors—red, blue, yellow, and green. When I introduced the riddle to the class, I presented the clues, one at a time. Working in pairs, students analyzed the clue and then displayed with their tiles what they knew. Each successive clue narrowed the possibilities, until there was sufficient information to declare what's in the bag. The students later created their own riddles for others to solve. I've found this exploration to be appropriate for students in grades 3 and above.

MATERIALS

- 1-inch-square tiles in four colors, at least 20 of each color for each pair
- paper lunch bags, a large supply
- clothespins, 1 for each lunch bag
- lined paper, $8\frac{1}{2}$ inches by 11 inches, 1 sheet per pair of students plus extra
- paper bag filled with 4 blue and 2 yellow tiles, 1
- paper bag filled with 4 blue, 4 yellow, and 4 green tiles, 1
- Extra Riddle No. 1 on chart paper with a matching bag of tiles, 1 (see page 144)
- Extra Riddle No. 2 on chart paper with a matching bag of tiles, 1 (see page 145)

INTRODUCING THE FIRST RIDDLE

Allow time for free exploration with the color tiles.

Because students hadn't yet had time to explore the color tiles, I began by giving them a chance to do so. I've learned from experience that if students' curiosity about a material isn't satisfied, they have difficulty focusing on the lesson being presented. Time for their own exploration is essential.

The amount of time students need for this free exploration differs from class to class. In this instance, I gave students fifteen minutes before asking for their attention. Then I told them I wanted them to try an activity I had planned with the color tiles. I judged from their responses that most were willing to stop their own exploring. However, if they had been so involved that they couldn't refocus, I would have allowed more time.

Give instructions for solving riddles.

Once I had students' attention, I asked, "What's a riddle?" The students had various thoughts to share. "It's something you have to guess." "You get clues." "Sometimes it's funny." "Sometimes they rhyme."

"I have a riddle about what's in this bag," I told the class. I had put four blue tiles and two yellow tiles into a lunch bag.

"My riddle has clues," I continued, "and I'll write the clues on the board, one at a time. After each clue, I'll ask you to think about what color tiles could be in the bag. Then your partner and you will talk about what information you have about the tiles in my bag and use your tiles to show what you know."

Write Clue No. 1 on the board. Have partners use tiles to reflect their thinking.

I gave the class the first clue. "I have fewer than ten tiles," I said, writing the clue on the board. "What could I have in the sack?"

Russell raised his hand. "Could it be ten tiles?" he asked. This gave me the opportunity to clarify what "fewer than" means.

The students talked with their partners and displayed possibilities with their tiles. I had them describe what the tiles showed and what they knew. There were various responses.

Neil explained for Stacy and himself why they thought there were nine tiles. "We put out ten tiles," he said, "and then took away one, so we think there are nine."

Ari and Jung had carefully laid out nine lines of tiles, with nine, eight, seven, and so on, down to a line with only one tile. "It could be nine or eight or seven or six or five or four or three or two or one," Ari explained.

No other pairs were so organized. Most displayed either a few possibilities, or showed just one prediction, as did Neil and Stacy. Elissa and Jason, for example, placed six tiles in a line. Elissa reported, "We think there are six tiles." When I asked why they had decided on six tiles, however, neither of them could supply a reason.

The different responses from the pairs didn't surprise or disturb me. I knew they would have a chance to reconsider with later clues.

I asked several students to repeat the directions I had just given. I find that asking stuents to revoice gives a better chance that they all understand what I expect.

Write Clue No. 2 on the board. Again, have pairs of students arrange their tiles and share their thinking.

I presented the second clue, "There are two colors," I said, then wrote this clue under the first one. "Talk about this with your partner and show with your tiles what you think I could have put into the bag."

Again, students discussed and reported what they thought. Some kept what they had had before, making adjustments so they had two colors. Some changed completely what they had. Busana and Lizette displayed just two tiles, one red and one yellow. They ignored the previous information about how many tiles, and merely focused on the colors.

Repeat the procedure for Clue No. 3.

I gave my third clue and wrote it on the board. "I have no green or red tiles," I said. The students scurried to make changes on their desks.

"What do you now know for sure?" I asked. Many hands went up.

I called on Sergio. "You only used blue and yellow," he said.

"What else do you know for sure?" I asked.

Fewer hands were raised. "There are less than ten tiles," Jennifer responded.

"What else do you know for sure?" I continued.

"You could have six tiles," Dalia said.

"I might," I said, "but you can't say how many tiles I have for sure yet. I'll give you another clue that will help you begin to figure out how many I have in the bag."

Repeat the procedure for Clue No. 4.

I then gave the fourth clue, "I have twice as many blue tiles as yellow tiles." After writing the clue on the board, I asked, "Who knows what I mean by 'twice as many'?"

Only two of the students in the class responded that they knew. Though both could show what they thought with their tiles, neither could verbalize what "twice as many" meant. Students need a great deal of experience explaining to develop language appropriate for describing their thoughts.

I explained the concept of "twice" to students by using other words—double, two times, that many again—and the color tiles. "Put out three red tiles and three blue tiles," I directed the students. "Now put out another three blue tiles. That gives you twice as many blue tiles. How many blue tiles do you have?" When they answer, I can say that six is twice as many as three. "It's double the amount." I did several other examples such as this one with the students.

There were murmurs of recognition. Students seemed to remember knowing about the idea of "twice."

Repeat for Clue No. 5.

I went on to my fifth clue. "I have two yellow tiles in the bag," I said, and added this clue to the list already on the board. "Now discuss with your partner what could possibly be in the sack."

Ari was eager to report his discovery. He was sure that there were two yellow tiles and four blue tiles in the bag and explained how he had figured it out. "I put two yellow and two blue down, and then I put two more blue," he said.

"That's what I think too," Darwin said. Several others nodded in agreement.

"So, you're willing to guess what's in the bag?" I asked Ari. He nodded confidently.

"Is anyone else willing to guess what's in the bag?" I asked the class. Only a few other students raised a hand.

"I think I know," Mia said, a bit tentatively.

"Do we get another clue?" Jason asked.

"What about Ari's idea?" I asked.

"I think we need another clue," Darwin said. Although he agreed with Ari, he still felt the need for a further check.

Write Clue No. 6 on the board to complete the riddle.

"I have six tiles," I said, writing this sixth clue on the board. That resolved it for the class. They watched eagerly as I emptied the bag and showed them the four blue tiles and the two yellow tiles.

The sixth clue resolves the riddle for the students.

5. There are two yellow tiles in the bag.
6. I have six tiles

STUDENTS WRITE RIDDLES

Explain the procedure for writing riddles.

I gave students directions for writing their own riddles. "Your partner and you will write a riddle together for others to solve," I explained. "For your riddle, use no more than ten tiles and only two colors."

I then outlined the procedure. "I'll give your partner and you one sheet of paper, a lunch bag, and a clothespin. First you decide together what to put into the sack. Then write clues so others can guess. Finally, attach your clues to the bag with a clothespin and put the bag on top of the bookcase. You can begin now and work until it's time for recess. You can continue working on your riddle tomorrow."

Circulate, observe, and offer help as needed.

The students had difficulty with this assignment. Most began by focusing on the colors they had chosen, giving clues for these. *The colors are dark. The colors start with a B and a Y. The colors are not red or yellow. The colors are kind of bright. The colors are in the room. There are some green.*

After this, however, most groups got into difficulty. "What do we do now?" was a common question. I let them work, however, as I think there is benefit in struggling a bit as long as the frustration doesn't become overwhelming and cloud students' interest in the activity. Also, watching students work helps me learn more about individual thinking processes and problem-solving abilities.

> "I think there is benefit in struggling a bit as long as the frustration doesn't become overwhelming and cloud students' interest in the activity."

The next day, read a few of the students' riddles to the class.

The next day, after all had done some work on their riddles, I called students together. I told them that I knew that all their riddles weren't finished yet, but that I wanted to talk about what they had done. "I'm going to have some of you read your clues to the class," I said. "Together we'll decide if you have enough clues or if you still need more."

We did this for several of the students' riddles, and it seemed to help students focus on the need to test their clues to see if the clues were sufficient. Still, it was clear to me that further experience was needed, and I planned to do another riddle with the class the next day.

A SECOND RIDDLE

Give Clue No. 1 and observe what students do.

The students were excited the next day when I told them I had another tile riddle for them to solve. I reminded them that after each clue, they were to talk with their partner, decide together what could be in the bag, and use tiles to show what they thought were possibilities.

I gave the first clue. "There are twelve tiles," I said, writing the clue on the board. The students immediately began talking and counting out tiles. They seemed much more comfortable this time. "I think it's all yellow." "I think it's six blue and six red." "It could be four colors and three of each."

Some pairs of students placed twelve tiles in a line. Others arranged theirs in an array. Some displayed just one possibility, while others showed several possibilities.

Have each pair of students explain their thinking, then give Clue No. 2.

Before presenting the next clue to the students, I asked them to share their thoughts. "One from each pair is to tell what you have in front of you," I explained, "while the rest of the class listens."

After this reporting, I gave the second clue. "I used three colors," I said, writing this clue under the first one. Again, students got busy arranging tiles and talking. Most made changes in what they had shown so their possibilities had three colors.

Ari and Jung tried to figure out how many different ways they could have three colors, filling their table with arrays of twelve tiles. Others still held to a single prediction. Busana and Lizette, for example, showed one line of twelve tiles with five blue, five red, and two yellow. Russell and Miles made the same prediction, but arranged their tiles into a row of five green, a row of five blue, and a row of two yellow.

Help students stay focused.

Getting students to stop work and refocus on a discussion was more challenging this time. Some were eager to continue exploring possibilities. Others had begun to play and build with the tiles. Even after several reminders, some students were distracted by the tiles when they were supposed to be listening to each other.

I instituted a system for bringing them to attention so they wouldn't continue to fiddle with the tiles during our discussions. "From now on," I said, "when I put a star on the board, that means no one can touch the tiles. I think it is important for you to listen to each other, and I think not touching the tiles will help. After we spend a little time talking, I will erase the star, and then you can go back to work with the tiles." I drew a star on the board, and all of the students took their hands off their desktops. This system turned out to be a tremendous help.

Write Clue No. 3 on the board.

After students reported their conclusions from the second clue, I gave the third. "I have no red tiles," I said. I wrote this clue on the board and then erased the star.

The students got busily involved making changes in the possibilities they had displayed, reminding each other that it had to be three colors and that there had to be twelve tiles. Most just eliminated the red tiles, replacing them with other colors. Russell and Miles were even more convinced that their prediction of five green, five blue, and two yellow was correct.

When I wanted to refocus them for a discussion, I walked to the board and drew a star. This time, it took little effort to get their attention.

Share with the class what you observed, then have students share their ideas.

Before having them share their thinking, I commented to the class what I was able to observe as I watched them work. "I could tell many things from looking at what was on your desks," I said. "I could tell who was working together. I could tell if you were using all the clues on the board. I could tell what your ideas were." Then I had students share what they now thought might be in the bag.

Give Clue No. 4.

I continued with the fourth clue. "There are the same number of blue tiles as green tiles," I said, and I wrote this clue on the board. The students looked at me patiently.

"You didn't erase the star," Elissa pointed out.

I erased it, and students got to work.

This clue helped some of the students more accurately define the possibilities. Once again, the number of possibilities they placed in front of them varied. A few pairs found all five possibilities, some displayed two or three, and a few still showed only one choice.

Ask students to report their predictions and record each one on the board.

I drew a star on the board and called students back to attention. This time I recorded their predictions as they reported them.

$$6y + 3b + 3g$$
$$2y + 5b + 5g$$
$$8y + 2b + 2g$$
$$4y + 4b + 4g$$
$$10y + 1b + 1g$$

"Are there any more possibilities?" I asked.

Ari raised his hand. "You can't have six blue and six green because that would be twelve already, and you wouldn't have any yellow," he said.

No one could think of other possibilities.

Then I put a loop around the column that listed the yellow tiles and asked students what they noticed about what I had circled.

$$\boxed{6y} + 3b + 3g$$
$$\boxed{2y} + 5b + 5g$$
$$\boxed{8y} + 2b + 2g$$
$$\boxed{4y} + 4b + 4g$$
$$\boxed{10y} + 1b + 1g$$

"They all are yellow," Renata said.

"They all are counting by twos," Jung said.

No one had any other comments. "What can you say about the numbers that tell how many blue and green tiles could be in the bag?" I asked.

"Those are just counting by ones," Miles said.

Give the fifth and final clue.

I then gave the class the fifth clue. "I have four yellow tiles," I said, and added this to the list of clues. This last clue told the rest of the story for all the students. After a few minutes, each pair had a single tile arrangement showing four yellow, four blue, and four green tiles. There were no doubts, and no one needed an additional clue.

A SECOND CHANCE AT WRITING RIDDLES

Once again present the guidelines for writing riddles.

"I'd like you to get back to writing your own riddles again," I said. "You can continue working on the riddle you started, or you can begin again and count that one as practice."

This time, the assignment was greeted with much enthusiasm. Again, I presented them with the same guidelines. "Remember, use no more than ten tiles and only two colors. First, agree on the tiles to put into the bag, and then write clues so others can figure it out. Call me over to check your riddle when you've finished it." There was less confusion this time as students began work on their riddles.

Elissa and Jason work together to write their own riddle.

Give a new riddle to students who finish writing their riddles quickly.

The students continued working on their riddles during math time the next day. To engage those who finished writing their riddles more quickly, I had prepared two sets of clues. This way, students who completed their own riddles had new problems to consider while those who needed more time to work could have it. I wrote each set of clues on large chart paper, clipping the matching bag of tiles to it.

> Extra Riddle No. 1
>
> Clue No. 1: There are ten tiles in the bag.
> Clue No. 2: There are three colors.
> Clue No. 3: There are three blue tiles.
> Clue No. 4: There are two more red tiles than blue tiles.
> Clue No. 5: There are three more red tiles than yellow tiles.

> Extra Riddle No. 2
>
> Clue No. 1: There are more than six tiles in the bag.
> Clue No. 2: There are three colors.
> Clue No. 3: There are four green tiles.
> Clue No. 4: There are half as many yellow tiles as green tiles.
> Clue No. 5: There is one more blue tile than green tiles.

Offer help to those students who need it.

Having the extra riddles made me available to help students who needed it. Russell and Miles, for example, had written a riddle with six clues. Their clues were:

1. We have more yellows then the other colore.
2. One is the colore of the sun.
3. One is the colore of the sea.
4. And it is dark.
5. The colores are around the room.
6. I bet you can't ges how many blues and yellows there are.

Russell and Miles were right. From their six clues, I wasn't able to guess how many blues and yellows were in the bag. I talked with them about also needing clues that gave me information about how many tiles there were, not just about their colors. I directed the boys to look at the clues I had written that gave hints about how many tiles were in the bag. I left them to work, and they added two additional clues:

7. There are 2 more yellow than blue.
8. There are 10 all together.

> 1. We have more yellows then the other colores.
> 2. One is the colore of the sun.
> 3. One is the colore of the sea.
> 4. And it is dark.
> 5. The colores are around the room.
> 6. I bet you can't ges how many blues and yellows there are.
> 7. There are 2 more yellow then blue.
> 8. There are 10 all together.

After Russell and Miles add the seventh and eighth clues, their riddle is complete.

I encountered the same situation with Elissa and Jason and handled it in a similar manner. The five clues they had written weren't sufficient. They were pleased with the sixth clue they added to their final version. They wrote:

1. There are ten.
2. There are six of one color.
3. We have some reds.
4. There are no yellow.
5. There are no green.
6. There are less blues.

Stacy and Neil wrote a sufficient set of clues without prompting:

1. We have no yellows.
2. We have 1 red.
3. There are more blues then red.
4. There is more then 2.
5. We have no greens.
6. We have more then 7.
7. We have 8 more blues then red.

> 1. We have no yellows.
> 2. We have 1 red.
> 3. There are more blues then red.
> 4. There is more then 2.
> 5. We have no greens.
> 6. We have more then 7.
> 7. We have 8 more blues then red.

Stacy and Neil's riddle provides sufficient clues for guessing how many tiles of each color are in the bag.

When students had completed their riddles, they took turns presenting them to the class. One or two pairs of students presented their clues each day until the class had deciphered all of the riddles.

> ### Riddles
>
> 1 There are ten tiles,
>
> 2 There are two colers.
>
> 3 The colers are kind of light.
>
> 4 There are no green and red.
>
> 5 There are more yellow than blue.
>
> 6 There are four blue;

Before presenting their riddle to the class, Jason and Jennifer added clues to clarify the colors.

CONVERSATIONS WITH MARILYN

Why Write in Math Class?

www.mathsolutions.com/welcometomathclass8

"The process of writing got me to reflect on my teaching in a way that I wouldn't have necessarily if I had just gone on to plan my next day's lesson . . . eventually I said to myself, 'Why don't we get kids to do this? And then, when I wanted kids to produce work so I could share their thinking, they got better at it. So I decided writing should be an integral part of math learning—so much so that I wrote a book called *Writing in Math Class*. Now that I do it, I can't live without it."

"I don't use the word *show*. It's *write*. If I want you to explain your thinking, you can use words, numbers, pictures, equations, anything that explains your thinking. In a way that may be showing your work, but show your work sounds like you did some work to get an answer. I'm asking you to explain your thinking. I'm interested in what's behind what you're doing."

Overview

In this conversation with my longtime Math Solutions colleague Patty Clark, I share the benefits of and expectations for making writing a part of students' math learning.

Making Connections

Writing has become so integral to my math teaching that I can't imagine it not being a regular element of my instruction. I've tried many ways to use writing. Sometimes I ask students to do a quick-write on a half sheet of paper so the assignment doesn't seem so daunting. Sometimes I have students write letters to me or someone else in class so they have an immediate audience for describing their thinking. Other times I structure math writing as a persuasive argument, ask students to write directions for a game, or ask them to give their suggestions for strategies. I encourage you to draw ideas from the assignments you give students when teaching writing and make the shift into math class.

14
Sharing Cookies

Connecting Fractions and Division

Taught in Grades 3–5

Students have had many experiences with fractions before they receive formal instruction in school. They drink half their milk, they give a friend half of their snack, they fold paper into four equal parts, they learn that four quarters make a whole dollar. From these types of experiences, in which they explore fractional parts and the language of fractions, students begin to develop understanding of fractional concepts.

Their understanding, however, may be limited. It's not uncommon for students to say, for example, "Your half is bigger than mine" and not notice any mathematical inconsistency. Also, their experience most likely has not helped them learn about the symbolic notation we use for fractions or about the idea of equivalence of fractions. *Sharing Cookies* describes an introductory classroom experience with fractions.

OVERVIEW

This lesson, *Sharing Cookies,* was taught to third graders in December and was the first instruction in fractions the students had during the school year. The lesson models how a problem-solving approach using concrete materials can develop students' understanding of a new concept.

In small groups students were presented with the problem of sharing cookies equally. The use of paper circles to represent the cookies provided students the opportunity to deal concretely with fractional concepts. After their concrete exploration, the students' experience was connected to the standard symbols for writing fractions. The notion of equivalence was also introduced as an extension of students' concrete investigation.

For a description of how I used this lesson with fourth graders, read my blog post: "What Is 5 Divided by 4? So Many Answers!" (www.marilynburnsmathblog.com/what-is-5-divided-by-4-so-many-answers/).

MATERIALS

- construction-paper circles, 2 inches in diameter, at least 20 for each group
- *Sharing Cookies* (**REPRODUCIBLE S***), at least 6 for each group
- scissors, a large supply
- gluesticks, a large supply

PRESENTING THE ACTIVITY

Explain to the class that they are going to investigate sharing "cookies."

Before I started the lesson, I organized the class of twenty-five students into six groups, five groups with four in each and one group of five. After settling the students, I gave them a general idea of what they would be doing.

I explained, "I'm going to explain a math activity for you to explore in your groups. It involves sharing cookies," Their eyes lighted up. I then gave them the bad news. "We won't be using real cookies—we'll be using make-believe cookies." They looked a bit disappointed but were still curious about what I would have them do.

"I've cut small paper circles for cookies that you'll be using for this activity," I explained, showing them the circles. I had cut the circles, each about two inches in diameter, from buff-colored paper so they would be easier to see when pasted on white paper. "You'll also have recording sheets for your groups to record your work."

Ask, "If four students share four cookies equally, how much would each person get?"

I continued, "Before I give you any materials, here's a question I'd like you to think about. If I gave a group of four students four cookies to share equally, how much would each person get?" As I had predicted, this was obvious to students. But it gave me the chance to discuss sharing equally, an important concept for dealing with fractions. I then shared with students that they would have a similar problem to solve in their groups.

Give the task: *With your group, figure out each person's share if four people share six cookies equally. Then do the same for five, three, two, and one cookie. Record on the recording sheets* (**REPRODUCIBLE S**).

"Your first task will be to figure out how to share six cookies equally among four people. You are to use the circles I've cut as the cookies and actually share them. Use scissors and paste each person's share on the recording sheet." I made sure that the recording sheet had space for group members' names at the top and was divided into four spaces in which students could paste the "cookie" shares. I had written a question at the bottom of the recording sheet beneath the four spaces: How much did each person get? (This recording sheet is available as **REPRODUCIBLE S.**)

SHARING COOKIES

Names _____   _____

          _____   _____

Share _____ cookies equally among 4 people. Paste each person's share in a box.

How much did each person get?

"When you've shared the cookies," I explained further, "discuss together how to answer the question at the bottom of the sheet."

I also let students know that when they had solved the problem with six cookies, they should come and get another recording sheet and solve the problem with five cookies. And after that they would get additional recording sheets to solve the problem with three cookies, then two cookies, and finally with one cookie.

The goal of this lesson was to provide students with a problem-solving experience in which they would interact with fractional concepts. The cookies gave them the opportunity to learn from physical materials. Rather than focusing on the abstract symbolization of fractions, students could verify their thinking with the actual material they were using. Asking them to record how much each person got would give me the opportunity to learn what, if anything, the student knew about how to write fractions. I was curious how they would answer that question on their recording sheets.

I asked that one member of each group come up for the group's materials, and I gave each of them six circles and a recording sheet.

DURING THE WORK TIME

Circulate, observe, and offer help as needed.

When students began their explorations, all groups were able to work with ease. I worried a bit that perhaps this activity was too easy for them, however students were involved and interested. Not only did they focus on the mathematics in the activity, some groups also decorated their cookies—some added chocolate chips and others drew raisins.

Students worked without interruption for about half an hour. In that time, each group of four did all the problems, with six, five, three, two, and one cookies, and several groups asked for more to do. (As an extra problem for groups who finished first, I asked them to share seven cookies among four people.)

When I presented the seven-cookie problem to one group, Stephanie commented that it was too easy to do. "Let us do eight cookies," she said. And then she continued thinking aloud, "But that's easier—it would be two cookies." And then the group started to think aloud together. "What about nine cookies?" "Easy, two and a fourth." "Ten would be two and a half." Since they seemed involved and self-directed, I left them without their even noticing.

I gave one particularly interested and speedy group the problem of sharing seven cookies again, however this time I said that I was also planning to attend their party, so they needed to divide the seven cookies equally among five people. They did not think the problem was difficult. Though they were satisfied with their solution, it revealed that they were unable to deal with these particular fractional parts. They had pasted my share on the back of the paper and had recorded: *Evrywon get 2 halfs 1 quarter and one sliver.*

The group with five students had difficulty that I was not immediately aware of. They began by assuming that each person in their group needed a share, a decision that is commendable for its sense of fairness. It meant, however, that they had to tackle the problem of sharing six cookies among five people as their first problem. It was difficult for them, and once I noticed their struggle, I suggested they include me as well and share four cookies among the six of us. They did fine with that, but it was the only problem they had time for during the half hour. Because of their different experience, the summarizing discussion was not very valuable for them.

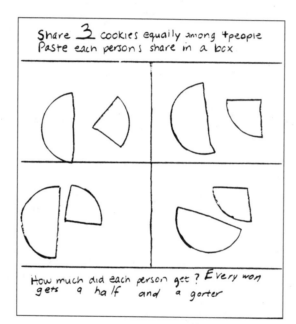
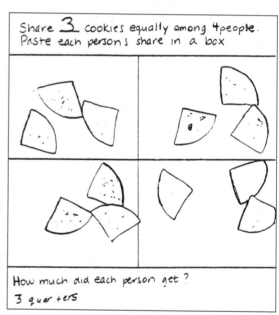

Groups find different ways to solve the problem of sharing three cookies among four students.

DISCUSSING THEIR WORK

Have groups share how they organized themselves to work.

The lesson was a rich one for summarizing. First, I discussed with students how they had organized themselves for working. The students reported the different ways they divided up the jobs of cutting and pasting the "cookies," how they decided who would do the writing, how they took turns, and how they helped each other. The students had worked cooperatively in a totally natural way because their regular teacher had developed a classroom atmosphere that supports such behavior, working hard to develop students' attention to the social skills needed for cooperation.

Discuss the results of the six-cookie problem, then the five-cookie problem.

Then I began a discussion of the fractions with the six-cookie problem. Students had all reached the same conclusion—each person gets one and one-half cookies. Four groups wrote the answer in words and two groups used symbols. "So," I concluded, "you all agree on each person's share. Here's how we write it." I wrote $1\frac{1}{2}$ on the board, and most students nodded that they were familiar with those symbols. In this way, I connected the standard symbolism to their thinking in this situation.

With the five-cookie situation, a student from each group read what they had recorded to indicate each person's share. "A whole cookie and a quarter of a cookie." "One and a quarter." "Everyone gets one and a quarter." None of the groups used symbols in the recording, however.

Introduce and explain what each part of a fractional symbol means, using $\frac{1}{2}$ and $\frac{1}{4}$ to illustrate.

I took this opportunity to talk about mathematical representations for fractions. "Does anyone know how to write the fraction for one-fourth?" I asked.

Jorge volunteered hesitantly, "Three over one?" This response did not surprise me. Students do not always think that the symbolism is supposed to make sense and often resort to guessing. Or perhaps Jorge was thinking that if he divided a cookie into fourths, there was one fourth and three other pieces.

I decided this was a good time to explain fractional symbols to the students. "Let me explain to you why one-half is written as a one over a two," I said, writing $\frac{1}{2}$ on the board. I took a circle and cut it into two equal pieces. "The two," I said, pointing to the denominator, "tells us that we cut the cookie into two pieces. The one on top tells how many pieces I have. If I have half a cookie, I have just one of the two pieces." I did not introduce the words *numerator* and *denominator*. Instead, I pointed to the cookies as reference and drew a diagram of what I had just done on the board next to where I had written $\frac{1}{2}$.

I continued with fourths. "Here's how you divided a cookie into four equal parts," I said, cutting a circle into quarters. "To write how much one piece is, I need to write a four on the bottom. Who can explain why?" Several students volunteered. "And what do I write on top?" I continued. In this way, I presented the symbolism for one-fourth. I used the language of one-fourth and one-quarter interchangeably as I talked. Again, I was connecting their experience to the standard fractional notation.

"One of four equal pieces is one-fourth of a cookie."

As groups report sharing three cookies, introduce the idea of fractional equivalence.

When I asked the groups to report how they had shared three cookies among four people, most agreed that each person got a half and a fourth, and I wrote those on the board as $\frac{1}{2} + \frac{1}{4}$. One group, however, reported that each person got three fourths. They had cut each of the three cookies into four quarters. Each student had taken one of the quarters from each cookie, so each had three quarters. This explanation gave me the opportunity to introduce the symbolism for three-quarters and to introduce the idea of fractional equivalence, again using "fourths" and "quarters" interchangeably.

"Though the answers are different," I asked them, "did each group divide up the cookies equally?" There was some initial disagreement and confusion. Dusty finally blurted out, "They're just the same amount of cookie, except some people get more pieces." I took a half and a fourth of a cookie and showed how I could cut the half and wind up with three pieces, each one a quarter. I also drew a diagram of this on the board as another way to show that $\frac{1}{2} + \frac{1}{4}$ is the same amount as $\frac{3}{4}$.

Continue to connect fractional symbolism to students' findings as groups report on sharing two cookies, then one.

As I continued to discuss each problem, I wrote the fractions on the board to connect the students' findings to the symbolism. The most interesting variation came from Claire, Jamie, Nina R., and Stephanie's solution to sharing two cookies among the four of them. Most groups had solved this problem by giving each person half a cookie. But this group cut each of their halves into smaller pieces. First, they cut each half in half and knew they had two quarters. Then they cut each quarter in half. Their final conclusion stated: *Each person gets 4 halves of a quarter of a cookie.* Complicated, for sure, but understood clearly by the group.

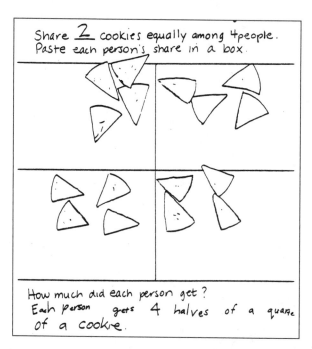

Though most groups share two cookies by giving each child half a cookie, this group cuts each of their halves into smaller pieces.

I was pleased with the quality of students' thinking during this lesson. Not only did students seem to learn, I also gained insights into their understanding.

15

Things That Come in Groups

Introducing Multiplication with Real-World Contexts

Taught in Grades 2–3

When learning about multiplication, it's helpful for students to experience multiplication in contexts, relate it to problem-solving situations, and investigate patterns. This lesson addresses all of these and it's become a standard part of my teaching repertoire. The initial lesson is followed by a collection of activities designed to support students' continued development of understanding multiplication. This lesson is appropriate for introducing multiplication or for reinforcing what students have already learned.

OVERVIEW

The lesson described here wasn't students' initial introduction to multiplication. I taught it to third graders after the middle of the school year. At the beginning of the lesson, to assess their current understanding, I asked students what they knew about multiplication. I followed with a multiplication problem in a context for them to solve, again to assess their understanding.

Then I asked students to focus on the idea that multiplication involves thinking about equal groups of objects. Working in small groups, students were asked to identify groupings of objects from the world around them that occurred in twos, threes, fours, and so on, up to twelves. We used the lists they generated for further experiences with multiplication.

MATERIALS

- paper, 12 inches by 18 inches, 1 sheet for each group
- paper, 6 inches by 9 inches, a large supply
- chart paper, 1 sheet
- counters, a large supply
- 0–99 chart or 1–100 chart (**REPRODUCIBLES T–U***), 1 for each student

*REPRODUCIBLES are available in a downloadable, printable format. See page xii for directions about how to access them.

BEGINNING THE LESSON

Ask the class what they know about multiplication.

"I'm interested in hearing from you what you know about multiplication," I asked students. "What can you tell me about multiplication?"

Several hands went up. After waiting a bit to give more students a chance to collect their thoughts, I called on students.

Damian
"Sometimes you have to carry."

Fatima
"What you do is when you have a problem like 42 times 3, you times the 2 by the 3, and then you times the 4 by the 3, and that's how you get your answer."

Emily
"You don't have to use paper and pencil all the time. You learn your times tables, and then you know those."

Nicholas
"You get big answers. Multiplication makes numbers get big faster."

Kamala
"Multiplication is when you are counting groups of things, and it helps you find out how many things you have altogether."

Yasser

"Suppose you were buying something, like potato chips, and they cost so much each, and you were buying three of them, then you could use multiplication to tell you how much it all costs."

Soo-Min

"Some of the times tables are easy to remember, like the fives because they all end in a five or zero. But some are hard to remember, like the sevens, because they're not gular."

(Soo-Min focused on multiplication facts.)

I continued, giving all the students who wanted to contribute the opportunity to do so. The students' understanding of multiplication ranged widely, from Kamala's and Yasser's explaining the meaning of multiplication to other students focusing on the procedural aspects of the operation.

INTRODUCING A SITUATION FOR MULTIPLICATION

Have students explain how many chopsticks are needed for two people, three people, then four people.

I was interested in presenting an activity in which students would focus on multiplication in contexts. Because students seemed comfortable with the times tables, I asked the class some questions that dealt with multiples of two in order to prepare for a larger investigation of multiplication in contextual situations.

"If I were eating a meal and using chopsticks," I asked students, "how many chopsticks would I need?" They all knew that I would need two chopsticks. (If I didn't think students would relate to this context, I could have used another context that made more sense for them, maybe wheels on bicycles, or how many mittens we'd need. Then I'd change the situations below to match the contexts, using the same numbers.)

I continued. "Suppose I invited three friends to dinner, and all four of us were going to eat with chopsticks. How many chopsticks would we need?" More than half the class raised their hands. Before accepting any responses, I added a direction, "When I call on you, along with giving your answer, I'd like you to explain how you figured it out."

"How many chopsticks would we need if four of us were eating dinner?

I called on Sunil first. "It's eight, because you go two, four, six, eight for the four people," he explained, using his fingers to show how he kept track of the four people.

I wrote *2, 4, 6, 8* on the board and asked the class if this made sense. "Can someone else explain why what I wrote on the board tells how many chopsticks I'd need for four people?"

I called on Holly. "He just counted by twos for the chopsticks and did that four times for the people," she explained. Other students nodded their agreement.

"Does anyone have a different way to figure the answer?" I asked.

Soo-Min offered, "You do four times two, and that's eight."

I wrote *4 × 2 = 8* on the board. "What do the four and the two have to do with my dinner party?" I asked.

Soo-Min explained, "Because you have four people, and they each need two chopsticks, and that's four times two."

Nicholas had another way. "You could add up the chopsticks, two plus two plus two plus two, and that would give you the same answer."

I wrote *2 + 2 + 2 + 2 = 8* on the board. "What do the twos stand for?" I asked.

I received a chorus of answers, "The chopsticks."

"And why did Nicholas add four twos?" I continued.

I called on Rosa to answer. "Because there are four people."

It's important to relate numerical symbols to situations as often as possible. In this way students come to understand that the numbers they use can be explained in relation to the contexts they describe.

"Here's another question," I continued. "Suppose I plan to come to your class and bring a meal for everyone. Then I'd have to figure out how many chopsticks to bring. How many students are there in the class altogether?"

"Twenty-six," Rusty said.

"You'd have to bring some for Mrs. Uyeda and for you, too," Kamala commented.

I agreed and asked, "So how many of us will be eating in all?"

We agreed that there would be twenty-eight of us in all. I asked, "How can I figure out how many chopsticks to bring?"

"You have to multiply," Damian said, making it sound as if it was an exhausting thing to have to do.

"Multiply what?" I asked.

Several students responded, "Twenty-eight times two."

"You need paper and pencil to do it," Damian continued.

I nodded in agreement and switched the focus to an activity in which students would search for other real-world contexts for multiplication. I would return later to the computations needed to find answers.

EXPLORING CONTEXTS FOR MULTIPLICATION

"Multiplication is a way to find out how many you have altogether when things come in groups, such as chopsticks," I told students in preparation for this activity. "What I want us to do now is to brainstorm together as a class what other sorts of things come in twos, as chopsticks do, so we can explore other situations that call for multiplication."

"I'm going to record what you think of on a chart," I continued, and wrote on the top of a large sheet of chart paper: *These things come in twos.*

The students volunteered many suggestions. "Eyes." "Ears." "Hands." "Feet." "Legs." "Eyebrows." "Lips." "Nostrils." "Thumbs."

Finally, I interjected, "Can you think of things that come in twos that aren't on our bodies?"

Students offered more suggestions. "Bicycle wheels." "Pedals on bicycles." "Bicycle handlebars." "Shoes." "Socks." "Gloves." "Twins." "Opposites."

The students raised questions about some suggestions. When "hands on a clock" was offered, Emily said that some watches don't have hands, showing the digital watch that she was wearing. Ben added that some clocks have three hands, like the clock in the classroom, which had a second hand.

"Hands on a clock come in twos only sometimes," I said. "This is an important idea to pay attention to as we make our list. What I want to include on our list are things that always come in twos, not those that only sometimes come in twos. So, I'm not going to include hands on a clock on our list."

The same sort of discussion arose when someone suggested "earrings," since they aren't always worn in pairs.

When Sunil offered "dice," I asked him to explain. "Because when you play games, you use two dice," he said.

"What about when we play our fraction games?" I asked. "How many dice do you use then?"

Several of the students responded that we use only one then, so I didn't add dice to the list.

The students continued to offer other examples. "Lenses in glasses." "Slices of bread in a sandwich." "Contact lenses." "Pairs of anything." "Wings on a bird."

"Could I write *tricycle wheels* on our list?" I asked.

I received a chorus of nos.

"On what list would it belong?" I asked, knowing this was an easy question for the class. I gave a few other examples of things that would belong on different lists. "Where would I have to write *legs on spiders*? What about *eggs in a dozen*?"

Explain the task: *With your group, think of things that come in threes. Do the same for fours, fives, sixes, sevens, eights, nines, tens, elevens, and twelves. Make a separate list for each number.*

Then I presented an exploration for students to do in small groups. I explained, "Now you'll think about things that come in groups other than twos," I said, "such as the examples I just gave about tricycle wheels and legs on spiders and eggs in a dozen. I want you to think about things that come in threes, fours, fives, sixes, sevens, eights, nines, tens, elevens, and twelves." I wrote the numbers on the board as I said them. We counted to determine that there were ten different lists that students would need to investigate.

Direct each group to record all their lists on one large sheet of paper.

I continued with the directions. "You'll work together in groups. I'm going to give each group one sheet of large paper." I had 12-by-18-inch paper ready. "I want you to work together in your groups to organize all ten lists on this one sheet of paper and think of as many things that would fit on as many of the lists as you can. After I've given you some time to do this, I'll interrupt you, and we'll compare what different groups have come up with."

After answering a few students' questions, I gave each group a sheet of paper, and the students got busy.

DURING WORK TIME

Circulate, observe, and offer help as needed.

It was fascinating to watch groups grapple with the problem of how to organize their papers for the ten lists. I was curious about how they would handle this task and realized quickly that it was a complicated spatial problem for students. Though giving students a photocopied form or telling them how to set up their paper might have saved ten minutes or so, the students would have been robbed of the opportunity to solve this problem. And I would have missed the chance to watch them as they struggled to organize their papers.

It was a delight to watch. It was a reminder not only of the problem-solving benefit of having students responsible for organizing their own work, but also of the creativity and uniqueness of students' thinking. The groups solved the problem of organizing their papers in a variety of ways.

Several groups folded the paper in half, folded it again, and folded it again, each time opening it to count how many spaces there were. After three folds, there were eight spaces, in a 4-by-2 array. This was perplexing to them, and they dealt with it in several different ways.

In one group Soo-Min came up with the solution of putting eight of their lists on one side, then turning the paper over for the last two lists.

In another group, Yasser folded the paper once again and opened it. The rest of the group seemed annoyed with Yasser when they counted and found they had sixteen sections. Yasser, however, came up with a solution that satisfied them: he labeled ten of the sections for their lists and ignored the other six.

Another group, determined to find a way to get ten sections, continued folding the paper this way and that until the paper was a mass of folds and the group was discouraged and frustrated. Finally, Nicholas drew lines, eyeballing it, and divided the paper into a 5-by-2 array of sections somewhat the same size.

One of the other groups folded the paper in half, half again, and half once more, with all folds in the same direction. They got to the stage where they had eight columns and were stumped. Sofia solved the problem for this group by folding the first two columns in half, saying he would write small enough for these narrower spaces.

Another group had the problem solved fairly quickly because Rusty seemed to be the only one interested in organizing the paper. He drew lines to get ten columns, stopping several times along the way to count how many columns he already had, looking ahead across the sheet to make the columns as close as possible to the same width.

The last group was hesitant to fold or mark the paper until they had a plan. They got some smaller sheets of paper, and each student experimented by folding the smaller sheets. They came up with all sorts of solutions, dividing sheets of paper into six, eight, nine, twelve, and sixteen sections. They were totally stymied, and I finally intervened. "How about if I help you organize your sheet so you can get started making your lists?" I offered. They agreed with grateful sighs. I penciled their large sheet into ten sections and focused them on finding entries for the ten lists.

Interestingly, it was not apparent to students that ten sections could be made in two rows of five each. It would seem to me that students who had been studying multiplication would see that as obvious. This reminded me that it's important to be careful when making assumptions about what students understand. It also reaffirmed how valuable problem-solving situations are for assessing students' understanding, even when incidental to the goal at hand. Also, I could see that it would benefit students to have experiences in which they would relate multiplication to rectangular arrays, so they had a way to see multiplication in a geometric context.

Once the groups had each organized their papers, they eagerly concentrated on finding entries for their lists. As with organizing their papers, groups worked differently on this part of the task. The students in some groups worked together, first thinking about things to write on the threes list, then the fours, and so on. Other groups worked together, however they also thought about things that could be written on any list, their ideas sparking other ideas. The members of one group worked independently, each writing items on the appropriate list, with little group discussion.

One group began wandering about the room, looking for possible things. Holly excitedly reported a find, "Rulers! There are twelve inches on each ruler. There's something for the twelves list."

"Sh!" Rosa, one of Holly's group members, said. "They'll hear you and put it on their lists." Rosa is often competitive in class, so her response didn't surprise me.

Groups also differed in how they handled the recording. In some groups, there was one recorder, while in other groups, students took turns.

Finally, I interrupted the class so we could investigate what they had found.

SUMMARIZING THE ACTIVITY

Explain how students will share their work.

I explained the procedure I wanted to use to report students' entries. I wanted students to listen to each other and to think about others' ideas.

"Here's what I want us to do now," I began. "We'll go around the room, group by group. Each group will report just one thing from any one list, without telling which list it's on. Then the others in the class will have the chance to decide where it belongs. Once we agree, I'll write it on the board under the correct number.

3's	4's	5's	6's	7's	8's	9's	10's	11's	12's
Tricle Wheel lights on a Stoplight canned tennis balls triangle Sides I am has Three letters	Sqare rectange Sides wheels on trans cars truck bikes whith traning wheeds Seas has four letters legs on a dog	fingers toes	eyes ona Spider Trever has six letters incets have 6 legs	seven red lins on flag	SP leg s plc eye		decads have ten years		OZ eggs

Working together to learn about multiplication, students identify groupings of real-world objects.

Give groups a chance to choose several items from their list that they want to share.

"Also," I continued, "I want you to report something that hasn't already been suggested, so take a moment now to choose several items you'd like to report, so that you'll have an alternative if the item you chose has already been mentioned."

My goal here, as well as investigating things in the world that occur in groups as a basis for exploring multiplication, is to involve the class in a way that encourages them to listen to each other, and also to have the opportunity to classify suggestions.

Create a list for items that cause disagreement.

The groups tried to report those things they thought were unique. They seemed disappointed when they reported something and someone from another group announced, "We've got that on our list, too." The offerings reported included quintuplets, players on a baseball team, wings on a butterfly, cans in a six-pack of soda, red stripes on the U.S. flag, pennies in a nickel, letters in the word *car*, balls in a can of tennis balls, legs on an octopus.

Some offerings caused disagreement. The first to do so was "sides on a stop sign." The class was divided as to whether there were six sides or eight. I wrote *stop sign* off to the side as an item to be questioned later. This list of questionable items grew. "Members on a soccer team" was included because students said when they played in school, the size of teams varied because sometimes students were absent. "Eyes on a spider" was another dispute. These would have to be verified later with research.

Some of the offerings didn't fit any list because they were similar to Sunil's suggestion that dice be included on the twos list. For example, "legs on a stool" was offered by one group, but students said a stool could have three or four legs. "Sails on a sailboat" was suggested, but some of the students knew that not all sailboats have the same number of sails.

Other offerings had to be clarified. "Points on a star" was offered by one group. Nicholas commented that not all stars had the same number of points, so the group changed its suggestion to "points on the stars on the American flag." "Numbers in a telephone number" had to be further clarified as to whether or not it included the area code.

Some offerings were surprise stumpers, even to me. "Holes in a shirt," Fatima offered for her group. Some of the students figured out that it belonged on the 4s list. I was still perplexed. Fatima explained, pointing out four openings—at the neck, at the bottom, and one for each sleeve.

When the sharing is complete, have the class post their lists so they can be seen by everyone.

It was time for recess, and I asked the students to post the group lists so that everyone could have the opportunity to read the rest of the ideas later. I told them that the lists would be used for further activities and that it would be useful for them to be familiar with the ideas that others had had.

GENERATING MULTIPLICATION PROBLEMS

Use the lists to pose problems that can be modelled physically on the students such as number of eyes on eight students. Connect each solution to the appropriate multiplication equation.

The lists are a rich resource for generating problems for students to solve. One way to begin is to choose something from a list that can be counted on the students—eyes, for example. Pose a problem: How many eyes are there on eight students? The purpose here is not only to arrive at an answer, but also to link the problem to multiplication and to connect it to the standard symbolization. Though this problem would be simple for these third graders, who have studied the times tables, it's still valuable to reinforce the connection between the situation in the problem and what they've learned about multiplication. I find it useful to ask eight students to come to the front of the room and together count their eyes. Count by ones. Count by twos. Write the appropriate multiplication equation on the board: $8 \times 2 = 16$. Relate this equation back to the situation—eight students have two eyes each, with eight students there are sixteen eyes altogether.

Counting eyes is one way to use the students to generate multiplication problems.

How many eyes?
$8 \times 2 = ?$

Pose other problems using the students and handle them in the same way: How many ears on seven students? How many toes do six students have? How many fingers in the room altogether?

Use the lists to pose problems for other contexts. Offer counters to students to model the problems and connect each solution to the appropriate multiplication equation.

Introduce problems that don't reference students but use other entries from their lists. Give students counters to use to figure the problems out. And be sure to connect every problem with its appropriate multiplication equation, each time having students relate the numbers in the equation back to the situation. For example, ask: How many cans of soda in three six-packs? Students can use counters to show the cans in the six-packs.

Ask students for the corresponding multiplication equation to write and write it on the board. For example, for cans in three six-packs, write *3 × 6 = 18* on the board and ask: What does the 6 tell us? What does the 3 tell us? What does the 18 tell us? How do you know that 18 is correct? Other examples: How many wheels on six tricycles? (Notice that the equation for the tricycles is *6 × 3 = 18*, rather than the order the same numbers are written for the cans of soda.) How many legs on five cats? How many eggs in two dozen? How many years in four decades?

Use the lists to pose problems that can be solved with drawings such as the number of points on five stars. Connect each solution to the appropriate multiplication equation.

Some problems can also be solved with drawings: How many points on five stars? How many tennis balls in three cans? How many legs on four spiders?

Have students make up their own problems, writing and illustrating a problem on one side of a paper, and the multiplication equation on the other side.

When you've done a number of these problems and feel students have a sufficient understanding, ask students to create problems. Ask them to write the problem and illustrate it on one side of the paper, then turn it over and write the corresponding multiplication equation on the other side. That way, students can read each other's problems, solve them and then check their solutions. Make sure the problems students write are correct, but after that, if students get a problem wrong, direct them to go to the person who wrote the problem for an explanation.

Once there was a turtle with 20 children. She wanted to buy them some shoes but she didn't know how many shoes to buy. Help mrs. Turtle.

Students write and illustrate multiplication problems for others to solve.

It's important to note that the solution is more than the answer that results from the multiplication—it's the entire multiplication equation. The emphasis here is on relating multiplication equations to problem situations to develop and cement students' understanding. Too often the goal is learning multiplication facts and procedures before students fully understand the concept.

> "The emphasis here is on relating multiplication equations to problem situations to develop and cement students' understanding. Too often the goal is learning multiplication facts and procedures before students fully understand the concept."

INVESTIGATING PATTERNS IN MULTIPLES

Use the lists to generate a list of multiplication equations as students count, for example, the number of ears on one person, then two people, and so on.

The lists the students make are useful for generating a study of patterns in multiples and a way to introduce the students to the idea of functions. For example, use the students to investigate patterns as they count ears.

Have one student come up and record *1 × 2 = 2* as the equation that describes that one student has two ears, and that is two ears altogether. Have another student come up; then ask for an equation that tells how many ears these students have altogether. Relate *2 × 2 = 4* to the situation that two students each have two ears, and that makes four ears altogether.

Continue for another student, and then another, until you've written equations to account for at least a dozen of the students:

1 × 2 = 2	4 × 2 = 8
2 × 2 = 4	5 × 2 = 10
3 × 2 = 6	6 × 2 = 12

Have students describe the patterns they see and record the multiples on a 0–99 or 1–100 chart.

Investigate the pattern of the numbers in the ones place as the multiples increase. Investigate the pattern of the numbers in the tens place. Ask students what other patterns they notice. Have them color in these multiples on a 0–99 or 1–100 chart (**REPRODUCIBLES T–U**) and describe the visual patterns.

Do a similar investigation for other multiples, each time choosing something from their lists as a way of relating the investigation to some context from the real world.

Working in groups, have students choose something from any list and investigate the patterns of its multiples.

When you think students are ready, have them work in groups to investigate the patterns in another situation. Post the directions for them to follow:

> 1. Choose something from a list to investigate.
> 2. Write a list of at least twelve multiplication equations, for 1 times, 2 times, 3 times, etc.
> 3. Look for patterns in the multiples. Write about the patterns you find.
> 4. Color in the multiples on a 0–99 chart. Continue the pattern to the end of the chart.

WRITING MULTIPLICATION STORIES

Write a multiplication equation on the board and tell a story that ends with a question and can be answered by the equation.

Students benefit from additional experiences relating situations to multiplication. Besides exploring multiplication from the lists, students can write stories that fit multiplication equations. Each story should end with a question that can be answered by the multiplication equation.

As with all tasks, it's important that the teacher model for the students what they're expected to do. To introduce this experience, write a multiplication equation on the board; *7 × 3 = 21*, for example. Tell a story that ends with a question that can be answered by this equation. Following is a sample.

> Elijah was sick and his dad took him to the doctor. The doctor gave Elijah pills and told him to take three pills each day for one week. How many pills would Elijah have to take?

Have each student write a different story for the same multiplication equation that you used, then share it with their group.

Then have each student write a different story for that same multiplication equation. When they are finished, they should read their stories aloud to each other in their small groups. After each student reads a story, the others in the group verify whether the story ended with a question and if the question could be answered by the multiplication equation. After groups finish, allow time for students who wish to do so to read their stories to the entire class.

Have students create their own multiplication equation and write a story that ends in a question and can be answered by the equation.

To follow up this activity, have students write stories for other multiplication equations, either ones they choose themselves or ones they draw from an envelope. Again, model a story for students.

> Celina was making party favors for the six guests who would be attending her birthday party. She figured she needed eight inches of ribbon for each party favor. How many inches of ribbon does Celina need to buy?

You can use these stories in several ways. Students can read their stories aloud in their small groups so others can try to give the equation that matches. The stories can be used as activity cards or at a learning center for others to try. Also, you can display the stories on a bulletin board for students to read.

ANOTHER INVESTIGATION OF MULTIPLICATION IN CONTEXTS

Revisit the chopsticks problem: *How many chopsticks do we need for the entire class to eat together?*

When I was talking with the class about chopsticks and presented the problem of how many chopsticks I'd need for all twenty-eight of us, I wasn't as interested in the answer as I was in developing the idea that multiplication is useful for counting things that come in equal groups. However, developing ways to find the answer is important, and it's valuable to return to the chopstick question.

Before resorting to paper-and-pencil computation, however, I think it is important to deal with multiplication mentally, before introducing an algorithm.

Tell the class that with you, they'll solve the problem without paper and pencil.

I tried this with the students. "Remember when we were talking about chopsticks a while ago?" I asked. I continued after they nodded. "We never did figure out that day how many chopsticks I would need if all twenty-six of you plus Mrs. Uyeda and I were going to eat together. I want to think about this problem together, but without using paper and pencil. I'd like you to think along with me before we do any writing."

Pose smaller problems such as how many chopsticks for ten people, how many for ten more people, how many for eight more people. Record students' responses.

After getting their attention, I asked students for how many people I needed chopsticks, and several answered, "Twenty-eight."

"Hmmm," I said, "that's a bit tricky. If there were only ten of us, that would be easy for me. Who knows how many chopsticks I'd need for ten people?"

Most of their hands went up, and I asked students all to say the answer softly together.

"What if I got chopsticks for another ten people?" I continued. "I'd need another twenty chopsticks. So how many altogether for the two tens?" This time I had individual students respond and explain their answers.

Nicholas said, "You'd need forty, because twenty and twenty more makes forty."

Kamala answered, a bit impatiently, "You can multiply that in your head, twenty times two gives you forty."

"OK," I said, "if I have forty chopsticks, then I have enough for twenty people. But there are twenty-eight of us altogether. How many more people do I need chopsticks for?"

Some of the students volunteered that there were eight more people. Because I felt that some of the slower students had just gotten lost, I asked the class to help me do some recording on the board. I wrote:

> For 10 people, I need 20 chopsticks.
> For 10 more, I need 20 more chopsticks.
> So, for 20 people, I need 40 chopsticks.
> But there are 28 people altogether.
> So, I still need chopsticks for 8 more people.

This recording helped some, but I suspected a few were still lost. However, this was the first example, and I decided to continue, knowing that there would be other opportunities for students to think about similar problems when I got them working in their small groups.

"How many chopsticks will I need for the last eight people?" I asked. Because they had been studying their times tables, they knew that sixteen chopsticks were needed.

Some of the students excitedly called out the answer, having figured that 40 plus 16 is 56. I continued, however, recording on the board as I spoke. "See if this makes sense. I need sixteen more chopsticks for the last eight people, and I needed forty chopsticks for the other twenty people, so altogether I'll need fifty-six chopsticks."

Reasoning in this way involves the application of the distributive property, a help when doing multiplication calculations mentally. However, I knew that this one example did not provide sufficient experience for the students to grasp the concept.

Use the same procedure to figure out how many legs are on 36 dogs.

Next, I wanted to figure out how many legs are on thirty-six dogs. I led into the problem gradually, beginning by asking students if they knew how many legs there were altogether on ten dogs. This was easy for them.

"What about for one hundred dogs?" I asked. "Is this too hard to do?" It wasn't hard for them, and they answered with a chorus of 400.

"There are four hundred what?" I said.

I called on Emily. "There are four hundred legs on one hundred dogs," she said.

"What about for twenty dogs?" I asked next.

Rusty answered, "That would be eighty legs, forty for ten dogs and forty for ten more dogs."

"What about for thirty-six dogs?" I continued.

We worked this out as we had done for the chopsticks, figuring that there were 120 for 30 dogs and 24 more legs for six dogs.

FURTHER EXPLORATIONS FOR OTHER DAYS

Offer more problems for small groups to solve without paper and pencil.

I planned to do other such examples on future days, then give students similar problems to solve in their small groups, just by discussing, without using pencil and paper. I present these to the students as "hands on the table" solutions rather than using paper-and-pencil solutions.

Following are some other examples:

If I promised to give each student in the class five markers, how many markers would I have to buy?

If a company manufactures twenty-five tricycles a day, how many wheels a day are needed?

If you will each get three tickets for our class play, how many tickets will our class use altogether?

If a company has to paint the word *Stop* on sixteen signs, how many letters will be painted?

It's beneficial to establish comfort with solving these types of problems mentally before presenting an algorithm. The problems provide students experience with splitting two-digit numbers into ones and tens and figuring partial products, which relates to written procedures.

For older students, offer similar problems but with larger numbers.

Also, for older students, present the same sort of problems, but with greater numbers. For example, if a company has twelve buses that seat forty-two people each, how many passengers can be traveling at one time? In this way, you build some beginning understanding of the partial products with two-digit multipliers.

16
The Two-Dice Sums Game

Reinforcing Basic Addition and Introducing Probability

Taught in Grades 2–5

The goal of this lesson is to engage students in playing *The Two-Dice Sums Game* that involves adding numbers that come up when rolling two dice. The game provides students informal experience with probability as they confront a situation where outcomes are not equally likely. Playing the game helps prepare them for later encounters with these mathematical ideas. A follow-up activity, *Two-Dice Sums*, has students collect data about the sums in order to investigate how often each sum occurs. The students are then asked to analyze the data, make inferences, and apply their analyses of the probability to their game strategies.

OVERVIEW

Most students are familiar with dice, having used dice to play games at home, generally for moving counters on board games. Through playing these games, students may have developed some intuitive ideas about which sums come up more often than others. In *The Two-Dice Sums Game*, students are taught to play a game with two dice and then are asked to devise a winning strategy for it. The follow-up activity, *The Two-Dice Sums*, focuses students on investigating the probabilities of the sums that come up when two dice are tossed.

I taught the lesson described here to third graders. Following the description of the lesson are a synopsis of the results from the same lesson conducted in a fifth-grade class and a surprising result when it was introduced to a class of third and fourth graders. If you're interested in more information about using menus, read my blog post: "Using Math Menus: Some Nuts and Bolts" (www.marilynburnsmathblog.com/using-math-menus-some-nuts-bolts/). And if you're interested in reading about how I taught the game again and what I learned, read my blog post: "One of My All Time Favorite Games" (www.marilynburnsmathblog.com/one-of-my-all-time-favorite-games/).

MATERIALS

*REPRODUCIBLES are available in a downloadable, printable format. See page xii for directions about how to access them.

- dice, 1 pair for each student
- number line 2–12 (**REPRODUCIBLE V***), 1 for each student
- counters or interlocking cubes, 11 for each student
- *Two-Dice Sums* recording sheet (**REPRODUCIBLE W***), at least 2 for each student
- chart paper, several sheets (for class charts as needed)

INTRODUCING THE LESSON

Have the class share what they know about a pair of dice.

I began the lesson by holding up a pair of dice. "What do you know about these?" I asked. Many of the students were interested in responding. "They're dice." "They have dots on them—one, two, three, four, five, or six." "They're square." (In response to this comment, I rephrased using the correct language, "Yes, each of the six faces are squares.") "You use them to play games." "You roll them."

Ask, "When rolling a pair of dice, what is the smallest possible sum? The greatest possible sum? Other possible sums?"

I continued, "If I roll two dice and figure out the sum of the dots that come up, what's the smallest sum I could get?" This question elicited a chorus of 2s. I wrote *2* on the board.

"What's the greatest sum that could come up?" I asked. This time I received a chorus of 12s. To the right of *2* I wrote *12* on the board, leaving room to fit the numbers from 3 to 11 in between.

2   12

I then asked about 3. "What about three? Is a sum of three possible? How could you get it?" It seemed obvious to students that you get a sum of 3 if you rolled a 1 and 2. I continued with 4, 5, 6, 7, and 8, writing each number as we verified it was possible to come up as the sum of rolls on two dice.

2   3   4   5   6   7   8   9   10   11   12

Asking students to verify that these sums were all possible outcomes when rolling two dice gave them the opportunity to think about the addition combinations for each number. Because the main contributors were students who were confident and quickest with the combinations, I had them turn and talk with a partner about whether the remaining numbers—9, 10, and 11—were also possible. Talking in pairs gave others a chance to voice their ideas. I added these numbers to the board.

> "Because the main contributors were students who were confident and quickest with the combinations, I had them turn and talk with a partner. Talking in pairs gave others a chance to voice their ideas."

"Let's see how many possible sums there are," I said. As I pointed to the numbers from 2 to 12, we counted that eleven sums were possible from rolling two dice.

TEACHING HOW TO PLAY THE GAME

Show one of the number lines with the numbers from 2 to 12 (REPRODUCIBLE V) and tell students that, in pairs, they'll place eleven counters on it.

I showed them a sample of the number lines I had duplicated with spaces between numbers so that counters would fit.

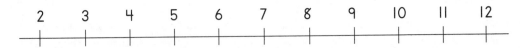

I explained to the class, "I'm going to teach you a two-dice game that you'll play with a partner. I'm going to give each pair a number line with the numbers from two to twelve on it and eleven counters. You and your partner should decide together how to place your eleven counters on your number line any way you like. For example, you may put one counter on each number, you may stack all the counters on one number, or you can arrange them in any other way you'd like."

Explain the rules for playing and share with students that the object of the game is to be the first pair to remove all their counters.

I explained the rules, "Once you've all placed your counters, I'll begin to roll the dice. When I roll the dice, I'll call out the sum that comes up. If you have a counter on that number, remove it. For example, if I roll a five and a three, I'll call out the sum, eight. If you have a counter on eight, then you take it off. If you have two or more counters on eight, you can take off only one of those counters. The idea is to be the first to remove all your counters. Together with your partner decide how you'll arrange your counters to try to be the first team to take them all off."

Distribute the materials, then observe how students place their counters.

I distributed the number lines and counters and then circulated and watched as students talked with their partners about where to place their counters. I clarified the directions for those who weren't sure what to do. Finally, all pairs had placed their counters on their number lines. Many had spread out the counters, putting one on each number. This strategy was so pervasive that a few of the students who had begun to do something different changed their minds when they saw what most of the others were doing and rearranged their counters.

I didn't give any suggestions or coaching. My plan was to play the game several times as a class, and then give opportunities to play in pairs. I wanted students to rely on their experience playing the game to make decisions about where it was best to place counters in order to remove them as quickly as possible.

From watching students arrange the counters for this first game, it was clear that they weren't aware that when two dice are tossed, some sums come up more often than others. The idea that some events are more likely to occur than others is basic to probability, and while the students may have had some experience with this idea from playing games with dice, few were transferring their experience to a strategy for playing this game. I was curious to see if and how playing the game would change their ideas. I also wanted to see if students could develop any understanding of why particular sums are more likely than others.

PLAYING THE GAME

Roll the dice and announce the sum. Repeat until most students have only a few counters left on their number lines.

When all pairs had placed their counters, I began to roll the dice and call out sums. I observed a few pairs rearranging their counters, so I stopped and explained that students weren't allowed to rearrange their counters in the middle of the game. I told them that I was pleased that they were thinking about improving the placement of their counters. "Please leave your counters where you placed them," I said. "After this game, you'll have the chance to think about what you'd do differently and try a different arrangement for the next game." I continued rolling the dice.

Stop and ask students what numbers they are waiting for and what number had been called most often.

When I noticed that most students had only two or three counters left on their number lines, I stopped rolling and asked one pair of students, "Which numbers are you waiting for?" They reported that they were waiting for 2, 11, and 12. I asked another pair, and their answer was the same. A third pair also gave me the same response.

"Is everyone waiting for two, eleven, or twelve?" I asked the class. Most nodded and seemed a bit surprised. I commented, "Maybe it wasn't such a good idea to put counters on those numbers. Or maybe it's just poor luck that those numbers haven't come up."

I then asked, "What sums did I call most often?" They called out what they recalled had come up most frequently. "Five." "Seven." "Eight." "Six." "Ten."

Start a new game, but first have students record how they arranged their counters.

Rather than opening up a class discussion at this time, I told students that we'd end this game and start again. "This time," I told them, "after you place your counters and before I start rolling the dice, I want you to record how you arranged the counters. That way we can compare and see what we can learn from a winning arrangement." I distributed paper to students who didn't have any available.

Play until there's a winner, then have the winners share their winning arrangement.

The students' arrangements of counters were varied this time. Few put any counters on 2, 11, or 12. We played the game until we had a winner. I asked the winners to report on how they had arranged their counters.

After playing the game one time, few students put counters on 2, 11, or 12.

Distribute additional materials so pairs can play on their own. Encourage them to discuss the arrangement of their counters.

Instead of continuing to play as a class, I gave each pair of students an additional number line, eleven more counters, and two dice so that they could play the game against each other. I encouraged them to discuss their arrangements with each other and share ideas about how they arranged them. I wanted them to play in pairs for several reasons: They would have the practice of figuring out the sums themselves, they would have more opportunity to talk about arrangements, and they could play at their own pace.

Some of the students recorded their arrangements again, doing it in several different ways. Also, several of the students kept track of the sums that came up as they played, although I hadn't suggested that they do so.

EXTENDING THE GAME

Introduce the recording sheet (**REPRODUCIBLE W**) on which students will record the sum each time they roll the dice. Have them continue until one column is completely filled, then record this sum on the class chart.

After pairs had time to play a few games, I told them I wanted to take a break from the game and try a different, but related, activity. I had prepared worksheets for this activity (**REPRODUCIBLE W**) and modeled for students what I wanted each of them to do. I rolled the dice and recorded the sum with an X in the proper column. I did that for about half a dozen sums.

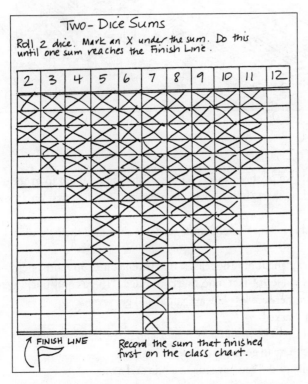

The sum of 7 reaches the finish line more often than other sums on students' worksheets.

"When you record on your own *Two-Dice Sums* recording sheet" I explained, "you'll continue until one sum reaches the bottom of its column, the finish line." I also listed the numbers from 2 to 12 on a sheet of chart paper and called students' attention to it. "When you're done, come and make a tally mark on this chart to mark the sum that reached the finish line on your sheet."

Circulate, observe, and offer help as needed.

The students were eager to begin. They liked having their own dice and recording sheets. Watching the students in this setting revealed differences in how they worked, and now I had the opportunity to assess how individuals determined the sums. Some knew the sums immediately from inspecting the two dice, chose to start with the number on one die and found the sum by counting on the dots on the other die, and a few had to count all the dots. Watching them work was a way to assess their basic number skills.

The sum of 7 came up most often on the students' papers.

Discuss the results on a class chart.

Most students completed two or three sheets before I interrupted them to examine and discuss the results on our class chart. The class chart showed that the number 7 finished first on an overwhelming majority of papers.

"Why do you think this is so?" I asked. Some students shrugged their shoulders. One said that seven was his lucky number.

Nina offered a clear explanation. "The reason that seven comes up more often is that there are more ways to get seven," she said in a matter-of-fact tone. She continued, "There's only one way to get twelve because you have to roll both sixes, but there are lots of ways you could get seven."

"What are the ways?" I asked.

Several others volunteered. "Five and two." "Four and three." "Six and one."

"How many ways are there to get a sum of two?" I asked.

"Only one way," Emilio said. "You have to get a one and a one."

"What about to get a nine?" I asked.

Ian responded, "Lots, eight and one, or seven and two."

Several of the students interrupted him to object. Jania explained, "You can't do that. There's no eight on the dice. There isn't a seven either."

"How can you get a sum of nine on the dice?" I asked Ian, giving him another chance to respond.

This time he told me that 5 and 4 would work, and so would 6 and 3.

"What other sums finished first?" I asked, drawing students' attention back to the class chart. Though there were many more 7s, there were a fair number of 5s, 6s, 8s, and 9s.

I was interested to learn how students would use the information from their experience to devise a strategy for playing the game, or even if they would use the information. I decided to give a writing assignment. I told students to think about how they would now arrange the counters to try to win the game. "But before you play again," I said, "please write a description of the arrangement you would use and explain why you made those choices." There was a good deal of a variety in their thinking.

Andres

I would put the most on seven because their are more ways to make seven than any other number. But not to many. And I dare you to put them on 12 or 2 because they have only one combination.

> Lucky: 5, 6, 7̃8,
>
> I would put the most on seven beaaause their are more ways to make seven than any other number. But not to many. And I dare you to put them on 12 or 2 because they have only one combi'nati'on.

Andres understands that some sums have a greater probability of being rolled than others.

Danitza

I would put the most on 7. Because it has the most waes to make it. Then I would put 3 on 8 because I keep getting it. And two on 6, 3, 5, 10, and one on 11 because sometimes I get them.

Megi

I would put one on each number because on you're first turn any number that you would roll you could take off one cube.

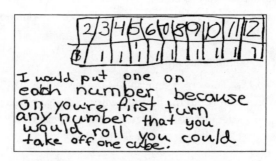

> I would put one on each number because on you're first turn any number that you would roll you could take off one cube.

Megi seems most interested in ensuring that she will be able to remove a cube on the first roll.

Valeria

Odd numbers are easyer to roll because there are more ways to make them up.

Jamie

I'd put one on eight, one on nine, one on six, one on four, two on five, one on three, one on ten, and three on seven because I won when I did it that way.

Lee

[Lee's math understanding surpassed his writing ability.]

five won a lot for me. but on the chart seven. why is becuse there is more ways to make seven than the other wons. I would poot fore on 7 and five, two on nine and one on for.

Give students time to continue playing the game.

I made dice, number lines, and a supply of additional recording sheets available for students to use. My plan was to give them more time during class, and then have the game included on our math menu. If you're interested in more information about using menus, read my blog post: "Using Math Menus: Some Nuts and Bolts" (www.marilynburnsmathblog.com/using-math-menus-some-nuts-bolts/).

RESULTS FROM FIFTH GRADERS

Students' thoughts about their initial experience.

Stephanie Sheffield presented a similar experience to her fifth graders. After she introduced the game to the class, she gave her students time to play it multiple times in pairs. She then gave a writing assignment for them to do in pairs of explaining how they would arrange the counters, based on their playing experience. As with the third graders, the students' thinking was quite varied.

Janik and Shuyin

Our conclusion is that to win the game you must put the counters or beans on numbers seven eight, ten and six. Most of your counters or beans should be on numbers seven and eight.

Thuy and Tanya

[A competitive view!] We think 7, 9, 6, and 5 are rolled the most. If your opponent puts three on one number, you would put one less than that person did. Then put the extra counters on the numbers you think are rolled the most.

Lawren and John

[A terse but noncommittal conclusion] John and I found out that if you put the counters on the numbers between 2 and 12, you might have a good chance of winning.

Students' thoughts after discussing the class graph.

Stephanie then distributed *Two-Dice Sums* recording sheets and gave students the individual assignment of rolling two dice and seeing which sum got to the finish line first. She also posted a class chart on which students recorded the winning sums. After discussing the results from the class chart, she asked them to write, in pairs, about why the results on the class chart came out as they did.

Janik and Shuyin

It turned out that way because six, seven, and eight have more addends than the rest of the numbers. Example: addends of 7 = 3, 4, 1, 6, 2, 5, addends of 2 = 1. Seven can come out more than two.

Thuy and Tanya

The smaller numbers have less number to add up to. Examples: 2 + 1 = 3, 1 + 2 = 3. The larger #'s have less #'s, 6 + 5 = 11, 5 + 6 = 11. 7 has more #'s to add up to 7 such as 4 + 3 = 7, 6 + 1 = 7, 5 + 2 = 7.

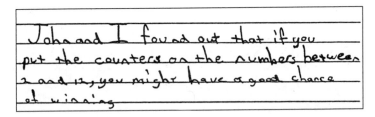

John and I found out that if you put the counters on the numbers between 2 and 12, you might have a good chance of winning

The initial reaction from these boys pays no attention to probabilities.

Students' thoughts after playing the game a few more days.

The students were interested in the game and continued playing it over the next two days. After that time, Stephanie gave them an individual writing assignment, asking them to explain what they had learned from playing the game.

Tanya
I learned it's better to put your counters on 6, 7, and 8 because those three numbers have a lot of numbers that will add up to 6, 7, and 8. Also that you shouldn't put any on 2, 12, or 11 because they don't have many numbers to add up to them.

Namthong
I learned that seven came out the most on the two dice games because there are many number that make sevens. We drew this on the board. [And Namthong included a listing of all the different ways to make each of the sums.]

Jack
I learned that for playing the counters game you should put most of the counters on 7. But I think you should put them on the numbers 5–9. You need to have other numbers for the game. You should put most of them on 7 because it has more combinations of rolled dice. But the dice won't equal 7 every time. So put some counters on the numbers 5–9 so you have a better chance of clearing your board. The numbers 5–9 are good because they have a more likely chance of being rolled than the numbers 1–4 and 10–12.

Heidy
I think that when I play this game again I think that I would put 4 on number 7 and 2 on number 6 and number 8 and 1 on number 5 and number 9 and 1 on number 4. I would put my beans on these numbers because I learned that 7 is rolled most often and 4, 5, 6, 8, and 9 are rolled often because these numbers have more numbers that = these numbers.

Lawren
Now I have understood how 6, 7, 8, and 9 are rolled often. They are rolled often because they have more sums and numbers that add to be them. Now I will put my counters on 8, 7, 5, and 9. [Lawren drew a number line and indicated three counters on 7 and two each on 5, 6, 8, and 9.]

Now I have understood how 6,7,8,and 9 are rolled ofter, They are rolled ofter because they have more Sums and numbers that add to the them. Now I will put my counters on 8,7,5,and 9.

Example:

2 3 4 5 6   7 8 9 10 11 12
    2 2 3 2 2

After further exploration and class discussion, Lawren's understanding of probability grows.

Carman

[She took a different approach when writing her explanation of what she had learned from the game.] In this game I've learned something. I have learned that Math is possible. I meen that I used to think that it all couldn't be done because it would take too long that it was not interesting. But in this game I have found out that it is not long and that it is interesting. And to tell you the truth, I think it was fun. And in this game I found that the 6, 7, and 8 would be the best numbers. But I think that I would still put my counters on the 3, 4, 5, 9, 10, and 11 because there is still a chance for those number to be rolled.

Two Dice Game

In this game I've learned something I have learned that Math is possible. I mean that I used to think that it all couldn't be done because it would take too long that it was not interesting. But in this game I have found out that it isn't long and that it is interesting. And to tell you the truth, I think it was fun. And in this game I found that the 6,7,and 8. would be the best numbers. But I think that I would still put my conters on the 3, 4,5,9,10,and 11 because their is still a chance for those number to be rolled.

Carman explains what she learned from The Two-Dice Sum Game lesson.

A REACTION FROM THIRD AND FOURTH GRADERS

Students react to *The Two-Dice Sums Game* as the fifth graders did.

Students in Sandra Nye's combination class of third and fourth graders responded in a similar way to *The Two-Dice Sums Game*. They came to the conclusion that the sum of 7 comes up more often when two dice are rolled and reported their strategies accordingly. And as with the other classes, the experience was one that got them involved and kept them interested.

Students react to playing the game with only one die.

As a follow-up activity several days later, Sandra asked the students how they would arrange counters on a number line for a game that was played with only one die. For that game only the numbers 1 through 6 were on the number line. Most of the students responded with the same strategy as for two dice—they chose to heap more of their counters in the middle, with most on the number 3 and least on the numbers 6 and 1.

After playing the game, they realized that their strategy hadn't been a sensible one. Their new understanding developed from their own experience with the game. The students' faulty strategy for the one-die game served as a reminder of how careful we need to be as teachers in making assumptions about what students understand and learn from the lessons we present. And it was a testimony to firsthand experience being the best teacher of all.

CONVERSATIONS WITH MARILYN

Why Play Games in Math Class?

THE VALUE OF GAMES WHEN TEACHING AND LEARNING MATH

www.mathsolutions.com/welcometomathclass9

"Mostly, math for me is playing with ideas, and if games can engage kids and get them playing with ideas, then yes, I think there's a huge place for games in the math classroom."

"Games that are most successful are ones that have some strategy involved, though they also can involve some luck so there's a little tension . . ."

"Sometimes, I've actually stopped in the middle of a game and switched to a writing assignment: 'Right now, what number are you going to guess next, and why?' Everything is about communicating. Everything is about thinking, reasoning, and communicating."

Overview

In this conversation with my longtime Math Solutions colleague Patty Clark, I share the value of math games, the role a teacher has in playing games, and a few "clues" about my favorite games. As part of our conversation, we play a round of *Race for 20* together.

Making Connections

I think that my interest in using games in math class stems from my personal memories of playing games as a child—board games, guessing games, card games, games we played outdoors. When playing games, I was totally involved, spending time with friends, honing my skills, enjoying the surprises. I've tried to bring the qualities of those memories into the classroom so that students can engage with math with the same involvement and gusto that games provided me. And I've found that math games work to support learning, including *The Two-Dice Sums Game, Multiplication Bingo,* and *Four Strikes and You're Out.* My book *Welcome to Math Class* features some of these games as well as others.

REPRODUCIBLES

The following reproducibles are referenced throughout the text. These reproducibles are also available in a downloadable, printable format. For access, visit www.mathsolutions.com/myonlineresources and register your product using the key code **WTMC**. See page xii for more detailed instructions.

THE BORDER PROBLEM

CENTIMETER-SQUARED PAPER

TENS AND ONES MAT

ONES

TENS

EXPLORATIONS WITH FOUR TOOTHPICKS

½-INCH-SQUARED PAPER

EXPLORING MULTIPLICATION WITH RECTANGLES

1. Which rectangles have a side with two squares on them? Write the numbers from smallest to largest.

2. Which rectangles have a side with three squares on them? Write the numbers from smallest to largest.

3. Do the same for rectangles with four squares on a side.

4. Do the same for rectangles with five squares on a side.

5. Which numbers have rectangles that are squares? List them from smallest to largest. How many squares would there be in the next larger square you could make?

6. What is the smallest number that has two different rectangles? Three different rectangles? Four?

7. Which numbers have only one rectangle? List them from smallest to largest.

1-INCH-SQUARED PAPER

Five-Tower Game

<u>You need</u>: Unifix cubes
2 dice
a partner

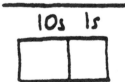

<u>Do</u>: Roll the dice and take that many cubes. Snap them into a tower. Take turns doing this until you each have 5 towers.

 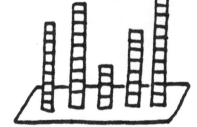

<u>Snap</u> your 5 towers together. <u>Compare</u> with your partner. Break your long train into 10s and record.

<u>Record</u>:

Names _____

	10s	1s

	10s	1s

Write who has more and who has less.

Digit Place

You need: a partner

Do: One person picks a 2-digit number. (The digits should be different.) The other person tries to guess the number. For each guess, the first person tells how many digits in the guess are correct <u>and</u> how many of the correct digits are in the correct place.

A chart helps:

Guess	Digit	Place
27	0	0
13	1	1

Do not tell which digit is correct — just <u>how</u> <u>many</u>.

Play again with the other person guessing this time.

☆ Stars ☆

You need: a partner
a way to time 1 minute

Predict: How many stars do you
think you can draw in
1 minute? Write your
prediction in your
note book.

Do: Make stars while your
partner times 1 minute.

Count: Circle groups of 10 stars.
How many 10s? How many
1s? Record in your
note book.

Extend: Repeat. What would you
do to get better results?
Write this in your
note book.

Pinch a Ten

You need: Kidney beans

Predict: If you take 10 pinches of beans, how many times can you pinch exactly 10? Write your prediction in your notebook.

Do: Take a pinch and count. Was your pinch less than, more than, or exactly 10? Do this 10 times.

Record: (Tally like this ⑷ II.)

Less than 10	10	More than 10

Extend: Repeat and see if you get better at pinching 10s. Or pinch popcorn.

Make a Shape

<u>You need</u> : a crayon
Color Tiles
a partner
white paper

On the white paper, draw a shape that you both think can be covered with 32 tiles.

Use 10 tiles of one color, then 10 of another, and so on, until your shape is covered. <u>Record</u> the number of tiles you used.

Now draw another shape that you both think can be covered with 32 tiles. Again, <u>cover</u>, <u>count</u>, and <u>record</u>.

Tape or staple your shapes in your notebooks. (Put one in each of your books.)

0-99 Patterns

<u>You need</u>: 0-99 charts
Crayon
directions (in envelope)
partner

Pick a strip from the envelope. With your partner, read the directions and decide which numbers to color. (Each colors on your own sheet.)

Tape your chart in your notebook. Write a description of the pattern.

Pick another strip and do the same.

<u>Directions</u>

Color all the even numbers.

Color all the numbers with double digits.

Color all the numbers with digits that add to 8.

Color all the numbers with first digits larger than second digits.

Color all numbers that have a 4.

0	1	2	3	4	5	6	7	8	9
10	11	12	13	14	15	16	17	18	19
20	21	22	23	24	25	26	27	28	29
30	31	32	33	34	35	36	37	38	39
40	41	42	43	44	45	46	47	48	49
50	51	52	53	54	55	56	57	58	59
60	61	62	63	64	65	66	67	68	69
70	71	72	73	74	75	76	77	78	79
80	81	82	83	84	85	86	87	88	89
90	91	92	93	94	95	96	97	98	99

Fill the Cube

You need: a Unifix cube
popcorn
lentils

Predict: How many kernels of popcorn do you think will fill the cube? Record in your notebook.

Do: Fill the cube. Put the popcorn into piles of 10. How many 10s? How many 1s? Record.

Repeat: Now do this with lentils.

Record:

Prediction: Popcorn ___
Lentils ___

Count:

Popcorn
10s   1s

Lentils
10s   1s

Handfuls

You need: Place Value board
beans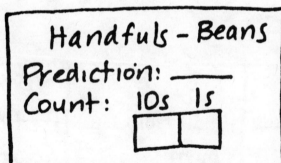
cubes
counters
small cups

Predict: How many beans do you
think you can hold in a handful?
Record in your notebook.

Do: Take a handful.

Count: Use cups to group the beans
into 10s. Put your cups on the place
value board, along with the extra
beans.

Record:

Handfuls – Beans
Prediction: _____

Count:

10s	1s

Repeat: Do the same for cubes
and counters.

Fill the Boxes

You need : Unifix cubes
boxes

Predict : Choose one box. Predict how many Unifix cubes can fit inside so that the cover can be put on. Record your prediction in your notebook.

Do : Fill the box.

Count : Snap the cubes into trains of 10. Count 10s and 1s. Record.

Repeat : Do the same for the other 2 boxes.

Box A	Box B	Box C
Prediction ___	Prediction ___	Prediction ___
Count	Count	Count
10s 1s	10s 1s	10s 1s

Number Puzzle

<u>You need:</u> paper with 100 squares
(10 x 10)
scissors
envelope

Write the numbers from 0 to 99 on the squared paper to make a 0-99 chart.

Cutting only on lines, cut the chart into 7 interesting pieces. Write your name on the back on each piece.

Put the pieces in an envelope. Write your name on the envelope.

Try and put your puzzle together. Then place it in the puzzle box.

Choose someone else's puzzle to put together. Sign your name on the back of the envelope to show you solved it.

SHARING COOKIES

Share _____ cookies equally among 4 people. Paste each person's share in a box.

How much did each person get?

From *Welcome to Math Class, Grades K–6* by Marilyn Burns. © 2020 by Houghton Mifflin Harcourt Publishing Company. Permission granted to photocopy for nonprofit use in a classroom or similar place dedicated to face-to-face educational purposes. Visit www.mathsolutions.com/myonlineresources to register your resource and download the reproducibles. See page xii for the key code.

0–99 CHART

0	1	2	3	4	5	6	7	8	9
10	11	12	13	14	15	16	17	18	19
20	21	22	23	24	25	26	27	28	29
30	31	32	33	34	35	36	37	38	39
40	41	42	43	44	45	46	47	48	49
50	51	52	53	54	55	56	57	58	59
60	61	62	63	64	65	66	67	68	69
70	71	72	73	74	75	76	77	78	79
80	81	82	83	84	85	86	87	88	89
90	91	92	93	94	95	96	97	98	99

1–100 CHART

1	2	3	4	5	6	7	8	9	10
11	12	13	14	15	16	17	18	19	20
21	22	23	24	25	26	27	28	29	30
31	32	33	34	35	36	37	38	39	40
41	42	43	44	45	46	47	48	49	50
51	52	53	54	55	56	57	58	59	60
61	62	63	64	65	66	67	68	69	70
71	72	73	74	75	76	77	78	79	80
81	82	83	84	85	86	87	88	89	90
91	92	93	94	95	96	97	98	99	100

TWO-DICE SUMS GAME

2　3　4　5　6　7　8　9　10　11　12

TWO-DICE SUMS

Roll 2 dice. Mark an X under the sum. Do this until one sum reaches the Finish Line.

2	3	4	5	6	7	8	9	10	11	12

↑ FINISH LINE   Record the sum that finished first on the class chart.

Index